The British Racing Hero

Stanley Paul

London Sydney Auckland Johannesburg

THE BRITISH RACING HERO

From Moss to Mansell

DERICK ALLSOP

TO

Mum and Dad

Stanley Paul & Co. Ltd
An imprint of Random Century, Random Century House,
20 Vauxhall Bridge Road, London SW1V 2SA

Random Century Australia Pty Ltd, 20 Alfred Street, Milsons Point,
Sydney, NSW 2061

Random Century New Zealand Limited, 191 Archers Road, PO Box 40-
086, Glenfield, Auckland 10

Century Hutchinson South Africa (Pty) Ltd, PO Box 337, Bergvlei 2012,
South Africa

First published 1990

Typeset in Linotronic Palatino by SX Composing Ltd, Rayleigh, Essex

Printed and bound in Great Britain by Butler & Tanner Ltd.

British Library Cataloguing in Publication Data
    Allsop, Derick
    From Moss to Mansell: British racing heroes
    1. Great Britain. Racing. Drag Cars. Racing
    I. Title
    796.720941

ISBN 0 09 174491 1

Contents

Acknowledgements

This book would simply not have been possible without the good will, generosity, patience and friendship of many, many people. More than twenty individuals have given their time and memories in extensive interviews. Other publications, such as Mike Hawthorn's *Champion Year*, Graham Hill's *Graham* and David Hayhoe's *Grand Prix Data Book*, have proved invaluable sources of information. My thanks to Aston Publications Ltd for allowing me to quote from *Champion Year*, which, along with *Challenge Me The Race*, is still available. Everyone who has co-operated with this project has been an invaluable source of inspiration. To all the following, I offer my sincere thanks:

Kate, Natalie and Sue Allsop (not least for enduring the incessant rattling of my typewriter), Julian Bailey, Derek Bell, Ann Bradshaw, Tony Brooks, Martin Brundle, Peter Collins, Malcolm Folly, Peter Gethin, Maurice Hamilton, Haynes Publishing Group, Johnny Herbert, Bette Hill, Christopher Hilton, James Hunt, Innes Ireland, Nigel Mansell, Allan McNish, Pat Mennem, Stirling Moss, Jonathan Palmer, Tim Parnell, Stan Piecha, Alain Prost, RAC, MSA, Dave Sims, Jackie Stewart, John Surtees, Stuart Sykes, Trevor Taylor, Ken Tyrrell, Rob Walker and Derek Warwick.

Photographic Acknowledgements
The author and publishers would like to thank the following for allowing the reproduction of copyright photographs: *Allsport* p.63, p.73, p.105 (Pascal Rondeau), p.146 *left* (Tony Duffy), p.148, p.169 (Pascal Rondeau); *Associated Press/Topham* p.16, p.20, p.31, p.33, p.56, p.92, p101, p.103; *Colorsport/SIPA p.7, p.81, p.85, p.97, p.108, p.119, p.137, p.143, p.146 right,* p.170;*Bette Hill* p.114; *Hulton-Deutsch Collection* p.2-3, p.9, p.11, p.14, p.18, p.22, p.25, p.27, p.37, p.41, p.58, p.69, p.74, p.77, p.83, p.87, p.91, p.98, p.127, p.149; *LAT Photographic* p.24, p.35, p.47, p.60, p.82, p.86, p.111, p.126; *Dave Sims* p.95; *Sutton Photographic* p.155, p.157, p.166, p.168; *Trevor Taylor* p.61; *Zooom Photographic* p.167

Opposite page: Record-breakers . . . France's Alain Prost and Britain's Jackie Stewart

Foreword

If motor racing is successful at the moment it is because of British teams and British drivers. Just look at the number of teams based in Britain. I spent six years with one of them, McLaren. During that time I won the World Championship three times. Ferrari is a legend in Italy, a very special case, but England is the true base of the sport.

When you are a young boy, of course, you are more interested in the drivers than the teams – unless, that is, you are a young boy in Italy! When I was a youngster in France I followed the exploits of many British drivers: Jim Clark, Graham Hill, Jackie Stewart. There were other great British drivers before them and there have been great drivers since. I am sure there will be more in the future.

Maybe there is something about the way British drivers are brought up that makes them competitive. They are fighting in a difficult environment all the way through. In Formula Ford and Formula Three they have tough competition. They have to fight from the very beginning if they hope to be successful in motor racing. It makes them stronger and that part of their character shows when they progress in the sport. I am certain they will go on proving tough opposition.

Alain Prost
World Champion 1985, 1986, 1989.

Introduction

One hundred and thirty-two British drivers competed in the first 40 years of the Championship that gave Grand Prix motor racing organised global status. Thirteen of those men won a combined total of 132 races. Six of them achieved the ultimate accolade of world champion driver. Between them they won ten titles. But statistics alone convey little of the drama of the World Championship and the contribution of the British contingent. Theirs is a story of emotion and conflict, excitement and commitment. Many more than the six titled men became heroes, gladiators in an arena where courage is never questioned. They were driven by the will, even the obsession, to compete, to go faster. The spectacle, spiced with controversy, has been unrelenting.

There is a further statistic which reveals the other side of this heroic story – the sombre side. Eighteen of those 132 Britons have lost their lives in pursuit of their ambitions. Others, including champions Mike Hawthorn and Graham Hill, were killed in accidents not involving racing cars shortly after retiring. Tragic irony, too, is part of the story.

The forerunners of Britain's World Championship heroes were men like Sir Henry Segrave, who delighted in setting land and water speed records as well as racing. He won the French Grand Prix at Tours in 1923 and when he repeated his success in the San Sebastian Grand Prix the following year the nation was moved to lobby for its own *Grande Epreuve*. The story of the British Grand Prix started at Brooklands in 1926.

The first Monaco Grand Prix was held in 1929 and history records the first winner as W. Williams, GB. W. Williams appears elsewhere from time to time, such as in the list of winners for the Belgian Grand Prix. With all due respect to Williams (or William Grover to give him his actual name) the great British hero of the thirties was Dick Seaman. He honed his skills on the Continent and drove a Mercedes-Benz to victory in the 1938 German Grand Prix. He was leading in Belgium the following year when he crashed and sustained fatal burns.

Donington staged Grands Prix in the 30s but after the Second World War Silverstone presented itself as the home of the *Grande Epreuve* in this country. There was also a new generation of drivers: Bob Gerard, Reg Parnell and Peter Walker. Gerard was third in the 1948 Grand Prix, second in the 1949 event. Parnell was third in the inaugural World Championship race at Silverstone on 13 May 1950, but the early title years were dominated by men from foreign parts: Farina, Ascari and Fangio.

The golden era for British drivers dawned in the late fifties. Mike Hawthorn's World Championship triumph in 1958 was emulated by Graham Hill (twice), Jim Clark (twice), John Surtees, Jackie Stewart (three times) and James Hunt. This is not to say that all our finest drivers are to be found in the ranks of the title winners. Stirling Moss and Tony Brooks,

Dick Seaman . . . British hero of the thirties

contemporaries of Hawthorn, were more than worthy of the crown. Indeed many argue, as we shall discover, that Moss was the greatest of them all. More recently Nigel Mansell has established himself at the very pinnacle of the sport and he may yet grasp that elusive prize.

What they all share is the admiration of the nation. Each has struck a chord with the watching public. Each has thrilled and captivated the gallery. Champion or not, each has been a hero. Down the years there have been less obvious heroes, men who never really had the chance to fulfil themselves, for whatever reason. But they also served, they also belonged to the Bulldog Breed. The spirit and determination of the British Racing Hero demands to be saluted and celebrated along with the Championships of the chosen few.

1

Out of the Wings

Britain's enthusiasm for recreation, sport, escapism if you like, could barely be contained in the immediate post-war years. The old motor racing circuits had suffered for the cause as the rest of the country had suffered. They had been employed by the Forces or had merely crumbled through neglect. So the sport had to seek new playgrounds, adapt what could be adapted. An aerodrome near the Northamptonshire village of Silverstone proved perfectly adaptable. The track has been changed and improved over the decades since, of course, and now the authorities are planning a major reconstruction. The secret is to keep pace with the times and the demands of the times.

In 1950 the time was ripe for Grand Prix motor racing to be given a new status. Two years earlier the Olympic Games had been revived, and in 1950 football's World Cup would be contested again. The third Grand Prix at Silverstone was to be the first round of the first World Championship. In recognition of this auspicious occasion it was also honoured with the title *Grand Prix d'Europe*. The garlands didn't finish there. King George VI and Queen Elizabeth attended the event, which thus became known as Royal Silverstone.

But what chance a British victory for the Royal spectators and the scores of thousands more who converged on Silverstone? The answer was: virtually no chance at all. These were days when foreign cars and foreign drivers were in command. That day in May *the* car was the Alfa Romeo. Three Alfas would be driven by three of the greatest names in the business: Giuseppe Farina, an Italian, Luigi Fagioli, also Italian, and Juan-Manuel Fangio, of the Argentine. A fourth Alfa was to be driven by an Englishman, Reg Parnell.

It was made clear to Parnell that he was the No. 4 in this operation and he accepted his role. He was a highly respected driver, but he acknowledged that the other three represented Alfa's front-line force. They were men with international reputations and were treated accordingly.

Watching from the pits was seventeen-year-old Tim Parnell, Reg's son. He would go on to compete in Grand Prix racing himself, but for now he was content to share something of Dad's big day.

Tim recalls: 'It was a great occasion for my father. He'd been invited to drive for a foreign team, only the second British driver after Dick Seaman. And not just any foreign team, but Alfa Romeo. Their cars were the best. Then he was introduced to the King and Queen. It was all a great honour. He was a very proud man that day.'

But Reg was merely No. 4. His job was to support the others: 'His instructions were to run behind the other three. I don't think they wanted to take any chances, though, because they put him on higher axle ratios than the others!'

Reg Parnell dutifully made up the front row of the grid as everything went to plan in practice. The race, too, was following the script as Parnell ran an unruffled fourth. His only moment of concern was when he ran into a hare. His team-mates, meanwhile, were shuffling places at the head of the field. The Alfas were in total control.

The one hiccup for the Italian camp came when Fangio, having jousted with Farina for the lead, dropped out. Victory was then a formality for Farina, the man with the laid-back style. The winner of the first World Championship race would also go on to be the winner of the first World Championship. At Silverstone, Fangio's demise handed third place to Parnell. He gratefully and lovingly cradled it all the way home.

'He was well pleased,' says Tim, now a farmer in the East Midlands. 'It was a terrific day, a great occasion. It was something a bit special for him and he had come third in an Alfa Romeo. Of course, there was not the same media coverage of the British Grand Prix then. None of the build-up, the hype or anything. Normally we'd come back from races and people would ask how we'd got on. Today they all know what's happening, they're all experts. Not then.

11

The British Racing Hero

'After that British Grand Prix at Silverstone there was a celebration at Alfa's hotel in Northampton. Members of the team had dinner together, then gathered round a piano for a sing-song. It was a friendly atmosphere. Sport and comradeship were what mattered. Motor racing is a million miles from that today.'

That isn't the last such comment we shall hear along our journey with the British Racing Hero. It may be stating the obvious but sometimes the obvious requires to be stated. All sports and their participants, like life itself, have changed down the years. It is in the nature of all of us to harp back to 'the good old days', to our youth, to the time when we were at our most impressionable. But motor racing has changed in ways that separate it from other sports. The shape of the cars and the attire of the drivers are stark examples. The decision to make crash helmets compulsory met with considerable resistance. Now the fire-proof race suit and incredibly strong monocoque are taken for granted. So are barriers and run-off areas. Deaths and serious injuries are now mercifully rare. In the fifties and beyond they were not.

Above all, the driver has changed. He is a totally different animal. He is dedicated, fit, professional. He no longer makes for a piano but his own helicopter or plane to head back to his tax exile. The successful are megastars with mega-buck incomes. Even the not so successful earn more than most top executives in business and commerce.

Reg Parnell was no megastar and it would never have occurred to him to consider himself a hero. The men who attracted any attention in Grand Prix racing during the early fifties were foreign chaps such as Farina, Alberto Ascari – yet another Italian – and Fangio, who would go on to be the most revered driver of all time. But they were foreign.

Parnell and his British contemporaries were enthusiasts, club racers, fun racers. Any notion of fame and fortune belonged to another age, another world. Parnell had only five other Championship races. He was fourth in the 1951 French Grand Prix, fifth at Silverstone the same year. His love of the sport and competition took him into team management and endured until his death at the beginning of 1964. He was fifty-two.

The seemingly carefree environment of 1950s club racing was, ironically, to be the breeding ground for a generation of British drivers who would not only take on the foreign stars in their own backyard but topple them. Come 1958 Britain had its first world champion in Mike Hawthorn and five other drivers in the top nine. Stirling Moss was second, Tony Brooks third, Roy Salvadori fourth, Peter Collins joint fifth and Stuart Lewis-Evans ninth.

Hawthorn never lost his sense of mischief. He remained essentially an amateur. Gifted, on his day even unbeatable, but still an amateur. His great chum Collins was a kindred spirit. They were almost inseparable. Collins was a daredevil, a devoted team-mate and a total sportsman. Brooks was a quieter man, educated, articulate, immensely talented yet still very much the amateur.

The man who broke the mould was Moss. Fun-loving, always with an eye for the ladies, he was at ease with the likes of Hawthorn and Collins. But for Moss motor racing was more than fun, more than a sport. Much, much more. It was a world of opportunity. A world to be enjoyed, yes.

But also a world that would *pay*. It was a world for the professional.

Moss and Hawthorn were still in the wings when Parnell was flying the flag. Reg's four points from Silverstone gave him joint ninth place in that first Championship. The only other British scorer was Peter Whitehead, who also had a third place in the French Grand Prix at Rheims, driving a Ferrari. In 1951 Parnell was the sole Briton on the scoreboard. He was tenth with five points in this, Fangio's first title year. It was in 1952 that British drivers began to make their presence felt. Hawthorn was joint fourth with ten points, Ken Wharton joint thirteenth on three, and Alan Brown and Eric Thompson joint sixteenth with two points apiece.

Still not earth-shattering stuff, but significant nonetheless, this was an indication of strength and depth and genuine quality at the top end. Moss, in fact, made his World Championship debut before Hawthorn, driving a HWM in the 1951 Swiss Grand Prix at Bremgarten, near Berne, but it was Hawthorn who made a more immediate impact on the title contest, taking the fight to the formidable Italian and Argentine contingents.

Hawthorn had racing in his blood. His father, Leslie, who ran a garage in Farnham, was an enthusiast. Hawthorn junior soon demonstrated more than a mere lust for fast cars. He could drive them well, and he could drive just about anything he managed to lay his hands on – but then that was the way of it. The days when Grand Prix drivers raced nothing else were a long, long way ahead. Partnered by Ivor Bueb, he won the 1955 Le Mans 24-hour sportscar race in a D-type Jaguar. It was not, however, a day of celebration. Mercedes driver Pierre Levegh and more than 80 spectators were killed in the worst accident in motor racing history.

Tragedy always stalked Hawthorn and his contemporaries, yet most of the time he sustained the much-loved image of the smiling Englishman with the infectious sense of humour. Tall and blond (Moss was the short, dark and rapidly balding one), he insisted on wearing a bow-tie while he was racing. Out of the car he would add the flat cap, soon to be followed by a pipe in one hand, a pint of beer in the other. His races to the pub were as famed as his races to the finishing line.

Hawthorn was serious enough when he had to be though, as his successes in Formula Two illustrated. His 'have a go' bravado inevitably carried him into the tougher scrap of the World Championship. He made his debut on 22 June 1952 in the Belgian Grand Prix. The Spa-Francorchamps circuit, almost eight and a half miles of climbing, tumbling public road in the Ardennes, was one of the great challenges in motor racing. The shorter, modern version still is. But the old circuit, that was something else. Hawthorn responded to the demands of the track and the occasion by steering his Cooper-Bristol to fourth place behind Ascari's Ferrari.

His third Championship engagement took him to Silverstone for his first home Grand Prix. Moss was there, too, driving an ERA, and so was Collins, in an HWM. For Moss and Collins, however, it was to be a day of frustration. The former retired with engine trouble, the latter with ignition problems.

Hawthorn, on the other hand, was able to push on, his Cooper giving him an uncomplicated ride. As others came to grief, Hawthorn contentedly advanced until he found himself in third place. Victory again went to Ascari, by now securely on course for the title. But the young

The way they were . . .
Mike Hawthorn at
Silverstone, 1956

Englishman's impressive drive had not only earned him four points, it had caught the eye of Enzo Ferrari. Another fourth place in Holland completed a highly creditable first season at this level.

Hawthorn was flattered by the offer from Ferrari for 1953. The Scuderia, led by Ascari, had decimated all before them in 1952 and promised to do much the same the following season. Certainly there was no British car capable of threatening their status. Hawthorn, like Moss, was a fiercely proud Briton and was reluctant to export his services. But, unlike Moss, he came to the conclusion that he could take patriotism only so far. His heart urged him to stay, yet his head told him to go. Ferrari it would be.

Hawthorn completed a powerful line-up, joining Ascari, Farina and Luigi Villoresi. The main opposition for their 500s seemed likely to come from Maserati, led by Fangio. So it proved. Fangio was runner-up in the Championship. But Ascari kept his crown, Farina was third and Hawthorn fourth, ahead of Villoresi. The high point of Hawthorn's season came in the French Grand Prix at Rheims. It was also one of the high points in the history of the Drivers' World Championship.

The early season races had given a firm indication of Hawthorn's potential, even if Ascari was consistently leading the way home. The Englishman was fourth on his Ferrari debut in Argentina, and fourth again in Holland. Hawthorn and his colleagues were almost withdrawn from the French Grand Prix following a row over the disqualification of a Ferrari in the sportscar race. Talks eventually consoled indignant team

14

officials and their cars lined up on the Grand Prix grid. Ascari was on pole.

Froilan Gonzalez, in a Maserati, decided to start with half-full fuel tanks and his lighter car duly built up a considerable lead. At that stage the contest was behind him, with Fangio taking on the combined forces of Ferrari: Ascari, Hawthorn, Farina and Villoresi. When Gonzalez went into the pits to re-fuel his fellow countryman took the lead. Gonzalez re-joined in sixth place. The man now chasing Fangio was Hawthorn. The duel was on.

For 150 miles they exchanged places, thrusts . . . and smiles. It was a race that captured the spirit of the day. Fangio had the experience, the style, the cunning; Hawthorn had the dash and the motivation. Behind them, too, the racing was intense. Gonzalez and Ascari were disputing third place and had the leaders within their reach.

On the final lap it seemed Fangio must deliver the decisive blow. For all the exuberance of this obviously bright young man, surely the elegant master would put him in his place. But no. A slight slide by the Maserati enabled the Ferrari to accelerate clear and cross the line one second ahead. Fangio almost lost second place but just managed to hold off the charging Gonzalez. Ascari was fourth, Farina a distant fifth.

The man of the moment for Ferrari – and for Britain – was twenty-four-year-old Hawthorn. His win was the first by a British driver in the World Championship, breaking the Italian and Argentine stranglehold. Britain had served notice that its drivers were ready to take centre stage. Stirling Moss was also in the cast that day, but he had to be content with a bit part. His starring roles would come later.

Hawthorn maintained consistent form for the rest of the season, the reliability of the 500 proving a vital factor in the Championship. He was fifth at Silverstone, third at the Nurburgring, third at Bremgarten and fourth at Monza. It had been an eventful and productive first season with Ferrari.

Ferrari signed the burly Gonzalez for 1954 but lost Ascari to the charms of Lancia. It brought to a close one of the most dominant periods of the Championship. During 1952 and 1953 Ascari had a record run of nine consecutive victories (if the domestic squabble at Indianapolis is discounted). That sequence was concluded by Hawthorn's success in France. Ferrari still had a heavyweight line-up, particularly with Hawthorn now growing into the job. Maserati, however, were menacingly flexing their muscles. And they still had Fangio.

Maserati and Fangio started the way they meant to go on. They won in Argentina and underlined their superiority in Belgium. Gonzalez took the British Grand Prix, with Hawthorn in second place, only for Fangio to clean up in Germany, Switzerland and Italy, and confirm himself as champion.

Hawthorn's one victory of the season came in the closing race, the Spanish Grand Prix. It left him third in the Championship, just behind Gonzalez. His climb had been steady and encouraging, but now his fortunes were to take a dive. The mid 1950s brought him unhappy times. His father was killed in a road accident and he left Ferrari to join a Vanwall team still finding their feet. Hawthorn couldn't even find his way into the points in 1955 and mustered a meagre four in 1956 as he shuffled his cars:

Vanwall to Ferrari to Maserati to BRM to Vanwall.

His life would brighten again with a return to Ferrari for the 1957 season. There he found fresh enthusiasm, fresh optimism and a soul-mate called Peter Collins. Ahead of Hawthorn opened a road to the very top of Formula One motor racing. He was to enjoy two years of gathering success, outrageous escapades and quite touching friendship.

Fangio, having moved from Ferrari to Maserati again, was about to put together another – and final – Championship-winning season. His victory in the German Grand Prix at the Nurburgring was perhaps his greatest. A lengthy pit stop threatened to sabotage his race but he came from behind to take Collins, and then Hawthorn, with a breathtaking demonstration of car control. It was his twenty-fourth and last Grand Prix win.

Hawthorn had, earlier in the season, taken fourth and third places in the French and British Grands Prix respectively. Collins was third in France. Hawthorn finished the season fourth, on thirteen points, Collins joint eighth with eight points. Their campaign would be stronger in 1958 and Collins would pledge his support to Hawthorn's title bid.

Collins shared Hawthorn's zest for life and his bravery behind the wheel of a fast car. He admired and learned from his great pal. There were those who felt Collins fooled around a little too much. Even in the 1950s team officials weren't necessarily known for their *joie de vivre*. Just like Hawthorn, though, he was a serious man and an unflinching competitor when he had to be.

Collins was born at Kidderminster in 1931. A ready-made job and a comfortable living beckoned at his father's transport firm but he was

The British Racing Hero

Even Hawthorn had his serious moments, here in the BRM at Goodwood, 1956

16

lured by the thrill and challenge of motor racing. He was competing at the age of seventeen and soon made a reputation for himself in his 500cc Cooper. He graduated through the ranks and demonstrated the required talent and appetite for a variety of cars and races.

He was summoned to Grand Prix racing by the HWM team in 1952. He went on to drive the Vanwall and the powerful Thinwall Special Ferrari. In sportscar racing he distinguished himself with Aston Martin. Among his partners was Tony Brooks; another was Stirling Moss. Collins and Moss shared the driving of the winning Mercedes in the 1955 Targa Florio, the daunting road race in Sicily. That success probably provided Enzo Ferrari with the last piece of evidence he required. In 1956 Collins switched to the Scuderia.

It was his most successful season in Grand Prix racing. He did not quite make it to the Championship, yet at the end of the season he was hailed a hero by Ferrari, all Italy and all Britain. He shared with Fangio second place behind Moss' Maserati at Monaco and registered his first win in Belgium. He followed up with another victory in France and a shared second place at Silverstone. Here he was, two races from the end of the season, with the title in his sights.

Fangio won in Germany, however, while Collins spun out of action. It would all be decided at Monza. Collins or Fangio could bring the crown to Ferrari, but Moss could still take it to Maserati; unthinkable, unbearable – but true. When Fangio's steering broke it seemed his hopes were gone. But Collins came in and handed over his car. Moss won the race, but second place was enough to give Fangio the Championship.

Whether or not Collins was instructed to give his car to Fangio and thereby sacrifice his own title chance is unclear and scarcely matters anyway. Collins did not hesitate and, as we shall see, he remained a gentleman and a true team-mate to the end.

Moss, too, was to distinguish himself as a gentleman and a sportsman. He had already distinguished himself as one of the outstanding drivers of his generation. A talent for racing ran in the family. Moss was born on 17 September 1929 to parents with a relish for motor sport. His father, Alfred, was into racing, while his mother Aileen leaned more towards rallying. She was the 1936 women's English champion.

Stirling had sampled the joys of steering a car by the age of six. At ten he had his own car, an Austin 7, and at the venerable age of fifteen graduated to a Morgan three-wheeler. For all the reticence of his parents, the wheels – however many – were now in perpetual motion. Master Moss was a less than enthusiastic scholar and found equally little appeal in the chores of the family farm at Tring, Hertfordshire. He recalls: 'My father didn't really want me to go racing, but then he conned his father when he was studying dentistry. He told grandfather the best place for him was in America, the University of Indianapolis. So my grandfather duly sent him there but, of course, he went there to race. He did qualify, though, and became a dental surgeon. Once he was established I suppose it would have been right for me to follow him into dentistry, but I wasn't smart enough. Tony Brooks went through dentistry studies because he was much brighter than I was, and yet he didn't use his qualifications.

'Once my father realised I really meant to have a go in racing he didn't

Peter Collins . . . British hero, but still mother's boy

stand in my way. He let me get on with it. He said that as long as I worked my forty-eight-hour week on the farm it was okay. I used to have to go down and milk the cows and I can tell you, I didn't like it. The only warm thing in the morning was a cow's udder! But he made sure I worked and I can see his point now. At the time, of course, I couldn't.

'I was also a trainee manager with Associated British Hotels. I worked at the Ecclestone Hotel, Victoria, at the Queensway Hotel and at a restaurant in the City. I was a commis-chef, or an office worker, right the way through, so I had the complete training for the business. If you fail your exams the only thing to do is to go into the hotel trade, be an estate agent, or, I suppose, go into politics. There's not much else open, is there?'

There was, for Moss, one other option, the option he was determined to pursue. His talent for racing quickly became apparent and, although he had no great academic acumen, he acquired an acute business sense that was to serve him well.

In 1948, at the age of eighteen, Moss had a 500cc Cooper. It was small, light and nimble, and would take him on the sport's nursery slopes. Hill-climbing was the only way to go – except that he wasn't able to get going quite as quickly as he would have liked. He tried to enter for the Shelsley Walsh hill-climb but his name meant nothing to the organisers and he wasn't accepted. He had more luck at Prescott a week later.

The Cooper was transported to Prescott in a horse box – Stirling and little sister Pat were also accomplished riders – and, on its second run, set a class record. Moss was soon nudged from his perch but he finished his first competition a creditable fourth. The first of the knowing nods were in evidence. The first win came in his next hill-climb. He went on winning throughout the season. The teenager completed his first year with a total of eleven victories from fifteen events.

When Stirling continued winning in his second season at the wheel of a 1000cc Cooper, even Alfred Moss began to appreciate that here was a lad blessed with something hugely more than average ability. His son had something special, and he knew it.

Stirling says: 'Once I got into it my father became more and more involved. In fact my father and mother came with me every week to the races. They were a great support.'

But did Moss junior realise he had an exceptional talent? 'I suppose I realised to some extent that I was a cut above the rest but remember I was lucky because it was just after the war and there were no established stars. Those who did have experience had gained it eight years or so before. There were people like Bob Gerard and Reg Parnell, but not many more who were established. There were certainly no great numbers of up-and-coming drivers. There were no Nigel Mansells to compete against.'

Wherever there was competition Moss went to seek it out. He was soon racing in Italy, audaciously jousting with the Ferraris and laying the foundations of an international reputation. As we know, it was usual for racing drivers of the time to have a variety of cars and take part in a variety of events. Moss just tended to drive more than most – and better. His range and the standards he set were phenomenal. Sportscar classics, rallies (Monte Carlo and others), land-speed record bids and Grands Prix were all tackled with the same commitment and skill. He was, purely and simply, a racer. His career spanned almost 500 events. He won more than 50 per cent of those he finished.

Of all these successes one of the best remembered and most admired was his victory in the 1955 Mille Miglia, a 1,000-mile Brescia-Rome-Brescia lap of Italian roads. It was a victory for control, nerve, planning and team-work.

Moss and his navigator Denis Jenkinson had a Mercedes 300 SLR, a car perfectly capable of winning. But this race required much more besides. It wasn't just Italian territory, it was an Italian stronghold. Foreigners weren't supposed to win it. Local knowledge, experience and tradition were all against the English pair. They didn't know every twist and turn of the route, they couldn't possibly learn every twist and turn. So, on a series of reconnaissance runs and at the expense of a couple of shunted cars, they put together what were, in effect, pace-notes. One thousand miles of road came down to a seventeen-foot roll of paper. They also devised a system of hand signals for communicating since the open Mercedes travelling at those speeds tended to kill the art of conversation.

Their preparation and Moss' complete faith in Jenkinson enabled them to reach speeds of 186 miles per hour, launch from the brows of hills at 170 m.p.h. and hurtle through towns at more than 120 m.p.h. It was flat-out and near flat-out driving for 10 hours, 7 minutes and 48 seconds, at a record average speed of 97.7 m.p.h.

Curiously, though, Moss recollects the experience with an air of

Setting out on the road to stardom . . . Moss at 21

'Stirling would drive anything'

disappointment. He explains: 'It was strange. It was very satisfying and yet there was a feeling of anti-climax about it. The shortcoming of the Mille Miglia was that when you won you didn't know you'd won. You set off at intervals, of course. We were first in Rome but that worried me because there's a saying in Italy "first in Rome, never first home".

'We were in the lead for so many stages but when we finished I had to stand there on the finishing line looking up the road to see if Fangio or whoever was going to come through and beat us. It wasn't like crossing the line in a normal race and thinking "we've won". Afterwards, then yes, it was tremendous. But only afterwards.'

Moss, again partnered by Jenkinson, was hopeful of going better still two years later, but his race came to a scary end just seven and a half miles out when the brake pedal of his Maserati broke off. Such was the pattern of his career. He won a lot, he broke down a lot. His frequent retirements led to accusations that he was a car-breaker. He and those he worked with resented the accusations. Again, he was, purely and simply, a racer. Enzo Ferrari recognised that as early as 1951.

Moss says: 'I can remember Ferrari calling me and asking me if I wanted to drive his new 2½-litre, four cylinder car at Bari in Southern Italy. I said of course I did, I was thrilled. I was in my early twenties and here I was being called by Ferrari. So off I went, all the way down to Bari. I remember going up to the car, getting in and then this bloke coming up and asking me what was going on. I said I'd been asked to drive the car but he said no, sorry, but I wasn't. Taruffi was driving it.

'I was very hacked off and hurt. I'd never come across someone who said something like that and did not mean it. I vowed then that I would

20

never drive for Ferrari. Later, of course, in 1962, I went to see Enzo Ferrari, we kissed each other on the cheek and it was all set up for me to drive a Ferrari. But I had my crash and that was that.'

Moss was, and still is, an entrenched patriot. That early experience with Ferrari strengthened his resolve to take on the world with private British cars. It was a stand which, probably more than anything else, deprived him of the World Championship.

Those who watched Moss in the early fifties were convinced the title would fall to him. It was inconceivable that all that talent, all that dedication would not be rewarded. For Moss driving wasn't merely fun, it was a profession. Every £100 prize in practice was there to be won. He introduced to racing a new level of fitness, a new attitude. He didn't drink, though he did smoke a little.

At the old Le Mans-style starts, where the drivers ran across the track to their cars, he would crouch for the off like a sprinter. He is slightly irritated by the mirth that tactic caused, pointing out: 'It mattered, even at the start of a 24-hour race, to get away in front because there were a lot of shunts at the start of races and the one sure way of avoiding trouble was to be clear of it before it happened.'

Moss had the style and appeal of the modern sporting hero. One of his fans was a young Scot called John Young Stewart. The man who wrote his name in the record books as Jackie Stewart says: 'Stirling was a particular hero of mine. He looked, walked and behaved like a racing driver – or at least how a boyhood hero should. And, of course, he was the most exciting driver of that time. He dressed like a racing driver in the Dunlop blue overalls and even before that in the short-sleeved shirts and the helmet at a jaunty angle, and all that sort of stuff. He was the first British driver to be commercial as well as professional. He was doing adverts on the back of buses! Nobody had ever seen or heard of that sort of thing by a racing driver before.'

Stewart had to share his hero with much of the nation. Moss makes no bones about his appearance and style. He worked at it. He affected Farina's laid-back look in the car and made a point of waving to other drivers as he overtook them. He claimed, whenever he could, his lucky number – seven: 'I copied the laid-back driving style because I'd seen Farina and it looked good. I thought to myself "yes, I like that, I'll do it". It isn't the natural way but it became natural in time. It's what you develop, what you grow into. It becomes a habit. I can't sleep now with a pillow or drink tea with sugar in it. It's just habit.

'As far as the waving is concerned, I think it is fair to say that I have never, ever passed another driver without thanking him – or shaking a fist at him. If a driver gets over I say "thanks". It's no trouble. Particularly with the cars I drove. If someone's in the way you give him a different gesture. Seven was the family lucky number. My birthday is the seventeenth, my mother's the seventh of the seventh, my sister's the twenty-seventh.'

Just like his career on the hills, Moss' Grand Prix World Championship career had a false start: 'I was due to race in the Swiss Grand Prix at Berne in 1950 but didn't due to illness. I had Asian 'flu or something.' Moss was susceptible to illnesses as a child and into adulthood he appeared to be

Moss, Maserati, and lucky No. 7

more vulnerable to disease than most.

Even after making his debut, in the 1951 Swiss Grand Prix, it hardly amounted to lift-off. Over the course of the following three seasons he had only ten championship races, in British cars that could not compete with the might of the Continental machinery. He began with an HWM, moved on to an ERA, then Connaught, then Cooper. At the end of 1953 he still had not scored a point, let alone won a race.

It was at this stage that Moss's father and his business manager, Ken Gregory, decided he should make a concession to pragmatism: 'My father and Ken had heard that Mercedes were coming out so, unbeknown to me, they went to see the man, Alfred Neubauer. He agreed that I'd done jolly well but said he hadn't seen me in a winning car and that I needed a bit more experience.

'So again without my knowing, my father and Ken ordered a 250F Maserati. They contacted Maserati, asked if they would sell one and were told they would. So in 1954 I had the Maserati. I was third in Belgium and in Berne, in the wet, I put the car at the front of the grid. Neubauer then came along and asked me to join them the following year, which I did.'

Now, at last, Moss's Grand Prix career was on the move. The Mercedes challenge was led by Fangio, the reigning champion, and Moss was to prove himself a worthy partner. The young Englishman had a shared fourth place in the oppressive heat of Argentina and was runner-up to Fangio in both Belgium and Holland.

The next race was at Aintree, the first time a World Championship British Grand Prix had been awarded to a circuit outside Silverstone. Moss celebrated the occasion by becoming the first Briton to win his home race. He fought a rousing contest with Fangio before opening a decisive lead. To this day, no-one knows whether the Old Maestro decided not to get between the young lion and his feast that day – not even Moss. The only certainty is that the British gallery had a British winner, and they excitedly registered their approval. Moss says: 'At Mercedes we didn't have team orders as team orders go. It was simply that when you got half a minute lead over the rest they held out a REG (*regulare*) sign, which meant you were to hold your position. So, whoever was in the lead, be it me,

Fangio, Kling or Taruffi, would win the race. I was always happy to follow Fangio, but at the British Grand Prix we were going round together. Then, for some reason, traffic or whatever, I found myself in front of him. We came to a back-marker, I went by and left Fangio behind. I then went like hell. I can still remember coming round the last corner of the race, pulling right over to the right and, with my foot flat on the accelerator, waving him past. It was really a gesture on my part and he didn't pass me. I just managed to win.

'You can't tell if he was happy to let me win. Fangio was such a gentleman. I've asked him and he's said "No, no, you were on form and that was your day." He was that sort of man and we were fairly close. He's always said nice things about me. I think he was better than me in Formula One, but I could beat him in sportscars. Whether what he said that day at Aintree is true I don't know. It was obviously better for me to win the British Grand Prix from Mercedes' point of view and he was the sort of man to say "what the hell, I've won all the others".'

Fangio won four races that season and collected his third Championship. Moss completed the year a convincing second in the rankings. Alas for Moss, his arrival coincided with the departure of Mercedes-Benz from the sport. Moss tested the available British cars – BRM, Connaught and Vanwall – but much as he liked the handling of the Vanwall, he felt the home teams didn't offer a full season and so opted for Maserati. Fangio signed for Lancia-Ferrari.

Moss won at Monaco and again in the last race at Monza but Fangio, assisted by Collins, did enough to retain his crown. Moss had to be content with another runner-up position. The following year it was still the same story. Again, only the names of the cars had changed. Fangio had gone to Maserati, while Moss had come home to drive Tony Vandervell's Vanwall. Alongside Moss were two other gifted British drivers, Tony Brooks and Stuart Lewis-Evans.

Brooks took second place at Monaco but the team's breakthrough came in the British Grand Prix, held for a second time at Aintree. The build-up had done little to inspire confidence in the camp. It was doubtful whether either Moss or Brooks would be able to compete. Moss missed the French Grand Prix with a sinus infection caused by spray in a freak water-skiing incident. Moss was up and about again a few days before the meeting, but Brooks, lucky to escape serious injury when his Aston Martin overturned in the Le Mans 24-hour race, was on his feet again only the day before first practice at Liverpool.

Brooks recalls the accident at Le Mans: 'I took over at about three o'clock in the morning and it was stuck in fourth gear. I was busy mucking about with the gear lever and not looking where I was going. I suddenly looked up and realised I'd left my braking for the corner at Tertre Rouge too late. I almost made it round the corner but it would have been better if I'd hit the sandbank head-on. I would have just been shocked. Instead I went up the sandbank, the car flipped and trapped me underneath it.

'I was waiting for the next car to come round and run me over but in fact it was a Porsche, which kindly hit my Aston and knocked it off me. I was able to clamber out from under the car and I flew over the sandbank out of the way of the following cars. I had a few deep gashes and contusions so I was whipped off to hospital. They were jolly painful so I was in a bit of a state. I was flown back to England, went home to bed and got up the day before practice for the British Grand Prix. The first driving I'd done since Le Mans was driving over to Aintree.

'The object was really to get a third Vanwall started with a decent place. Obviously I was still in a bit of a state so the understanding I reached with Stirling was that if something happened to his car I'd bring in mine. We were still allowed to share cars then and there was no way I would have had the stamina to last the race anyway. I got some big packs of rubber put into the car to give me a bit of comfort and managed a quick lap in practice, a one-off really, to get me on the front row. We got three cars into the race, which is what we wanted. It was a team effort.'

Moss defied his problem to satisfy the demands of the British people and put the Vanwall on pole. He led the early part of the race until a misfire forced him into the pits and eventually out of his car. An exhausted Brooks was content to hand over his car. Moss was back in business. He was also back in ninth place.

The challenge was tailor-made for Moss. He set about it with a controlled ferocity that is the hallmark of the great – and for once, he had luck on his side. Others crumbled and retired as he advanced up the leaderboard. A throttle linkage failure denied Lewis-Evans second place and Vanwall a crushing one-two success. But they had their victory. Nothing was going to stop Moss now. Nothing was going to prevent the first all-British triumph of the British Grand Prix.

Fangio produced that magnificent drive at the Nurburgring to claim his last Grand Prix win and the last of his five World Championship triumphs. But before the season was over Moss had two more victories. He beat Fangio at Pescara (Italy was granted an additional race after the Dutch and Belgian Grands Prix had been called off) and put on a repeat performance at Monza. Now a British car was winning in Italy, too. The next objective for Moss and Vanwall had to be the Championship.

The British Racing Hero

Stuart Lewis-Evans . . . 'very, very quick' – in the Vanwall, 1957

Brooks also had good reason to be hopeful for 1958. It was just that fanfares never accompanied his ambitions. Slim and straight, quiet and intelligent, he never viewed motor racing as an all-consuming pursuit. Once in a car his commitment was assured, his concentration total. He had an outstanding talent for driving which had to be expressed, but he recognised there was a much wider world outside the racing car and that sense of values was to guide him through a career that undoubtedly touched on greatness.

Even when Brooks first made an impact on Grand Prix racing, he was primarily concerned about other matters. As Moss says, Brooks was bright enough to study dentistry. Coming up were his exams at Manchester. He went on to qualify, just as Moss would have expected him to. Little, however, was expected of him when he flew out to Sicily in 1955 to drive a Connaught in the non-Championship Syracuse Grand Prix. Brooks says: 'I certainly appreciated the great opportunity to go to Syracuse but I was obsessed with my exams and studied all the way there and all the way back. It was perhaps a good thing because it took my mind off the fact that I had never sat in a Grand Prix car, let alone driven one. I'd driven only F2 Connaughts.

'The interesting thing about the Connaught was that it hadn't got a good record for reliability. I was allowed to do only about fifteen laps in practice for fear of having some calamity and not being able to pick up the starting money. In fact we did make the start, the car proved reliable and I won the race. It was especially satisfying because it was a road circuit bordered by walls etc. and we were up against the works Maserati team in full strength.'

Tony Brooks . . . great talent

Brooks' ability was no longer a secret and the day of decision inevitably drew closer. He says: 'I was a house surgeon at Manchester Dental Hospital and my absences became more and more frequent. They were very considerate and encouraged me, but it was getting ridiculous. I didn't want to presume on their goodwill any longer. I realised I ought to retire from dentistry and go full-time motor racing, which I did.'

His World Championship debut, driving a BRM in the 1956 British Grand Prix at Silverstone, might have convinced him he should stick to dentistry. He manfully struggled to keep the car in second place behind team-mate Mike Hawthorn in the early part of the race and, after pitting for repairs to a broken throttle cable, resumed his charge.

He says: 'The car was actually undrivable. I was trying to compensate for it. I'd been taking Abbey flat but when I came back out I drifted on to the grass. In a decent car it would have been no problem. You could have just pulled on again because it was quite wide there. But this car was uncontrollable. It hit the bank, tipped over, threw me on to the grass and set itself on fire, which was probably the best thing that could have happened to it. After that I decided my strict policy would be to drive as fast as I could as long as the car was fit to drive.'

Brooks' fast, safe driving was to be a feature of the following few seasons of World Championship racing. In 1957 his strategy, at the wheel of the Vanwall, earned him eleven points and fifth place in the title table. The 1958 campaign promised more – more for Brooks, more for Moss, more for Hawthorn, more for British motor racing.

2

All Heroes, One Champion

1958 was no ordinary year in sport. In football's World Cup finals a boy called Pele gave an international audience the first indication that perhaps the greatest player of all time had arrived. His tears of joy, shed in Brazil's hour of triumph, touched the watching millions. But there were also tears of sadness that year. Eight players of Manchester United, perhaps England's greatest-ever club side, were killed in the Munich air disaster.

The year of glory and tragedy was reflected in motor racing. The World Championship produced one of its most inspiring seasons, particularly if you happened to be British. But it also gave harrowing reminders of the dangers that accompany drivers along that road to success and celebration. These were changing times in the sport, but the concerted campaigns for improved safety standards were still to come.

The 1950s had nurtured a fine crop of British drivers. British cars, too, were emerging to dispute supremacy with the powers of Europe. Mike Hawthorn and Peter Collins would lead the Ferrari offensive in 1958, but Vanwall would have, for most of the season, Stirling Moss, Tony Brooks and Stuart Lewis-Evans. Roy Salvadori would make his presence felt in the Cooper and an all-new, all-British challenge would be introduced: Lotus cars, driven by Cliff Allison and Graham Hill.

Brooks reasons: 'There were so many British drivers coming through because we had more club racing than other countries. There were more opportunities to race, for people to start with their own cars, as I did. There were weekends when there were club races all over the country. Grand Prix drivers came from the lower formulas and the 500s. Then there were the sportscar teams. There was Aston Martin, there was Jaguar. The number of meetings and categories gave more opportunities for drivers to come forward. In Italy and France there weren't club meetings where you could take along cars and have a bit of a go. Then, of course, if people are doing well in a particular sport it generates interest in that sport and on it goes.

'Quite apart from Stirling, Mike and Peter, there were a lot of very good British drivers at the time. Roy Salvadori was very quick. Despite his name, he was British through and through, and he was happiest on British circuits. Cliff Allison drove very well in the Lotus and made it into the Ferrari Formula One team.

'Stuart Lewis-Evans was very, very quick. He was, in my view, quicker than Cliff. But I think his problem was a lack of stamina. He wasn't a terribly well person. He was slight of build and I don't think he could sustain the effort for a full race. But he did put in some really quick practice laps.'

Moss endorses those opinions and adds: 'Roy was a particularly good sportscar driver. He was very competitive. Stuart had enormous ability, enormous ability. And there were others who didn't drive regularly in

Grand Prix racing. Archie Scott-Brown [a tenacious Scot who had a deformed arm yet drove a Connaught in the 1956 British Grand Prix at Silverstone] was a tremendous driver. Considering his disability he was amazing. Mind you, when you think of Douglas Bader and what he did . . .'

One of the journalists covering motor racing at the time was Pat Mennem, who convinced the *Daily Mirror* it really should have its own man on the scene. He remained on the scene for more than thirty years. Mennem says: 'Scott-Brown drove mainly sportscars, but they wouldn't have let him drive now.' Archie Scott-Brown was killed in a sportscar race in May 1958.

Mennem: 'So much about motor racing has changed since the fifties. I don't think the public really appreciated how special 1958 and those times were. Motor racing hadn't caught on as it has now, although the newspapers were giving more to it.

'It was still supposed to be a rich man's sport, which was no longer quite true, but it was still a case of the right crowd and not too many of them. At Goodwood on Easter Monday you'd never see anybody wearing jeans or anything like that. Everyone wore a jacket. It was the same at Silverstone. They never sold hot dogs or such like. It was a sport for the aficionados, I suppose. Brands Hatch started to change all that in this country. They catered for a different crowd, a wider audience.

'Drivers like Peter Collins and Mike Hawthorn were still very much part of the local motor club and the chaps from the local pub scene. I'm sure they used to drive a lot faster from Goodwood to the Spread Eagle at Midhurst than they did round the circuit. The first one to the pub was the chap who had to buy the drinks. Nevertheless they used to boast about

Best of British . . . Moss and Vanwall

27

who got there first. You'd never see the drivers now going to the pub after the race.'

It ought to be mentioned here that this is a subject close to Pat Mennem's heart. He, too, was very much a chap of the era: sports jacket, cravat, flannels and leather uppers. He could also stand his corner as a drinker and a raconteur. Above all he was, and still is, a gentleman.

Which reminds him: 'At Le Mans in 1953 Duncan Hamilton, who had been in the Fleet Air Arm, and Tony Rolt, who had been a regular soldier in the Rifle Brigade and had been in Colditz, were disqualified for infringing rules in practice, so the two of them went out on the toot. Their wives told them not to come back until they'd pulled themselves together. There wasn't much point in that because they didn't come back at all.

'They went out on the town, drank all night and were in Grubers restaurant the following morning when Bill Lyons arrived and told them he had paid a fine and they were racing at 4 p.m. that day. They could not find a Turkish bath, so resorted to hot baths and black coffee. About two hours before the race Duncan ordered – for medicinal purposes – a large brandy and immediately felt some improvement. So Tony tried the same, with more black coffee. They got in their C-type Jaguar and won the race. They were also the first drivers to average more than 100 m.p.h. The car was doing 160 down the straight when the windscreen broke and a bird hit Duncan in the face. It broke his nose, but they didn't worry too much about that sort of thing.'

From this distance it seems they didn't worry too much about anything. Mennem: 'It was then a very, very dangerous way of spending your time. Today it's nowhere near as dangerous. Twenty and thirty years ago Senna wouldn't have taken the risks he takes now. You only have to look at the casualty list in the 1950s, 1960s and even into the 1970s. It was fairly horrendous.

'The racing cars then were much more fragile than nowadays, but even so they were still jolly quick and on tyres that were minuscule compared with today's. If you went off at Spa, for instance, as many people did, you had little chance of escaping without some form of injury. People just accepted that it was dangerous. It always had been. If you went motor racing and you had an accident you were very lucky if you survived.

'There were far more casualties but there was much more fun. It was an attitude of mind. You did it because you enjoyed doing it. You weren't doing it because you were told to do it. It wasn't a business. It wasn't originally for the money although later on they were making reasonable amounts. They weren't being pressurised by sponsors to meet people.

'Like a lot of things, if it had a bit of a risk to it, it added some spice. Take Peter Collins, for instance, I doubt if he thought about dying. The only thing they were concerned about was the car falling apart or a wheel coming off or something like that. They never thought they would ever make a mistake. They always thought they were far too good to make a mistake. In the end, of course, dear old Peter obviously did make a mistake. But this was something they were prepared to take a chance with.

'Peter was a bloke I admired. He was a great friend of mine. I remember him driving me along the Corniche to Monte Carlo at about half past four in the morning. We were in an Aston Martin DB2 and as we got to this very big S-bend he said he could go through it absolutely flat in third. I said he didn't have to prove anything to me, I believed him, but he said he'd show me. He went through completely sideways. It was all very impressive stuff, except that if anybody had been coming the other way, we were on the wrong side of the road. They tended to do that sort of thing.

'He was very much the dashing Englishman with the Aston Martin or whatever it was. Wherever you went with Peter he had a girlfriend. We arrived in Lille at one time and he said he was going to give some girl a ring. Her father was an enormous industrialist in Lille and they had an enormous apartment. There was champagne and goodness knows what else. This was typical. Everywhere he just had to pick up the phone.'

Brooks also enjoyed Collins' company. He says: 'I admired Peter as a driver and as a man. He was very quick, and, in my view, much more of a natural driver than Mike. He was good fun, too. I used to room with him quite often.'

Moss and, of course, Hawthorn were two more who had their adventures with Collins. Moss recalls: 'I'd done the Alpine Rally a couple of times and I was asked by the Rootes Group if there were any more drivers who would be interested because we seemed to be good at this rally stuff. So I went to Peter and Mike and said "Look, you get five days playing around in the South of France getting acquainted, going scrutineering, and then you drive around the mountains, which is rather super. You get all expenses paid and you get fifty quid as well. What about it?"

'So they got Mike Hawthorn, Pete Collins and me, the whole team, for £150 to do the Alpine Rally, which took two weeks in all. It puts it all into perspective. We were doing it for fun. And the fun we had. We had a squeeze gun and used to shoot at girls' bottoms. Then, when they turned round, we'd try to pick them up.'

The pursuit of ladies by Moss and unnamed friends became an organised activity of international scale. He explains: 'We had what we called the Mouse Club. If, for instance, I met some cracking bird who was going to Nassau and we had a member of the club who lived there I'd suggest to her she might like to go out with him. If you were going through a place where we knew a girl, an introduction could be arranged. We all had the same eye. I admit I was in the club but never gave out how many members we had. We wanted to keep a certain mystique about it.'

In 1958 this happy-go-lucky bunch of Brits were lined up to contest the Drivers' World Championship. Moss was teamed up with Brooks and the Welshman, Lewis-Evans. Hawthorn was with his big buddy, 'mon ami, mate' Collins. That term of endearment had become a catch-phrase for Hawthorn, an indication of his affection for, and trust in, Collins. Their friendship was an integral part of the 1958 story.

A significant change in regulations meant that a driver had to use the same car through a race to score Championship points. Moss, of course, had taken over Brooks' Vanwall to win the 1957 British Grand Prix and Collins had handed his Ferrari to Fangio in the 1956 Italian Grand Prix to enable the great man to secure the title.

The change from dope fuel to aviation fuel was of more immediate concern to teams. Ferrari supported the switch and declared themselves ready for the first Grand Prix of the season, in Argentina, on 19 January. But the uncertainty over the status of the race – Championship or not – and the conversion work required to the engines threw Vanwall's plans. They would simply not be able to make Buenos Aires.

It seemed that Moss, runner-up for the previous three seasons, was up against it even before the off, but Rob Walker (a man we shall hear much more of) offered him a drive in his 2-litre Cooper Climax. Moss gratefully accepted the car and the services of mechanic Alf Francis, another of the characters of the day. Brooks and Lewis-Evans had to sit it out.

Only ten cars made the grid of the 2.4 mile No. 2 course at the Buenos Aires Autodrome. Fangio, on the verge of retirement, and Carlos Mendi-teguy had 1957 works Maseratis. There were also Maseratis for Behra, Schell, Godia and the Briton Horace Gould, three Dino 246 Ferraris for Hawthorn, Collins and the Italian Luigi Musso, and Walker's Cooper completed the field.

Hawthorn was in optimistic mood. He had not won a Grand Prix in 1957 but the prospects for 1958 looked brighter. He was much impressed with the new car, named in memory of Ferrari's son Dino, who had died after a complicated illness at the age of twenty-four. Fangio's expected retirement later in the year was another source of encouragement. Back home there had been considerable conjecture about a Hawthorn–Moss duel for the title and Hawthorn was fully aware of the threat posed by his compatriot – but not here in BA, not with the little Cooper.

Qualifying gave no indication that Moss and the Cooper might confound Hawthorn's calculations. Moss' task was made no easier by a damaged eye, the result of a little larking about with wife Katie. He had to wear a patch over the eye, which was causing him considerable discomfort. Moss managed only seventh fastest time. Fangio took pole, and Hawthorn and Collins would be alongside him on the front row.

Men and machines were spared the usual intense heat of Buenos Aires on race day, though for Collins it didn't matter anyway. He broke a half-shaft on the line and was instantly out of the contest. Behra was away first, followed by Hawthorn, Fangio and Moss, who made a good start. Moss' progress was soon hindered, however, by what he thought was a jammed gearbox. What he had, in fact, was a broken clutch but as he was about to pit a stone flew up into the mechanism and opened it up for him.

Hawthorn should have suspected right there and then that his rival was to have a charmed race. Moss' advance was irresistible. He climbed up to third place, behind Fangio and Hawthorn, who had led only to be hampered by a locking offside front wheel. Moss went ahead of Hawthorn and took the lead when Fangio stopped for fuel and tyres.

Moss planned to go the distance on the same rubber and he was relieved when Fangio began to slow rather than mount a challenge in the second half of the race. He could not afford to give his tyres any brutal treatment. Now the main danger was Musso.

Moss, seeing and feeling the wear on his tyres, carefully picked out the oily stretches of road and avoided wheel-spin. He had to conserve his tyres, because he couldn't change his wheels, which had 5-stud fixing.

His strategy worked perfectly. He crossed the line 2.7 seconds in front of Musso. Hawthorn was third, a further ten seconds behind. Moss had

ridden his luck and ridden it quite beautifully. It was the first World Championship victory for a Cooper and the first for a private entrant. It was a victory that stunned everybody, not least Ferrari.

Well done mon ami, mate . . . Hawthorn and Collins, Silverstone, 1958

There were angry scenes in the Italian camp as Musso was summoned to explain why he hadn't stepped up his pace and put more pressure on a car rapidly losing adhesion. His response was that he had been given no signals from the pit and that the team were preoccupied with Hawthorn's situation – all of which was naturally denied.

The Grand Prix was traditionally part of an Argentine racing festival called the *Temporada*. Before the next event, the sportscar race, the three Ferrari drivers took a trip to Uruguay. The fair-skinned Hawthorn returned with sunburn and suffered during the race. It was no fun for Musso, either. He crashed. Collins' victory was some consolation for his Grand Prix disappointment.

Hawthorn sought soothing female company during the second interlude. He recorded, in his book *Champion Year*: 'I met a very nice Argentine girl who had a Cadillac and she drove me to and from the circuit. Martha Pristerini, I think her name was. She had a little penthouse flat with the smallest swimming pool ever. You dived in and hit your head the other end immediately, all in one movement – no trouble at all.'

Meanwhile, back at the track, the series was completed with the City of Buenos Aires Grand Prix, a grand title for what was, in reality, an open free-for-all. Hawthorn steered clear of the 'Specials' and won the first heat. Moss, who looked a good bet in the wet, was not so fortunate this time. He was bumped off by an over-zealous local driver in a Chevrolet. Hawthorn's luck ran out in the second heat. Fangio won it and took the overall race.

All thoughts, though, were on the Formula One World Championship and the deliberations of the sport's governing body. Would the points from Argentina count, or wouldn't they? The RAC found themselves in a tricky situation, since they had protested on behalf of Vanwall and BRM, the British teams who said they had insufficient notice of the Argentine race. But now Moss' victory was at stake. Vanwall inevitably withdrew their appeal and when BRM did likewise the problem was effectively solved. Moss had his eight points, Hawthorn had four.

There was a four-month gap between Argentina and the next World Championship race in Monaco. Time enough for Vanwall to prepare their cars, for the drivers to earn a few bob in other races, to go partying, or, in Moss' case, to install a heating tank at his house in Nassau. There was time enough, too, for a bizarre incident in Cuba. Moss was among those who turned up on the island for a sportscar race. Fangio was also due to compete, but was kidnapped by rebels supporting Fidel Castro. They wanted to draw attention to the plight of the half million who were un-employed at a time when the government were putting money into motor racing. Fangio was released unharmed after the race, which was won by Moss.

There was also time to be reminded of the extreme dangers of motor racing. Archie Scott-Brown, the gutsy Scot, died after his Lister-Jaguar crashed in the Belgian Sportscar Grand Prix at Spa and burst into flames. Continental race organisers had been reluctant to accept his entry because of his disability.

Joy and sadness were never far apart. Moss, Hawthorn and Collins had successes during that spring. Collins also had his usual fine for speeding in America, and Hawthorn jumped into Collins' bath with his clothes on! That was all part of the game in the 1950s.

At last the scene switched to Monaco. The Principality brings out the best and worst in people. Vanity comes to the surface as glaringly as the boats in the harbour. Even for those with no interest in motor racing, the sense of occasion has an irresistible appeal. For the drivers it is a unique challenge. In 1958 the track was a little under two miles in length (today it is a little more than two miles). Then, as now, it was tight, twisty and un-forgiving. Many drivers, including some of the best, have hated the streets of Monte Carlo. Many, again including the best, have been caught out here. In 1957 Moss' Vanwall went straight on at the chicane, and Haw-thorn and Collins were ensnared by the debris.

For the 1958 Monaco Grand Prix Moss had his modified Vanwall, and two more of the cars were ready for Brooks and Lewis-Evans. Ferrari had four cars. Wolfgang 'Taffy' von Trips joined Hawthorn, Collins and Musso. The second practice session started at 5.45 a.m. on Friday which, as Hawthorn observed drily, was 'a convenient time if you happened to want to watch on your way home from one of the Monte Carlo night clubs'.

Moss was more concerned with his car. He was happier with Brooks' and, as No. 1 driver, felt entitled to have his engine put into his partner's car. The team resisted his demands and Moss found his own car rather more responsive on the Saturday. He made the third row of the grid with Lewis-Evans and Hawthorn. The other Ferraris were considerably slower. Brooks' Vanwall was on pole.

Salvadori led the charge into the Gasworks Hairpin but was a casualty of the familiar bumping and barging. Behra and Brooks went clear, soon to be tracked by Hawthorn and Moss. A spark plug unscrewed and cut short Brooks' race, while brake trouble forced Behra into the pits. Now it was a Hawthorn–Moss head-to-head. Moss took the lead and set a lap record, only for Hawthorn to improve on the time.

On lap thirty-eight their duel ended. Smoke from the Vanwall's exhaust signified that Moss was in trouble and he duly retired. Before half-distance Hawthorn, too, was out. The Ferrari's fuel pump had dropped off. Hawthorn found consolation on his way back to the pits: 'Walking past the hotel near the station I looked up into one of the rooms and a lovely blonde girl looked out. I stopped and asked if she had a glass of water. She asked me to come in and I climbed through the window. I had my glass of water, several of them, and then returned to the pits in a much better temper.'

Moss the victor . . . 1958
Dutch Grand Prix

Hawthorn's colleagues Musso and Collins were now second and third respectively behind Frenchman Maurice Trintignant – in Rob Walker's Cooper. The Ferraris made ground but the Cooper was never under serious pressure. Walker had his second win in two races. Musso had another second place and that was enough to take him to the top of the Championship.

Collins and his wife Louise threw a party on their yacht in Monaco harbour that evening and Ferrari's two Englishmen joined the inevitable pilgrimage to the Tip Top Bar. 'I cannot recall who was there,' said Hawthorn, 'but my definition of a memorable party is one that I don't remember.'

Hawthorn had to gather his thoughts for racing again. The next Grand Prix was at Zandvoort, the Dutch seaside resort, just eight days later. He was in optimistic mood. The faster circuit would, he believed, suit the Ferrari, while the Vanwall didn't appear as menacing as the Italian camp might have feared. That view changed during practice. Lewis-Evans claimed pole, and Moss and Brooks completed Vanwall's front row takeover. Hawthorn was again on the third row.

A chill wind welcomed the drivers to the first Championship race around these sand dunes for three years, and Moss seemed to be caught on it as he flew into the lead from the start. Both Brooks and Lewis-Evans ran into problems, leaving Moss alone to fend off the BRM of American Harry Schell. This he achieved with some authority. He also compounded Hawthorn's misery by lapping the Ferrari. Worse still for Hawthorn, he was also lapped by the BRM.

Moss took the race, and an extra point for fastest lap. British cars had their third successive win and Moss showed every sign of tracking down that elusive Championship, Hawthorn's wickedly-handling car could manage only fifth. A season of promise was crumbling around him. He went home to express his dissatisfaction in a letter to Enzo Ferrari.

Hawthorn looked to the sportscar race at the Nurburgring, his favourite circuit, for some relief. The old track threaded through Germany's Eifel Mountains for more than fourteen miles, its 187 corners providing a constant test of a driver's skill and concentration. Moss, eager as ever, was down and ready for the Le Mans-style start, only to see Hawthorn pound across the road before the off. Moss screamed, 'You bastard, Hawthorn,' but the joke backfired on his compatriot, who was giggling so much he fluffed his start. Moss was magnificent, driving the Aston Martin for thirty-six of the forty-four laps (his partner was Jack Brabham) and comprehensively beating Hawthorn, who was thankful to get his Ferrari going again after a spin.

The British Racing Hero

Awaiting Hawthorn on his return home was Ferrari's reply to his letter. The Old Man assured him much time and effort had been put into improving the car. That, he hoped, would be apparent in the next race, the Belgian Grand Prix. Some alterations had been made to the Spa circuit since the previous Championship event, in 1956, and the organisers had achieved their objective of eclipsing Rheims and making it the fastest track in Europe.

For 1958 this was the race accorded the title *Grand Prix d'Europe*, though the organisation hardly merited it. Hawthorn took pole but, much to his unease, found himself on the left side of the grid. From the start the track plunged down the hill and into a left-hander, so clearly the advantageous line was from the right. That privilege had been given to Moss, who was third fastest. Hawthorn made his point and the two Englishmen were switched. Between them was Musso.

That was not the end of the pre-race confusion. For reasons beyond the comprehension of the drivers, the starting procedure was prolonged to the point where cars and tempers alike were steaming. Collins' Ferrari was lost in a cloud. When they finally burst away Hawthorn was too concerned with his temperature gauge. Moss, typically, was unrestrained. He was away in the lead, followed by Brooks as he dipped left into Eau Rouge and swept right up the hill. But going through Stavelot Moss missed fifth gear, his revs launched and his car was crippled. The Vanwall limped back to the pits. Moss was out.

Brooks took over the lead, yet was soon challenged by Collins. Smoke appeared from the Ferrari, however, and it was the beginning of the end for Collins. Musso's race was also cut short. He had a lucky escape when a tyre blew and sent his Ferrari careering off the track. Brooks opened up a sizeable gap. Hawthorn was second, Lewis-Evans third. It stayed that way to the end, despite a charge by Hawthorn that yielded fastest lap.

All three were grateful to reach the line. Brooks' gearbox was jamming, Hawthorn's car blew coming out of the hairpin for the last time and Lewis-Evans' right wishbone had broken. The first healthy car home was the Lotus of Cliff Allison. That fourth place was a firm warning to Ferrari, Vanwall and the rest that a new force would be shaking motor racing in the not-too-distant future.

Meanwhile, 15 June 1958 was another day for the Vanwall team and for Tony Brooks in particular. He had shared victory with Moss in the 1957 British Grand Prix but now he had his first 'solo' success in the World Championship – and Spa was a fitting scene. He had won three successive sportscar races here, the fast, sweeping circuit suiting his smooth,

fluent style. He won the Grand Prix at an average speed of 129.93 m.p.h.

A word in your ear, old mate . . . Moss and Hawthorn

He says: 'I'm torn between the Nurburgring and Spa as my favourite because they are both great circuits. They both give the driver great satisfaction, they both provide tremendous challenges. But going round Spa is like poetry in motion. Especially with a decent car. The Nurburgring didn't have the broad corners that you could throw the cars into. You didn't have the sort of rhythmic swing you had at Spa. Yes, Spa was a great circuit.'

Hawthorn's second place and the extra point for that frantic last lap pushed him up to fourteen points and second place in the Championship. Moss led with seventeen. Hawthorn was more content, but not satisfied. Four races into the season Ferrari still did not have a win.

Before the next Formula One Championship race, the contenders had dubious diversions. At Le Mans, Moss blew up and, deep into a wet night, the sick Hawthorn–Collins car also retired. Hawthorn was none too distressed. It was, in his opinion, the most dangerous event on the calendar. Neither Hawthorn nor Moss was happy about the prospect of competing in the Europe–America Monza 500-mile race on the banked circuit. An assortment of unconvincing 'specials' lined up to take on the Indianapolis cars. Moss' worst fears were confirmed in the third heat.

Moss calmly recalls what happened when the steering of his Eldorado-backed Maserati sheared: 'I was going round the banking flat-out at 165 m.p.h., about five or six feet down from the Armco. Suddenly my arms crossed. There was nothing I could do. I thought that was the end. I was sure I was going to go over the top. You see the Armco coming towards you and think it can't be strong enough to stop you. It was. It threw me back down, I spun, lost a wheel or two and was shaken, but really wasn't hurt apart from a few cuts.'

Hawthorn had a share of third place and an aching body at the end of the ordeal. The two great rivals were in agreement: it would be good to get back to Grand Prix racing.

They were rivals, but friends too. Drivers of their generation socialised together, threw parties, lived for the moment. Perhaps the perils of their racing served as a bond that is nowhere near so strong in the modern sport. After a night out at the Crazy Horse Saloon in Paris, the rivals drove together down to Rheims for the French Grand Prix, a race that would underline those perils.

Hawthorn reckoned the acceleration of the Ferrari might prove decisive, and practice reinforced his theory. So did the 300 bottles of champagne he earned. He was on pole and Musso was also on the front row, while Brooks and Collins were on the second. Moss and Fangio, making his farewell Grand Prix appearance, were on the third row.

Hawthorn took an early lead and held it, with immense conviction, for the duration of the race. Moss emerged from the squabble behind to take second place. Hawthorn's third Championship victory – and his first for four years – had given him joint top place in the table. But for Hawthorn and Ferrari this was not a joyous occasion.

Hawthorn recorded what happened as, ten laps into the race, Musso pursued him through the fast right-hander beyond the pits: 'I looked into my mirror to see if I had gained anything on Musso. To my horror I saw him sideways across the road. Then he disappeared backwards and out of my view. A great cloud of dust went up and that was all I saw. There was nothing I could do but press on.

'Next time round I saw the helicopter flying over – a little one carrying two stretchers on the outside – and I could see the place where Luigi had gone off. I could not see the car, which was hidden in the cornfield beside the track. I was terribly worried. I remembered his crash at Spa and how he got away with that. I just hoped he had been lucky again.'

It was a hope shared by everyone, but when Hawthorn and Collins went to the hospital their colleague was dead. The great Italian line of succession had ended. Musso carried an enormous burden of responsibility on his shoulders and that, ultimately, probably proved too much.

The Championship was perfectly poised for the British Grand Prix at Silverstone: two home drivers sharing the lead on twenty-three points. Their 'rivalry', enhanced by their contrasting characters and physical appearances, made good newspaper and magazine copy. It all amounted to good business. The country braced itself for the Hawthorn–Moss showdown.

Hawthorn was apprehensive. His Ferrari was a handful in practice and he feared that in reality it would come down to a Vanwall–BRM duel. The ever faithful Collins offered to risk his own car by setting a hot pace in the hope that the Vanwalls would take up the gauntlet and blow up in the process – anything to help his pal win the title.

Moss was entitled to be confident. He had pole position for the Grand Prix and warmed up for the main event by winning the sportscar race in a

Lister-Jaguar. Out of the first corner, however, he was perplexed to see the disappearing rear of Collins' Ferrari. True to his word, Collins surged ahead and, just as expected, Moss chased him. Hawthorn settled into a comfortable third place.

On the twenty-sixth lap a broken connecting rod forced Moss out of the race. He drove straight into the paddock, tormenting himself with the thought that he might well be out of the Championship too. This should have been a Vanwall circuit. It was not, it was Ferrari's. Hawthorn was able to stop for oil and reassert himself in second place with the fastest lap. Salvadori beat Lewis-Evans in the splendid scrap for third place. The Moss–Hawthorn race hadn't materialised, yet British drivers occupied the first four positions in the British Grand Prix.

More important to Hawthorn was a seven-point advantage in the World Championship. He took the flag and instantly celebrated. He accepted a pint from the marshals stationed at Becketts and drank as he completed his slowing-down lap. Now when did you last see that? Hawthorn, and Collins, had a few more pints that evening. Moss had no time to drown his sorrows. The following day he ran in the non-Championship Caen Grand Prix and won the Formula One event in Rob Walker's 2.2-litre Cooper.

The battle for points resumed in Germany at the formidable Nurburgring. A shortage of engines limited Vanwall to two race cars, one for Moss, the other for Brooks. Ferrari had Hawthorn, Collins and von Trips. The pressure was on Moss. Not only did he trail Hawthorn by seven points, he was now only nine ahead of Collins and could not afford to ignore him.

The front row line-up heightened the tension. Hawthorn was on pole, alongside him Brooks, Collins and Moss. Brooks, however, felt ill-prepared to play a full part. He explains: 'I wasn't allowed to do much practice with Vanwall because if I did a quick lap Stirling would keep going

Bravo, Peter . . . Collins wins for Ferrari, Silverstone, 1958

round till he beat it! So David Yorke would try and keep me short on practice time as a general policy to save the cars. I was still wet behind the ears. What with school and university this real world was all foreign to me. I'd been brought up with the public school attitude that in sport it's the team that matters. I did resent it, but not too strongly. I just thought it would be nice to explore my full potential.

'Anyway, this had been one of those occasions when I hadn't been allowed out to practise with full tanks, so when I started the car was an absolute pig. You couldn't drive it quickly on full tanks – or at least I couldn't. So, in the early part of the race I was down on the leaders.'

Hawthorn had woken up early on race morning and, as was his wont, wandered along to Collins' room. They stayed at a hotel conveniently situated for the circuit. He wrote: 'Louise was already awake but Pete was still asleep, snoring his head off. I looked at him sleeping there and, for some reason, I felt happy looking at him. He is one that won't die, I thought. Then he woke and saw me standing there and swore at me for waking him!'

Collins had been preoccupied that weekend with a wooden puzzle he'd bought and an hour before the race had triumphantly announced its completion. Hawthorn said: 'I am glad he completed it. It had meant so much to him.'

Despite Collins' win at Silverstone, he again insisted that his intention was to help his friend win the Championship. Hawthorn was hopeful, too, and although the Vanwalls were quickly away, the Ferrari pair were soon able to take Brooks. As Moss was contemplating a rapid course to victory his engine suddenly stopped. A broken magneto had caused a short, which in turn cut off the power. The Ferraris were out in front, half a minute ahead of Brooks. As in 1957, though, Collins and Hawthorn came under attack. This time the assailant was not Fangio but the mild-mannered, 'wet behind the ears' Brooks.

Brooks takes up the story: 'As the tanks started to empty the car began to handle as it had in practice. The gap diminished and I overtook them round the back of the circuit, first Mike, then Peter. But as soon as we came to the straight again, which is quite long at the Nurburgring, Peter flew by. So what I had to do round the back of the circuit was to build up a sufficient lead so that when it came to the straight Peter would be out of my slip-stream and not be able to come up and get me. I was going like the clappers trying to get this lead. I got to about a hundred feet ahead.'

Collins was equally committed as he strained to stay in touch. According to Hawthorn: 'He was driving as well as he had ever driven. But then he put his foot right down in the heat of the moment and did not turn into the corner early enough. When he did turn, it was obvious that he was going too wide. The car slid, drifting out. His back wheel hit the bank and the car lifted. God, I thought, the silly fool, we're both going to be involved in this. I thought he would spin off the bank across the road and I would hit him.

'I was just thinking up some choice words to say to him as we climbed out of the two bent Ferraris when, without the slightest warning, fantastically quickly, his car just whipped straight over. I could not believe that it had happened. There was a blur of blue as Pete was thrown out. I put the brakes on hard and almost stopped as I looked round. I saw the car bounce upside down in a great cloud of dust before it came to rest.'

Hawthorn was in a state of anxiety and confusion. He felt he should do something, but what? If he stopped at the pits to tell the team it would only fill Louise with fear – perhaps unfounded fear. He decided to go round again. He drove past the pits but about three miles on his car failed him. He asked marshals to contact the pits and inquire about Pete. They were told he was not seriously hurt.

Hawthorn sat out the rest of the race where he was. He was given a drink and a cigarette, but best of all was the news of his friend. The race belonged to Brooks, yet to Hawthorn that did not matter at all. He was given a lift back to the pits and, at the scene of the accident, asked the German driver to stop. The Ferrari was upside down. By it was his friend's crash helmet, a shoe and a glove. Red Cross people gave him contradictory reports. One said Pete was badly injured, another that he had merely broken an arm. Now he did not know what to believe.

He persuaded police officers to let him take the helmet, shoe and glove to the pits. His friend had been taken by helicopter to Bonn, so he stayed in his hotel waiting for news. When it came, it wasn't good. Peter was seriously injured. Hawthorn gathered his and the Collins' bags and was driven on the long, tedious journey to Bonn by Harry Schell. They arrived to be told that Hawthorn's 'ami, mate' Pete was dead. 'Louise was being very brave,' said Hawthorn. 'There was nothing to say. It would not have done any good if there had been. Pete was gone.'

The deaths of Musso and Collins inevitably led to widespread press and public debate about the safety and morals of motor racing. From some quarters, including the Vatican, there were calls for an end to the sport. The drivers, on the other hand, responded much as they always respond. All of them – Hawthorn, Moss, Brooks and the rest – knew their friends and colleagues died doing what they wanted to do. If they stopped racing it would not bring them back. They accepted the risks yet each comforted himself with the belief that he minimised those risks.

Collins' death obviously overshadowed Brooks' marvellous drive that day: 'When I heard that Peter, a friend of mine, had been killed it took the enjoyment out of it. Worse still, poor Peter lost his life chasing me.'

The show went on, just as it always went on. Vanwall had again upstaged Ferrari, and Brooks had again played a leading role at a great motor racing theatre. He says, 'There was the satisfaction of having put together a good drive at the challenging Nurburgring after Vanwall's problems the previous year, and achieving the first British car-and-driver victory in the German Grand Prix.'

The next stage was a new one for Formula One: Oporto, Portugal. It was 4.66 miles of true road, complete with tramlines, cobbles, kerbstones, lamp posts and trees. Rain added to the hazards on race day.

Moss, Hawthorn and Lewis-Evans occupied the front row, Brooks was on the second. This, though, was not to be Brooks' show. He was never in contention and eventually had a spin and stalled. Hawthorn led during the early part of the race but had to give way to Moss as his brakes began to fade. He then lost second place to Behra's BRM as he stopped to have his brakes adjusted. Fortunately for the Englishman Behra, too, ran into problems. The Ferrari not only regained second place but also established a lap record.

Moss' pit immediately gave him the signal HAW-REC, which he misread as HAW-REG, or regular. He therefore maintained a controlled pace and even backed off to spare Hawthorn the indignity of being lapped. The Ferrari's brakes had almost gone again but as third placed Lewis-Evans had been lapped Hawthorn had only to negotiate the final tour to be second. It proved a troublesome task.

Hawthorn, furiously pumping his brakes and changing down, realised he could not make a corner and took the escape road. As he tried to turn the car he stalled. He jumped out to push the Ferrari and angrily swung at a Portuguese spectator who tried to help. That, of course, would have meant disqualification. Moss, on his lap of honour, witnessed his rival's struggle and shouted to him to push the car downhill. Hawthorn did so, got it going, and carefully completed the course.

By this time he had given up on any points yet, to his amazement, he was told he had six for second place plus an extra one for the fastest lap. A marshal, however, reported that he had pushed his car in the opposite direction to the circuit and was consequently liable to be disqualified. The stewards summoned Hawthorn and also heard Moss' version of events. Moss says: 'I gave evidence on Mike's behalf. I said he wasn't pushing his car on the actual circuit so he shouldn't be disqualified. They agreed and Mike got his points.'

Two years later the Portuguese Grand Prix was back at Oporto. Late in the race the brakes of Moss' Lotus failed and he stalled – at precisely the point where Hawthorn had been in trouble. Moss pushed his car downhill and was disqualified. No-one spoke in his defence and the decision stood. 'That's life,' he says.

Moss' remarkable gesture – remarkable by modern standards, anyway – had left him five points behind Hawthorn with only two rounds of the Championship remaining. Not that Hawthorn was feeling secure. He asked for disc brakes instead of drums to be fitted before the Italian Grand Prix. Ferrari agreed, and discs were switched from Collins' road car to support his friend's cause. Moss tried a Vanwall fitted with a perspex cockpit cover, on the first day of practice, though he decided not to persist with it. Both men were anxious to gain whatever advantage they could.

Moss took pole and was joined on the front row by Vanwall team-mates Brooks and Lewis-Evans, as well as Hawthorn's Ferrari. The title contenders were relaxed and in good humour, which was evident in the BBC interview they gave. That night before the race Moss was in bed as usual by ten, while Hawthorn was seen rather later drinking at his hotel bar. 'Stirling's approach to motor racing is no doubt the right one, but mine is much more fun,' he said.

Moss and Hawthorn were together again in the early laps of the race, slugging it out for the lead. But then the Vanwall's gearbox broke and the Ferrari was on its own, out in front. If it stayed there, the Championship would be Hawthorn's. It was not, alas, to be as simple as that. Hawthorn's clutch began to slip and there was nothing he could do to resist the advancing Brooks. Moss' Championship hopes were still alive thanks to his partner's third win of the season, but to take the crown he had to win

the last Grand Prix, in Morocco, and register fastest lap. At the same time he needed Hawthorn to finish no better than third.

British pride . . . Brooks and the Vanwall win the 1958 Italian Grand Prix

It was a tall order, made no easier by the five-week wait. Both men – one the fun-loving amateur, the other an assured professional – found the tension nearly unbearable. Hawthorn occupied himself working at the garage, judging a beauty contest and accepting an award of his own. The Guild of Motoring Writers voted him their Driver of the Year. Moss won the Tourist Trophy sportscar race at Goodwood and busied himself in his office. But it was a long, long five weeks and the two drivers were thankful to be heading, at last, for Casablanca. Hawthorn's nerves were not soothed, though, when he saw the Ferrari entry list. He had car No. 2, the American Phil Hill No. 4 and the Belgian Olivier Gendebien No. 6. Both Musso and Collins had had the No. 2 on their cars when they were killed. Hawthorn could not cope with that. He was given the No. 6 instead.

Casablanca's Ain Diab circuit measured 4.724 miles. It had some fast and tricky corners, and a straight that ran parallel with the Atlantic Ocean. Hawthorn was fastest through the sea mist to take pole position. Then came Moss, then Lewis-Evans.

The deciding Grand Prix race in the Formula One World Championship began amid chaos and fraying tempers. The race was delayed and then, as the starter waved a dead Cooper off the grid, the restless remainder took that as the signal for battle to commence. Moss, naturally, was away first, to be hounded by Hill's Ferrari. Hawthorn, sensibly watching and waiting, inherited third place when Brooks' Vanwall blew up.

Brooks had set out to support Moss, but Vanwall's attempt to improve his car rebounded: 'They'd put a slightly lower gear ratio in to try and get a bit more performance, but it proved no good because the engine went. In those days they didn't really consult me about that sort of thing. I would never have asked for that lower ratio.'

Moss knew then that his chances were remote. With Lewis-Evans well down, he had no-one to keep Hawthorn out of second place. All Moss could do was march on. Twenty-fourth time round he set the fastest lap.

He was heading for a maximum nine points, but it would almost certainly not be enough.

Fourteen laps from the end Hill dutifully moved over, gave Hawthorn the second place he required, and then covered his partner's back. Even now, with the Championship settled, tragedy would still darken this extraordinary season. Lewis-Evans crashed and his Vanwall ignited. He scrambled clear of the fireball only to run away from his would-be helpers. He died of his burns six days later.

The British Racing Hero

Moss says: 'Stuart was a tremendously good driver but he was too fast. I had a great job making myself take a corner flat out. Stuart would do it and if he found he went over the edge he'd do it a bit slower next time. I didn't have the courage to do that. He was very quick and had he been stronger he would have been quicker still.'

The frail Welshman's accident and Moss' disappointment hung over the Vanwall camp. They had flown the flag with distinction, becoming the first British team to win the Constructors' Championship. But this was a sour victory. Ferrari had lost two of their drivers yet here was another crossing the line in second place, to become the first British World Champion. Both teams had achieved success at a horrendous price.

Hawthorn was engulfed by Ferrari mechanics as he returned to the pits and Moss, whose sportsmanship in Portugal had effectively surrendered the title, graciously congratulated him. But this was not the feeling Hawthorn had dreamed about. The loss of his friend Pete had left him with an emptiness not even the Championship could fill. He decided this was the end of his motor racing career. Ferrari officials did not believe him – but he meant it.

He returned home to a hero's welcome and sacks of fan mail and invitations. Nothing could dissuade him, though. On 7 December he announced that a career which had started eight years earlier at the Brighton Speed Trials was over. He had fulfilled his ambition and wanted to go out at the top. 'Why have you retired?', he reasoned, was a much nicer question than 'Why don't you retire?'.

That, however, was not quite the end of the chapter. On 22 January 1959, Hawthorn was driving his 3.4-litre Jaguar towards the Guildford by-pass, bound for a lunch appointment. Travelling in the same direction was a 300 SL Mercedes, driven by Rob Walker. He recalls: 'I saw a Jaguar coming up behind me and had no idea who it was until he came along-side. We were absolutely dead level for a while, through all the gears, but I thought "this is my limit". It was pouring with rain and he was the World Champion, so I let him pass me.

'Mike's car suddenly went five degrees out, hit the kerb and did a complete circle. Then he went backwards, over the other carriageway.'

The Jaguar plunged off the road and hit a tree. Walker, meanwhile, was fighting his own car: 'I got mine to a standstill, having run over Mike's bumper. I ran over to his car and was going to say "that was a bloody silly thing to do, Mike," but he wasn't in the driving seat. I saw him lying full length in the back seat. His eyes were open and as I looked at him they just glazed over.

'I was told later that the wet tyres he had never gave a sign of when they were going to break away. They suddenly go. Like that.'

Mike Hawthorn was twenty-nine.

3

Who Needs a Crown?

Stirling Moss was in Bangkok when he was woken up at seven o'clock in the morning to be told of Mike Hawthorn's death. Moss, compatriot, friend and rival, was affected by a sense of loss as all motor racing folk were. The past year had been tragic enough. Luigi Musso, Peter Collins and Stuart Lewis-Evans had been killed in the quest for the World Championship; Archie Scott-Brown and Peter Whitehead had lost their lives outside Formula One. Now Mike – and like this, just when he had given up racing. The irony. The cruel, savage irony.

Moss tried not to dwell on the subject of death. It is part of the driver's defence mechanism: 'The only way you could cope with the number of deaths was to feel that it wouldn't have happened to you. You had to have complete confidence in your own ability. You had to know that you had kept a safety margin.'

But perhaps now, after Hawthorn's death, subconscious forces were at work. Certainly, he concedes, he began to develop a very diferent attitude towards the World Championship. For four consecutive seasons he had been runner-up, three times to Fangio and once to Hawthorn. Losing to Fangio was no problem. He was, after all, Moss reckoned, the greatest Grand Prix driver of them all. Fangio was almost thirty-nine when the Championship was launched and retired at the age of forty-seven. He won a record twenty-four races and five titles, an achievement that may never be matched.

Much as Moss liked and admired Hawthorn, he was not Fangio. Hawthorn won only three Grands Prix in his career. In 1958 he won one, compared with Moss' four and Brooks' three. Where was the reward for winning? What does the Championship mean? Moss could find no satisfactory answers. His perspective was changing. Moss says: 'At the time I was very upset because I did feel I deserved the Championship more than Mike did. I'd won more races and I was quicker than he was, but there you are. In hindsight, though, I'm very pleased I didn't get it. The only thing to do with the World Championship is to try and win it six times and be another Fangio, which I don't think I was. If you win it once, twice or three times you just become a year.

'If only Nigel Mansell would get his finger out I'd be the only one people say should have won it but didn't. At the moment Nigel and I are put together but when he wins it, as he must do, I'll still be the only one who never won it. It can be embarrassing and amusing because I'm often referred to as a former World Champion. A lot of people don't realise I never was.

'So, after 1958 I realised the Championship wasn't all that important. I was doing fifty-two races a year and the most important race I ever did was the one today. Not yesterday's, not the one next week, because today

I can get killed or I can win or I can lose. My reputation is on the line. Last week's has gone and next week's may not arrive. Even if it was only a small race at Brands it was still more important today than any other one.

'After I'd accepted that I hadn't got the Championship when I thought I should have, I realised what mattered was the respect of the other drivers as the person to beat. Today Senna is in the position where he is the one they want to beat because he is the fastest. To be in that situation is the best you can ask for.'

The British Racing Hero

In the late 1950s and early 1960s, Moss was the man they wanted to beat. The first concern for him, and for Brooks, in 1959, however, was to find a car. Tony Vandervell's machines had given them six victories in 1958 and won the inaugural Constructors' Championship. But Lewis-Evans' death deeply affected Vandervell and those close to him sensed that he had lost much of his appetite for the business. When Vandervell had a heart attack he made the decision to retire. Some voiced the opinion that the true reason for his withdrawal was the scheduled switch to 1500cc engines in 1961.

The upshot for Moss and Brooks was that they had to move on. Brooks, the 'third man' in that great Championship of 1958, had impressed Enzo Ferrari and received a call from Maranello. Moss was entrenched in his belief that British was best and private British was better still. He linked up with Rob Walker.

It is necessary here to paint a more vivid picture of Rob Walker, this privateer who dared take on the might of the factories and charmed the finest driver of the day into his comparatively modest stable. For that audacious stand and the capture of Moss alone he ranks as one of the remarkable individuals in British motor racing history. But there is more to him than that. Much more.

He had a privileged background, not least, he would consider, because his mother introduced him to the giddy world of racing at the age of seven. He recalls his first ride around a circuit – in a taxi: 'It was a very ill-advised thing to do because the taxi-driver got into the spirit of the thing and the circuit had melted quite a bit. We were going round in sort of four-wheel drifts and he was pointing out the different places where people had been killed. It was all very exciting to me. From then on I took an interest in motor racing.

'My mother gave me a car when I was ten. It was a Morris. A Bullnose Morris they called them. It cost her £10 and I think she was badly swindled. But it did go. We had a very long drive at our home in Wiltshire and I used to go up and down it. Then I went on to Austin Sevens, building up little racers. The second chauffeur was put to doing the work for me. I used to set my own record for going up and down the drive. I first competed in 1934, at speed trials at Lewis. My car blew up, of course.'

It was on his regular holidays in Paris that the young Walker became smitten with Delahayes: 'I got a trial run and it went through Paris very quickly – over 100 m.p.h. I was very taken by this.' He was positively seduced when he saw a beautiful creature of the racing variety up for sale. 'I happened to be walking down Park Lane and I saw it there. It was £400. Way above what I could spend. My total allowance was £360 and I had to pay my Cambridge fees out of that. So I learnt about hire purchase for the first time and walked out of the shop with my car. Without my mother knowing I entered it for Brooklands and I began racing there.'

In 1939 Walker took his Delahaye down to Le Mans for the 24-hour race. He was to partner Ian Connell, a driver of some repute. In fact Walker was to take on the lion's share of the work and become the toast of the French manufacturer. This is Walker's version of events that weekend: 'I started my first stint just as it was getting dark, so I thought I ought to wear a dark blue, pin-striped suit to be properly dressed for the affair. I drove until midnight. An exhaust gasket went and the exhaust was coming straight through the floorboards. Ian burnt his foot very badly and after four o'clock he couldn't go on. I had to drive for the rest of the race. I happened to have rope-soled shoes. I thought it was a good idea to drive in them. I jumped into a bucket of water and soaked my trousers and shoes. Daylight came and I changed into a check coat. I didn't have a helmet of any sort. Just goggles.'

As the factory Delahayes fell by the wayside French attention turned to the debonair Englishman: 'In the pit they were drinking champagne by the crate and suddenly, at about 2.30, they realised that this poor bugger was still out there. I was eighth and it was terribly hot. They thought he ought to be pulled in before the champagne ran out. So they called me in and while they re-fuelled and what have you, they gave me some champagne to go on with. Actually it was quite a long pit stop. Quite a few minutes. I had a couple of glasses of champagne and felt much better.

'I finished eighth, drove the car to Paris that night and went to a night club. All the boys who had been racing were there. We were drinking and what have you until eight o'clock in the morning.'

Walker gave up racing in 1940, a condition of his marriage. He agreed, reasoning that he wasn't really giving up anything. He explains: 'I was a Fleet Air Arm fighter pilot in the war. Things were pretty shaky then and I landed three hours before being married to Betty. I was given, with a lot of trouble, 48 hours' leave. I didn't think I'd ever see another motor race let alone drive in one so I willingly gave up. In fact, out of the 260 pilots who went on our three courses I think only twenty-five came out alive. Fortunately, I was one of them.'

His additional wedding vow limited him to hill-climbs and speed trials when he returned, but he yearned for the competition of the racing track. Management provided him with the right vehicle and took him into a career that was to stretch all the way to Formula One. Many of the leading drivers passed through his hands – Parnell, Rolt, Collins, Brooks, Brabham and, of course, Moss. Walker says: 'Reg Parnell's last racing was for me. He crashed at Crystal Palace and that finished his racing. He tried to beat Stirling and in those days he was not far off Stirling. Anyway, Reg stopped racing but he stayed with me. When Cooper brought out this little Formula Two car Reg told me I should buy one straightaway. He also said I should get Alf Francis.'

Walker had many drivers he admired, but Moss had him almost spellbound: 'We were at Goodwood with both the Formula One car and the Formula Two car. Stirling came up to me and said he wanted to buy a Formula Two car but didn't know whether to go for a Lotus or a Cooper. Could he try my Cooper? I said of course he could.

45

'They had a free-for-all at the end of the day and Alf, in fact, put Stirling in the Formula One car. Stirling went out, did one warm-up lap and then a flying lap. The circuit was full. There were MGs and goodness knows what else out there. Stirling came in after that one flying lap – he'd broken the out-and-out record. He didn't know it was the Formula One car. He was very, very impressed. So was everyone else.

'Stirling knew he was better than anyone else. And he *was* better than anyone else. He would race anything and he would be five or ten seconds quicker than anybody. Once, Pat, his sister, was with the Healey team practising at Silverstone and we were practising further up with the Formula One car. She came up to him and said he must try this car. She said these boys were so good, you wouldn't believe how quick they were. Stirling said he was busy but she kept on at him until he said "oh, all right". He went down to the Healey and was seven seconds faster than their quickest driver.

'This was always happening. People would go up to him and ask him to try their car, and he used to drive some terrible bangers. I remember in America he drove a dreadful thing but he was ten seconds quicker than anybody else. If Stirling didn't win a race it had to be my fault because the car wasn't right. He had five races at one meeting. He won three and had problems with the car in the other two.

'Tony Brooks was a magnificent driver but he was one of the last amateurs. He was an absolute natural, but if Stirling was in the race Tony would always sit behind him. If Stirling dropped out Tony would take the lead. And that was Tony. He just hadn't got that . . . whereas Stirling was a racer. He had to be first every time.

'Mike Hawthorn didn't drive for me but he was a good friend. Again he was an amateur. He used to drink a lot and party a lot. He'd have his very fine days when he was really good, but then he'd have his bad days. Stirling was quite different. He was a complete professional. He was also a tremendous friend and very loyal. He was committed to the team. The nicest thing he used to say was that I wasn't only a super boss but a really good friend.

'I couldn't tell Stirling anything. I learned from him. I was the go-between for Stirling and Alf and stopped them fighting. I provided the money for the team and saw that it was generally properly run. I would never tell Stirling anything, though. I would show him a pit sign and from that he would run his own race. I would never tell him to go faster or slower or anything like that.

'The importance of the driver was far greater then than it is now. We'd set up the car but it didn't really make any difference to Stirling. Sometimes he would have his own ideas that Alf wouldn't agree with. But Stirling's ideas would work because he'd make them work. He would just drive faster. In practice if anyone went faster than him he'd just jump in the car and go faster still.'

Moss' commitment to Walker's stable made, the task was to sort out the equipment for 1959. Walker negotiated a deal for a BRM-engined Cooper, to be constructed at Dorking. The new car wasn't ready for the Easter meeting at Goodwood, so Moss had his Cooper fitted with a 2½-litre Coventry Climax engine – and won. Moss tried the Cooper-BRM

Grand alliance . . . Moss and Walker

in practice for the Monaco Grand Prix but still was not happy with it. The car would not feature in his World Championship campaign after all. He would start his title trek with the Cooper-Climax.

Moss took pole position with the Climax but Behra's Ferrari beat him into the Gasworks Turn and frustrated him for twenty-two laps. Moss eventually had him going up the hill and built a comfortable lead only to be put out of the race by transmission trouble. It was to prove an all-too-familiar fate. Brabham's works Cooper stayed the course and he claimed victory. That would also prove an all-too-familiar feature of the season as far as the British boys were concerned. Brooks had a useful second place in the Ferrari and at least the Walker camp had a third place, delivered by Trintignant.

Moss made the front row of the grid again for the Dutch Grand Prix at Zandvoort but also there, ominously, was Brabham. Moss recovered from a sloppy start to work up to the front. Once more, however, his gearbox broke and he was left empty-handed. Brabham kept going for second place behind Jo Bonnier, who gave BRM their first Championship victory.

It had been a miserable start to the season and the old 'Moss jinxed' line was being dusted and lifted. Worse still, he was having to contend with

47

the 'Is Moss a car-breaker?' debate. The accusation hurt Moss and angered Walker. The team had faced a dilemma over the gearbox and decided to use the Colotti because there was little or no option. Moss recalls: 'The reason we had a Colotti was that Cooper wouldn't let us have one of theirs. The Colotti gearbox was a fabulous box made of very bad material. The accusations of being a car-breaker were very hurtful because I really didn't think I was. I don't think I deserved that. I think the fact that I could do 1000 kms at Nurburgring or the Mille Miglia and so on and finish with a decent car is proof enough. It hurts because if I hadn't been leading it wouldn't have meant anything.

'I said to Rob at Zandvoort the following year that I was fed up with all this and would follow Jack Brabham. So I followed Jack and what does he do? He runs over a paving stone, I collect the damage and burst my front tyre. I have to stop and change it. I told myself it was my own bloody fault. I should have played my own game. I'd listened to the things people were saying, that I was a car-breaker and so on and look what happened backing off. It was a lesson to me. I was a racer not a driver. That was a big difference.'

Walker: 'This car-breaker business was nonsense. He would have won the Championship easily if it hadn't been for this awful gearbox trouble we had. The gearbox broke time and time again when Stirling was comfortably in the lead. That wasn't down to Stirling at all. If the material had been good enough there wouldn't have been a problem. I was very sorry for Stirling because the things that were being said were totally unjustified.'

Walker felt, in fact, that he couldn't allow the situation to go on. He advised Moss to drive another car while he attempted to solve the problem. Moss switched to BRM for the French and British Grands Prix.

At Rheims, though, his luck was not to change. He was chasing second place when he stalled and, exhausted in the severe heat, settled for a little outside assistance. That meant automatic disqualification. This was Brooks' day. He was commanding from the start and strengthened his Championship prospects with a fine win ahead of team-mate Phil Hill. The consistent Brabham was third.

Brooks was soon to suffer a setback, however. Ferrari, confronted with strike action, withdrew their cars and Brooks had to take a Vanwall to the British Grand Prix at Aintree. He qualified well down the grid and Moss could manage no better than the third row. Brabham had pole. Brooks was never in the contest but Moss found himself chasing leader Brabham. He stopped for fresh rubber in the hope of applying more pressure and again for fuel, but the Australian stayed beyond reach. He had taken an important step towards the Championship.

British motor racing lost another driver and another friend that summer of 1959. Ivor Bueb crashed in a Formula Two race at Clermont-Ferrand and never recovered from his injuries. He appeared in only a handful of World Championship Grands Prix but regularly competed with the likes of Moss and Brooks in other events, and was one of the most popular drivers of the time.

Just hours before Bueb lost his fight for life Frenchman Jean Behra was killed in a sportscar race at the German Grand Prix meeting. The controversial Avus track – two parallel stretches of autobahn linked by a hair-

Opposite page

Above: Collins steers his Ferrari to third place in the 1957 French Grand Prix

Below: Clark on the victory trail, 1963 Dutch Grand Prix

pin and a brick-built, banked curve – had replaced the Nurburgring on the Championship calendar and Behra's death confirmed the drivers' fears. His Porsche lost grip and went backwards over the edge.

Against the backdrop of this double tragedy Moss and Brooks attempted to revive their title hopes. Brooks' Ferrari was on pole, Moss, back with the Cooper-Climax, alongside. Also on the front row were Dan Gurney's Ferrari and Brabham's Cooper-Climax. The contest would be over two heats.

Throughout the event Brooks was in imperious form. He established an early lead, holding the pack of Coopers at bay, and went on to win both heats. Moss made an early exit from the proceedings – yet another gearbox failure had scuppered his chances. It had not been a good weekend for him.

Moss desperately needed a change of fortune in the Portuguese Grand Prix, held for the first time on the Monsanto circuit near Lisbon. Brooks and the Ferrari contingent were much less effective on this track and Moss led a Cooper line-up on the front row. Moss was also in front from the first lap of the race and won with ease. Once Brabham had gone off he was able to nurse his car home and not endanger his first Championship success of a largely frustrating season.

Moss was buoyed, too, by a stirring sportscar win at Goodwood. It secured the world title for Aston Martin and broke Ferrari's hold on the Championship. Brooks was unable to resist the takeover but sought consolation in the Italian Grand Prix at Monza, where he headed a five-man Ferrari team. With two races left, the top of the Championship table read: 1st Brabham, 27 points; 2nd Brooks, 23 points; 3rd Moss, 17½ points.

The contenders duly assembled on the front row, with Moss fastest. Seconds into the race the contenders were down to two. The Ferrari's clutch had gone. Brooks: 'At the end of practice there had been a smell of brakes or clutch linings burning, probably the former as I had been working hard to get within a tenth of a second of Stirling's time. Ferrari decided to put in a new clutch, which was not bedded in. I got on the startline and moved 100 metres. That was it. My race was over.'

For Moss and Brabham it had only just begun. Moss led, followed by Phil Hill's Ferrari, then Brabham. Soon Hill launched a Ferrari attack but both Moss and Brabham figured they did not have to worry too much because the Maranello squad would surely have to stop for new tyres. One by one the Ferraris pitted and Moss found himself out in front. He rationed his rubber to win ahead of Hill and Brabham.

It meant a three-way contest in the final round of the Championship, the United States Grand Prix at Sebring, a full three months later. Brabham still led and victory would give him the title no matter what the others achieved. Moss would be champion if he won and set the fastest lap, giving him a slightly better chance than he had had in 1958. Brooks, now third, required not only the win but also failures from his rivals.

Moss was content with preparations for the decider in Florida. The gearbox now appeared to be reliable, suspension adjustments seemed to have improved the car and, after the nerve-racking experience of 1958, he had approached the build-up to this all-important race in a much more relaxed manner. If he became champion, fine. If not, it would not be the end

Who Needs a Crown?

Opposite page

Above: Hill completes his Monaco hat-trick, 1965

Below: Surtees and his Ferrari, 1966

of the world.

The opening practice skirmishes gave Moss a distinct advantage over Brooks and Brabham, though the Australian made ground by the end of qualifying. Schell was given the third place on the front row after a dispute over times. Despite Ferrari's protests, Brooks was pushed back on the grid. He should have sensed then that it was not to be his race or his Championship. He says: 'On the first lap von Trips, my team-mate, bashed me up the backside. I knew if I came in that was it. I had to win the race, but what if the car was unsafe? I'd promised myself I would never again drive an unsafe car. All these things were flashing through my mind and I had about a minute to decide. It was one of the most difficult decisions I ever had to make but I knew what I was doing. Those cars were quite strong as long as they received impact where it was intended, i.e. through the tyres, but if someone has knocked you at an angle you cannot be sure.

'So I made myself come in because I told myself I had not got the right, particularly now, as a family man, to take the risk of driving this car which may not be in a fit state to drive. In taking that decision I knew that I'd blown the Championship. I came in and they didn't find anything seriously amiss. I re-joined the race and ended up third, which of course was not enough.'

Fourth place was enough for Brabham. Moss established an early lead and the Championship came into sight – until the transmission broke. Walker blamed only the gearbox, but Ferrari was less understanding and sympathetic towards *his* English driver. Brooks recalls: 'I heard only secondhand, but I gather he did react against my decision that day. I think I saw Ferrari only twice: once when I signed and once when he came to practice at Monza. To Ferrari the race was everything, the car was everything. Drivers weren't supposed to be analytical. It was not for them to decide whether or not to take risks. His attitude, I think, was the schoolboy book attitude – win or bust and blow the consequences.

'So I think he probably reacted badly to my pit stop. The fact that there was no serious damage to the car didn't help. But that doesn't alter the situation. I didn't know at the time what state the car was in. I twice nearly killed myself trying to cope with mechanical defects in a car and if you don't learn a lesson from that . . . '

How, then, did he cope with the many deaths? The deaths of Peter Collins and Stuart Lewis-Evans, for instance? 'Obviously I was very sad, but my own confidence was never shaken. You see, I wasn't psyching myself up to produce my performance. I was fortunate to be a natural driver and whilst I tried my very best with the right equipment I never said "I'll stick my neck out" to try to be a little quicker. My intention was to stay on the circuit; I had no intention of flying off.

'Certainly motor racing is a risk. It's a question of where you draw the line. I wasn't prepared to take a totally unreasonable risk. It's like going beyond the limit on taking sleeping pills. I felt to take such a risk, to go into a corner or into a race thinking "I'm going to push myself to the point where I may finish up in a box" is going beyond that line. I believe some drivers had the attitude of mind – and I suspect some still do – that they were prepared to psyche themselves up and take serious risks whilst not mentally recognising the full potential consequences. To my mind that was taking unreasonable risk with a God-given life in what is only a sport. Risking life to save others, for example, is something else.

'I gave my all while I was behind the wheel. I would drive to the limits of my ability and that of the car. I wouldn't push harder for the audience because that would be loading the dice against me. I think some drivers had a go, on the British airfield circuits in particular, because they thought that if they got it wrong they could use the run off areas or escape roads. In the 1950s, however, as soon as they got to Europe, to the Nurburgring, Spa and the like, they were no longer serious competitors. I drove with the same attitude at Silverstone as at any other place. My intention was to go as fast as possible but to stay on the road.'

Brooks, like Moss, had taken a philosophical attitude towards the Championship. 'It almost seemed that I was fated not to win it. Motor racing is full of "if onlys" and bad luck, but if you run through the events of 1959 it really was a bit excessive.

'Ferrari didn't go to the British Grand Prix at Aintree that year because they had a strike, the first anyone could recall. Jean Behra and I had been first and second earlier in the year in the 200 race at Aintree so we at least had a good chance of some points as the car was very reliable. Then the Belgian Grand Prix at Spa was cancelled. I'd won every time I'd been to Spa and the Ferrari, of course, was made for that circuit. At Monza we had that business with the clutch and then, on top of everything, look what happened at Sebring. Nevertheless, we were only four points behind at the end of the season.

'So you have all this, all these incidents churning through your head and it does influence things. You think, maybe it's not supposed to happen, my winning the Championship. It was an unfortunate season. I can understand Ferrari's disappointment because we were capable of winning the Championship, but that's motor racing.'

Brooks left Ferrari at the end of 1959, but insists that his decision had nothing to do with events at Sebring: 'It was a difficult decision because Ferrari already had a 1½-litre car winning races and it was obvious to me that a Ferrari driver was almost certainly going to win the Championship in 1961 with the new 1½-litre formula. I finished up No. 1 driver at Ferrari so I realised I was giving up that very good chance.

'I enjoyed motor racing and was totally committed to it when I was driving, but it still wasn't all my life and I was beginning to look forward. I'd saved a bit of money from racing and if it wasn't going to be invested in a dental practice what else did I know about? It had to be cars. So I bought this small business, a garage, in December 1959. Well, four antiquated petrol pumps in Brooklands Road, Weybridge, to be more precise. It formed the basis of the business we have today. That's why I left Ferrari. I couldn't be based in Italy and start a business here. It was far too small to have a manager in. I had to run it myself. I realised what I was doing giving up Ferrari, putting my future and the business before motor racing, but I had a tremendous opportunity and an exciting offer from Tony Vandervell which would enable me to be based in England.'

In 1960 he signed to drive a sole rear-engined Vanwall, which was basically a Lotus with the 1958 engine. But then Vandervell decided not to race

51

the car, by which time all the other prime drivers had gone.

Brooks had won six races in the first half of his World Championship career and was runner-up to Brabham in 1959. Without a competition car, the second half of that career produced not a single victory. In 1960 he ended up driving a Yeoman Credit entered Cooper, apart from one race with a 1958 modified Vanwall. His best place was fourth, at Monaco. He scored a total of seven points and finished eleventh in the table. In 1961 he switched to BRM. He wound up the season, and his career, with third place in the United States Grand Prix at Watkins Glen, BRM's best result of the season, to double his tally and leave him tenth in the rankings.

'If you've ever tried driving last year's Grand Prix car this year, you'll understand what it was like driving that Cooper in 1960. And what's more, there was a dramatic technical step forward from the 1959 Cooper to the 1960 Cooper. Anyway, I put up with it and then went to BRM in 1961.

'You might think once bitten twice shy, but it sounded like a good car. It was supposed to be out for Monaco; instead it appeared for the first time at practice at Monza. That was the car I should have been driving all 1961 and in fact was the one Graham Hill won the Championship with in 1962. So the choice of car and team was right but the timing was somewhat awry!

'It was a disappointing two years on which to finish but then 1958 and 1959 had made me pretty philosophical. Stirling should have been champion in 1958 and I could have been in 1959. It's a travesty of justice that Stirling and I had seven wins between us in 1958 and the World Champion had one. The World Champion should be the guy who wins most races. Winning and coming anywhere else is as different as chalk and cheese.

'Mike was a great character and very good for the sport because he created interest in it when there was very little. But he wasn't, to me, a natural driver. You could say that developing his driving the way he did, and the way Graham Hill did, was more meritorious. But Mike wasn't in the same class as Stirling.

'It became clear to me that you could go on forever and still not get the right combination to win the Championship. I'd had five wins in fourteen months in 1958 and '59, but I needed to move the sequence a little. I had six wins in all and thought that in those days, when there were half as many Grands Prix per season as today, it was a fairly good score. There have now been five World Champions with the same number or fewer career wins. I thought I'd had a pretty good innings. I'd survived a very traumatic period in motor racing and I decided a good gambler quits while he's ahead. It would have been nice to have finished on a high in terms of results, but in terms of driving ability I knew I could still do it. Fastest lap in the 1961 British Grand Prix in the overweight BRM, with its secondhand Climax engine, was one of my major achievements, made possible only by the wet conditions.'

Apart from the philosophical, survival and business aspects, Brooks had a family to consider. He married an Italian girl, Pina, at the end of the 1958 season. They have raised five children and live in an elegant house within braking distance of the old Brooklands circuit. There are no photographs on the walls, no trophies on the sideboard or mantelpiece to flaunt his racing past. The pictures are of his family. 'There is more to life than motor racing and to me the quality of that life has been very important. I had to think of the business, which has gone well, and I had to think of the family. Many of my associates now know nothing about my racing career. We have a totally different life now.

'Stirling is still racing. He knows my view on that. I think it's a big mistake because people cannot see the real Stirling, the Stirling at his peak. But that's Stirling. He loves racing, whereas to me there were more important things.'

When the battalions regrouped for Formula One hostilities in February 1960, the sport had a pointer to the future, to the men and machines that would take over from Brooks and Moss, from Vanwall and Cooper. A rear-engined Lotus, driven by a Scot called Innes Ireland, made its first appearance in Buenos Aires, while Graham Hill's BRM joined it on the front row. On pole was the familiar figure of Moss in the Cooper-Climax.

Moss' pace and commitment were never in question, but that season the Championship drifted further from his reach. It opened with a shared third place in the Argentine Grand Prix, behind New Zealander Bruce McLaren's Cooper-Climax and Cliff Allison's Ferrari. Ireland's Lotus was a creditable and significant sixth.

Allison's second place gave him every right to look forward to a productive season. Instead he became a victim of motor racing's fickle nature. He crashed during practice for the Monaco Grand Prix and was put out of the Championship. (He was to crash at Monaco again the following year, and this time his career was over.)

Moss, now in a Lotus-Climax, ruled the streets of the Principality that weekend. He was fastest in practice and emerged from a chaotic, fluctuating race as the victor. He had given Cooper their first World Championship success in 1958, now he'd done the same for Lotus.

The new combination was quickest again in the scramble for grid positions at Zandvoort, but this was where Moss discovered the frightening way that the safest place was out in front. He tracked Brabham for the early part of the Dutch Grand Prix, only for the Cooper to throw up a stone which burst a front tyre of the Lotus. The wheel buckled and Moss missed a tree by inches. With a new wheel and the old strategy, Moss surged up through the field to finish fourth behind Brabham, Ireland and Graham Hill.

At Spa, in practice for the Belgian Grand Prix, Moss was to endure a still more frightening experience: 'A front wheel came off at flat 140-odd. Luckily I managed to go in backwards. I was thrown out of it because we didn't wear seat belts. I broke my back and both legs. Even now I can remember I was on my hands and knees. I can remember the cars coming up and the engines cutting out. I couldn't see and I couldn't breathe either.

'I was worried a rib might have punctured my lung or my heart or something. All sorts of things were going through my head. I was on my knees panting. It was quite a hot day and from somewhere they got a blanket to keep the sun off me. Quite a few of the drivers came up to see me. But I couldn't see. Whether that was because I didn't open my eyes I

Who Needs a Crown?

don't know. I just remember being very worried about my sight.'

The forecasts of the doctors were almost as gloomy. He recovered his eyesight, all right, but was told he would be in plaster for months. Moss knew he had to write off the Championship for another year. Brabham won in Belgium (a race which claimed the lives of two young, inexperienced British drivers, Alan Stacey and Chris Bristow) and followed up with victories in France and Britain. But for Moss there was still a lot of racing to be done that season – and soon.

He was driving little over five weeks later and won his comeback race, a sportscar event in Sweden. He returned to the Championship arena in Portugal. He qualified on the second row of the Oporto grid. On pole was another driver we shall hear more about – John Surtees. A spin put Surtees out of the race and handed victory to Brabham. The title was once again the Australian's. Moss was disqualified after a repeat of the 1958 Hawthorn incident. The leading British driver with third place that day was a young Borders farmer called Jim Clark.

The British contingent boycotted the Italian Grand Prix in protest against the use of Monza's infamous banking, so for Moss and the rest there remained only the United States round at Riverside, California. Moss did not waste it. He took pole and won the final race for the 2½-litre formula. Ireland was second. Moss had third place in the Championship, behind Brabham and McLaren.

Moss would again be third in 1961, his last World Championship season. He had two victories: in the German Grand Prix at the Nurburgring, and at Monaco on the opening day. His win at the Ring was one of the great ones. He defied the power of the Ferraris with his own force, the force of the true racer. His win at Monte Carlo was, he unhesitatingly declares, his greatest.

Formula One's 1½-litre era had arrived and only Ferrari were truly prepared. Rob Walker's Lotus-Climax should have been no match for them, but Moss was more than a match. He outstripped them in practice and then pushed himself to the limits of his skill and courage to win the race. The kerbs, the buildings, the harbour, all must have appeared to be closing in on him like the three Ferraris as he weaved his majestic path, lap after lap after lap.

Moss recalls: 'I'd say, without a doubt, that was my best race. I had to drive flat-out for all but about eleven of the 100 laps. And I mean flat-out. For the first few laps I was happy to pace myself, but when the others started to speed up I felt I had to keep with the pack. I wouldn't normally have gone for the lead so soon but it seemed the right thing to do.'

Moss took the lead from Richie Ginther's Ferrari and braced himself for reprisals. He'd anticipated the ordeal and had the side panels of his Lotus removed for the purpose of ventilation. Now it was Moss against the pride of Maranello: 'I had to drive at ten tenths to stay out there, and even then I was convinced the Ferraris were going to get me. I thought they were just playing around. First Phil Hill was on my shoulder, then it was Richie. One would have a go, then the other. When it got to the last lap I thought "here we go, this is where they put their foot down and take me". From what I heard they were given signals by the Ferrari pits to "give all" but I managed to stay in front.'

Moss took the flag 3.6 seconds ahead of Ginther. Hill was third and von Trips, in another Ferrari, was fourth.

In 1962 Moss made up his long-standing differences with Ferrari. The Old Man told Moss he needed him and made, for Ferrari, a quite staggering offer. Moss: 'He said "tell us what you want and I'll build you whatever car you'd like".' Even then, Moss wasn't prepared to turn his back on the Walker stable: 'I said I wanted them to maintain it but for Rob Walker to run it and for it to be painted in Rob Walker blue. He agreed. He actually built it, painted it in Rob Walker blue and delivered it. But I never drove it.'

Moss never drove that Ferrari because of what happened shortly after his visit to Maranello. He was to compete in the traditional Easter Monday meeting at Goodwood: 'The last thing I remember is reversing out of the pub I used to stay at called The Fleece. I had a Lotus Elite. I remember the gates closing. I think that was on race day, but I'm not sure. I remember taking round Paul Bates, a polio victim. I think that was race day, but again, it might have been practice. The next thing I remember was coming to in the hospital, which, it turned out, was about a month later, and seeing this very cute girl I'd met at a party . . . '

A flag marshal at Goodwood that day, 23 April, was a starry-eyed sixteen-year-old who would go on to become one of Britain's most successful racing drivers. Derek Bell recalls: 'I was pushing a handicapped person round in a wheelchair and Stirling came to talk to him. I was breathing heavily because my hero was right there. Stirling was a tiger if anyone was a tiger.

'At that time the closest I could get to racing cars was waving the bloody flags. I was marshalling two corners before the accident. I was shattered by the accident. Stirling was badly injured but one didn't know how badly. When anything like that happens the stomach goes and you think "Oh, I can't take this".'

Moss crashed as he hacked away at Graham Hill's three-lap advantage. He'd lost a lot of time in the pits for attention to a troublesome gearbox (the gearbox again!) and had no hope of catching Hill. But he was a racer and he could still race, he could still put on a show. He broke the lap record and made up one of the three laps. He came up behind Hill at about 120 m.p.h. as they approached St Mary's Corner.

Hill, in his book *Graham*, wrote: 'I was leading the race comfortably, with Stirling still two laps behind me, when he flew past on the outside of a bend. Normally Stirling would never have attempted to pass anyone there, and as he overtook me he was already off the grass. Then, for no apparent reason, he just ploughed straight on into the bank. When he passed me he seemed to be completely out of control. Just what happened no-one will ever know – but I'm absolutely sure it wasn't due to driver error.'

As a devastated nation sought an explanation, driver error had to be considered. Even the greatest are not infallible. Another possibility was that the engine cut out. More likely, though, was a jammed throttle. Whatever the cause, the effect was horrific. He was trapped in the wreckage of the Lotus for forty minutes. He was unconscious and gravely injured. Not merely his career, but his life was in danger: 'They didn't tell

me at the hospital how long I'd been out or about my injuries. The doctors didn't want to tell me I was paralysed down one side because of the shock it might cause me. But my best friend David Haynes knew and he told me. He said I was paralysed on one side because I'd banged my head. I said "don't be stupid" because I'd never heard of a bang on the head affecting you like that. So he told me to move my fingers and of course I couldn't. I couldn't speak properly, either.

'Technically the accident was not as bad as the one in which I broke my back and legs, and I was convinced I was soon going to be back in a car. I kept thinking it will be soon . . . and soon . . . and soon. It was quite a few months before I began to realise it was really quite serious and that perhaps I wouldn't drive again. Eventually I had to write off that year, anyway.'

On 1 May 1963, just over a year after the accident, Moss returned to a deserted Goodwood to put himself to the test. He had to know whether he could go on racing. He drove a Lotus for a little over half an hour: 'I went round in quite a reasonable time but I can remember thinking it wasn't the speed that was wrong. What was wrong was my concentration. It had gone. What I did automatically before wasn't automatic anymore. It was a great effort to do a lap.

'I decided it wasn't feasible to go on racing. I was going to hurt myself. So I decided to retire there and then. It was awful to accept and yet not that difficult because I could see that what I needed wasn't there any more. It wasn't until a lot later that I thought I'd rushed into making the decision, that I should have waited until my concentration returned. But two or three years on they were racing completely different cars, slicks were coming in, there were different people around, it was a different sport. It was unfortunate but that was it. It had just happened.'

Moss' top level racing career ended at the age of thirty-two. He won sixteen Grands Prix, a record for an Englishman that was not to be threatened until Nigel Mansell's arrival in the front-line. In truth he never really retired, of course, and his fame has scarcely diminished with the passing years. Now turned sixty, he still attacks life with a zeal that would shame a man half his age. He has property interests, remains in constant demand for personal appearances and, to the disapproval of Tony Brooks and other valued friends, continues to compete in historic sportscar events and the occasional rally.

Sitting at his desk in the ground-floor office at his gadget-rigged home in Mayfair, he says: 'I know Tony and David and others have a point because obviously I am nowhere near what I was. At sixty I can't be the same as I was at twenty-five, but then neither am I, probably, at anything else! I still enjoy racing, though. It gives me the chance to meet people and I think I drive with reasonable competence.'

But now, these many years on, does he have any regrets about his decision to stick with British cars? 'I am an Englishman and that was the era when it was great to be English. British was best. The only regret, I suppose, is that I didn't have a go at Indianapolis, but at the time it wasn't feasible. I certainly don't wish I'd joined Ferrari earlier because the fun for me was competing, being the underdog, beating the odds. To me that was more rewarding.

'But motor racing gave me so much more besides. There was a great sense of fun and camaraderie. On one of my birthdays we were down at a place near Brands Hatch for a dinner-dance. Lots of drivers were there because we were all friends. This stunning girl called Yvonne came over to me and said she was my birthday present. I thought that was a pretty decent gesture by the boys. I mention that incident because it simply wouldn't happen now. At my first wedding all my six ushers were racing drivers. Today the drivers wouldn't even go, never mind be ushers. It's a great shame. I wouldn't swap my time for now.

'Motor racing opens an awful lot of doors because it is, I think, socially acceptable. I've got fifty-seven scrapbooks of my career. The black ones are social, the green racing, and I have more black books than green. I'm still busy, I'm glad to say. I use a scooter to get around London. Wouldn't live anywhere else. I like to be where the pulse is. To me movement is tranquility. To be outside waiting for something to happen is terrible. I've had a country cottage and once you've done the wallpapering and plumbing, what else is there to do?'

Moss realised early in his career, of course, that he could get not only a good life but a living out of motor racing: 'I *had* to make a living out of it because I couldn't afford it as a hobby. And if you are going to be paid to drive you owe it to the people who pay to produce a certain level of performance.

'In my best year I made £32,700 gross. With the same sort of success now I'd expect to be making something like £10 million, I suppose. But I wouldn't swap it because of the quality of life. I remember getting 25 per cent of the £200 starting money. That meant £50 every other week and £25 a week was enough to live on.

'I'd go to a restaurant and just order a main course and then buy fruit outside because I couldn't afford a three-course meal. When I was at Mercedes they gave me $20 a day expenses, which was good. You could live well on $20. They also gave me one dollar a day to have the car washed, so

I used to wash it myself and put the dollar in my pocket. All that was part of growing up. It was all part of the learning and the pleasure of that time.'

Many have tried to learn from Moss and he has always been ready with a word of advice or a guiding hand. He had only one man to look up to – Fangio, of course: 'I think it's a rub-off rather than learning. I followed him very closely. You can't learn that much, but perhaps something of where to position the car, what he's doing on braking, etc.

'I could never go up to Fangio and ask him if he was taking a certain corner flat out. There was a corner I wanted to know about at Nurburgring, at the end of the straight. You come over the brow and I never knew if he took it flat out. I wouldn't ask him. It would be like asking a master chef how he gets a certain taste. It just isn't done. I did ask him, though, much later. He said yes – but only once!

'It's very difficult to analyse drivers – British or foreign – and say what made them outstanding. Why was Fangio so good, why was Clark so good, why is Senna so good? The requirements can change with the changing demands of the time. You cannot just label drivers according to nationality. Fangio, for instance: an Argentine with an Italian background, but he's not excitable.

Stirling Moss . . . a racer and a professional

'I think determination has to be one of the qualities of the British driver. In Graham Hill you had a man who was by no means a natural driver. His skill as a driver was good but it wasn't great. Tony Brooks had far more skill. But Graham won two World Championships, and all credit to him. He got there by sheer graft and determination. To win races you need a feeling of balance, concentration, dedication, determination and stamina, the stamina to lap and race consistently.'

Moss developed a braking technique which enabled him to go into a corner deeper – and through quicker – than most. But bravery, he insists, was not part of his make-up: 'In all my races I can remember only about twice being what people would call brave. To my mind bravery and stupidity amount to much the same sort of thing.

'I can remember quite clearly that at Syracuse there was a very fast corner, about 135 m.p.h., and every time I came into this corner I'd lift slightly. A confidence lift. But I was sure I could get round without lifting so I forced myself. Just before I got to the curve I glanced at the instruments and by the time I looked up it was too late to lift. I would have got oversteer. It was calculated because I knew if I had the courage to do it, it was possible. But it was also pretty stupid. Normally I maintained quite a big safety barrier.'

We have heard much of the good life motor racing has brought Moss, but there has been a cost to his private life. Two marriages have been broken by the demands and circumstances of his profession: 'My first marriage, to Katie, was a victim of the sport because we had to live out of a suitcase. There was no home life. I met my second wife, Elaine, when I'd just had a crash and retired. I was doing PR work in America and seeing her on holidays. It was my mistake.'

Moss was still married to Katie when he met his third wife, Susie. She was then five. They have a son, Elliot. 'I hope he doesn't go into motor racing but discovers tennis or golf or something. But if he did decide to go into racing I wouldn't be stupid enough to try to stop him because I don't think you can. In fact I know you can't.'

4

Heirs Apparent

The last World Championship race of Stirling Moss' Grand Prix career was won by Innes Ireland. The first World Championship race after Moss' Goodwood crash was won by Graham Hill. British motor racing had entered a new era and was about to acclaim new heroes. The glorious years of Hawthorn, Brooks and Moss had gone and the sceptical doubted we would ever again see the like of them. Sporting dominance tends to move in cycles. Britain enjoyed phenomenal ascendancy in middle-distance running during the 1980s but it is totally unrealistic to expect every generation to produce a crop the equal of Ovett, Coe and Cram.

In the world of Formula One, however, Britons would reach even greater heights of achievement through the 1960s. Hill, Clark and Surtees would all be crowned champion, and by the end of the decade yet another British driver, Jackie Stewart, would be king. Britain ruled the tracks.

Innes Ireland was not, alas, destined to join the ruling classes. That victory in the United States Grand Prix at Watkins Glen was his only Championship success. Despite the fact that he had given Team Lotus their first win (Moss, of course, drove Rob Walker's Lotus) his services were not required by Colin Chapman for the following season. Chapman had decided to build his plans around Clark and give Ireland's seat to an Englishman, Trevor Taylor.

It is perhaps not surprising, then, that Ireland does not enthuse about his solitary Grand Prix triumph: 'Brabham and Moss were there with the V8 Climaxes and I had only a straight four, but luckily they both blew up and I was the guy left. I had to get myself back from being thirteenth because Graham and I had a coming-together and went off. Passing Graham was not an easy task. I also had to back off in the closing laps because I was dangerously low on fuel. There wasn't much else to remember that race for.'

The connections between Ireland and Clark went way back. Ireland's father, a vet, frequently visited the Clarks' farm and a friend, Alec Calder, was Jim's brother-in-law. Innes set out on his racing career in a Riley he bought from Alec: 'I'd wanted to race from the time I was about ten. I read a book called *Full Throttle* and from then on I wanted to race cars. Family friends had a couple of old Bentleys and I weaved my dreams around those two cars and Le Mans.'

Innes and Jim were, however, very different characters. Jim was quiet, shy, almost an introvert. Innes was, well, not so quiet, not so shy and certainly not an introvert. Many who have known him say he should have been racing a decade earlier. He agrees: 'Yes, I'm sorry I didn't race ten years earlier than I did. I would have loved to have started when Stirling was starting. He and I are more or less the same age [Ireland is the younger by nine months]. He was racing when he was eighteen but I

Innes Ireland . . . first winner for Team Lotus, 1961 United States Grand Prix

was twenty-six when I started. Even so, there was still plenty of fun and comradeship in my time.'

And Innes had fun. He was a keen patron of Scottish wines, and ever-ready to meet a challenge on or off the track: 'After a race in Austria we had a good old party and somebody challenged me to climb this clock tower in Judenburg. I got quite a good way up but then the police showed up. They were always showing up at the wrong time. They told me to be a good boy and go home.'

More recently Innes and his lady were attacked by muggers on Rio's Copacabana beach. Not being the kind meekly to hand over his valuables, he and his lady – an equally resilient opponent, wielding a high-heeled shoe – gave their assailants a scrap for their credit cards.

He was similarly concerned about his valuables when he crashed in the tunnel during practice at Monaco in 1961. Stirling, who stopped to go to his aid, recalls: 'Innes was lying there and as I came up to him all he wanted to know was whether he was all right down the bottom because he was frightened he might have chopped something off. I was able to assure him everything was in order.'

Ireland: 'We were all much better chums in those days. These days you rarely see a bunch of drivers gathered in the paddock together having a bloody good laugh. I think the drivers today are all under intense financial pressures which didn't exist years ago. Pressures because of sponsors and because they have to perform and live up to the vast amounts of money they are being paid. I never had any financial pressures on me, or I never felt any. In 1962 I made, from starting, bonus and prize money, about £34,500, or at least my secretary told me that was how much I spent. So I must have earned it, I guess.

'But despite all the jolly chaps and japes image off the track we were all very serious on the track and applied ourselves. I can't think that anybody in a totally and utterly light-hearted manner drove a racing car to the limits of its adhesion or his own ability. I can remember the odd times closing my bedroom door in the morning before going to the track and wondering if I'd be around that evening to open it again. It was just a fleeting thought that you put straight out of your mind again. But in truth one did think about death and in those days it wasn't all that difficult to get killed.

Trevor Taylor . . . 'a bloody good lad'

'Something I believe quite sincerely is that the cars today are so safe, so strong, that the standard of driving has deteriorated. The drivers know they can have horrendous accidents and walk away from them. They are using them as bumper cars half the time. When I was driving we didn't have guard-rails all over the place. There were trees and houses and stuff like that. So one had a great deal more respect for what one was doing and for the other fellows. Nobody wanted to kill anybody.'

Ireland picked up five points with the Lotus during 1959 and advanced to a total of eighteen points for fourth place in the 1960 Championship. Clark joined him that year and the Scottish ship was a happy one. Lotus even had a third Scot, Ron Flockhart, on board for the French Grand Prix. Come 1961, however, Clark's talent was shining through and although Ireland's American win took him a point ahead of his partner, Chapman would not be swayed. Ireland was out of the team. Taylor, who had one Championship race in 1961, got a permanent place.

Ireland was convinced that Clark had, in some way, conspired against him, but Clark insisted he had nothing to do with his sacking. The bitterness between them would never be bridged. Ireland felt he had done nothing to warrant dismissal and was equally hostile towards Taylor. That relationship was, however, patched up.

Taylor, now considered by Ireland 'a bloody good lad', recalls: 'Innes was very upset when I was given his car. We had a row and it was all a bit unpleasant, but then we thrashed it out over a few drinks one night and shook on it. After that we got on fine together.'

Ireland was still driving a Lotus in 1962, but for the UDT Laystall team. He managed just two points that season. He continued in Formula One until 1966, though his competitive career at this level effectively ended with that victorious drive at the Glen, five years earlier. He toiled with out-of-date machinery and lost heart after his traumatic split with Lotus. He did, however, enjoy success in sports and GT cars.

These days Ireland, like Rob Walker, deploys his knowledge and experience as a journalist. He says: 'I often wonder, now that I'm having to write about Formula One, what I would be like in the situation the present drivers are in. You keep hearing all this talk about minute alterations here, there and everywhere, and the aerodynamics, and I wonder how much of it is bull and how much they really know. I can't think that all the drivers today are so damn clever that they all know exactly what they are doing with aerodynamics and roll bar settings and all that stuff.

'I certainly wouldn't. When I was racing it was pretty technical when I came in and said "put two pounds of extra pressure in the rear tyres" or "just alter the handling a bit". And today the driver's contribution to the final outcome or the lap time is far smaller than it was in my day.

'But again, we come back to all these financial pressures. People can't relax enough. Look at the state Senna gets himself into. You never got anybody like that when I was racing. I can't see it being worth it whatever he's earning. If that's what gives him pleasure, he's got a very curious idea of what pleasure is. I think he suffers. I think he goes through mental anguish. It's an ordeal and it cannot be healthy for a young man. He's won the World Championship, he's a magnificent driver and he should be able to enjoy it. I believe, away from the circuit, he's a very nice guy but how many of us know him away from the circuit? None of us, probably.'

Jim Clark was born on 4 March 1936 at Kilmany, Fife, but six years later his parents, who were farmers, moved to the Borders. That is where Jim's heart always belonged. He would go on to be acknowledged as the supreme driver of his generation, a man totally at ease, totally in control, totally in command at the wheel of a car. Yet, stripped of his armoury, he was, certainly until his later years, coy and vulnerable; a stranger in a world of growing commercialism and increasing numbers of sycophants. He remained, essentially, the wee boy from the Borders.

He was a pupil at Loretto School, but at the age of sixteen was working on the family farm, Edington Mains, between Chirnside and Berwick-upon-Tweed. He had four sisters, all of whom married, and it was brother-in-law Alec Calder's interest in motor sport that led young Jimmy down a one-way track. His parents were not at all happy when he indicated his intention to take up racing, but then whose parents were? It was, by then, obvious to his chums at the young farmers' club that the course was inevitable. He could make his dark green Sunbeam Mark 3 saloon talk and if he did have the occasional spill, well, that was part of the fun, wasn't it?

He drove his trusty Sunbeam in his first event, a sprint, in June 1956. He won. Later that month he had his first race, driving a DKW Sonderklasse owned by a friend, Ian Scott Watson. He was only eighth but the contest was a mismatch and he had given a glimpse, up at wind-swept Crimond, of a gift so rare.

The following year Scott Watson bought a Porsche 1600, previously owned by Billy Cotton, who was no mean driver but enjoyed greater success leading bands than in races. That Porsche presented Clark with the opportunity to give further expression to his talent, and he ended the season on a high note Cotton would have approved of.

In 1958 Scott Watson and friends revived the Border Reivers team to project their budding star. Clark, now armed with a D-type Jaguar, obliged by becoming the first sportscar driver to register a lap at more than 100 m.p.h. on a post-war British circuit. The triumph of Full Sutton opened the door to Europe – and the other side of motor racing.

He was entered for a sportscar race at Spa, the awesome monster of a circuit in Belgium. He found it intimidating, and his dislike of the place remained with him for the rest of his life. Four Grand Prix wins could not change his opinion. An accident in that first race left an indelible impression. The monster claimed the life of Archie Scott-Brown, the Scotsman, and for the novice Clark it was a shattering experience. He finished the race eighth, but he had finished. He was content enough with that.

Clark had his first test drive in a Lotus Formula Two car that year, but was not impressed. The Lotus Elite, however, was a different matter. The Reivers ordered him one for the Boxing Day meeting at Brands Hatch. The intervention of a hapless backmarker denied Clark his victory over Colin Chapman – then a formidable figure *on* the track – but the Lotus boss had noted the name of this bright young Scot.

In 1959 Clark had regular success with the Elite and a Lister-Jaguar, and was also introduced to Le Mans. He and John Whitmore drove their Elite to tenth place. By now, though, there was talk of Formula One, and he linked up with Reg Parnell to drive the planned Aston Martin Grand Prix car with Roy Salvadori. That venture crumbled, but, having joined the Lotus stable for Formula Junior and Formula Two events, Clark was the obvious choice to replace John Surtees when he had to miss the 1960 Dutch Grand Prix because of a motor cycling commitment. Thus began one of the most enduring and successful associations in the history of the sport.

It was not a fairytale start. Gearbox trouble forced Clark to retire on the forty-third lap. He had, however, been involved in a joust for fourth place with Graham Hill. It was a preview to a contest that would stir the sixties. To Clark's dismay the next race took him back to Spa, and more tragedy. That Belgian Grand Prix weekend Stirling Moss was badly injured in practice and two other British drivers, Chris Bristow and Alan Stacey, driving a Lotus, were killed in the race. Spa, it seemed, would never shed its black cloak.

Yet Clark came away with fifth place and his first Championship points. The following weekend he was driving an Aston Martin with Salvadori at Le Mans. They finished third. Clark continued to compete in Formula Junior and Formula Two events that year and even when he was an established Formula One driver he raced other models from the Lotus stable. His three-wheel antics in the Cortina were almost an art form and he submerged his early abhorrence of the American way of racing life to conquer the 500 classic in Lotus' Indianapolis car. He took on all-comers, in all sorts of competition, in twenty-three types of Lotus. Not all were great cars. Many were. But whatever the quality of the car, the driver demonstrated sublime skills.

Jim Clark preparing for action

Clark completed the 1960 Formula One World Championship with eight points. He was fifth again in the French Grand Prix and third in Portugal behind Brabham and McLaren. Already he was attracting the interest of other teams, including Ferrari, but his faith in Chapman was absolute. Chapman, in turn, was to pamper his golden boy, ensuring him the best of his attention and equipment.

The British Racing Hero

In 1961 Clark, like Moss, relished the challenge of taking on the more potent 1½-litre cars of Ferrari. He took the Lotus 21 to third place at Zandvoort and, after capitulating at dreaded Spa, was third again at Rheims and fourth at the Nurburgring. Monza was ready to acclaim as champion a Ferrari driver. Phil Hill could win it, but Wolfgang von Trips was favourite. Clark was to be involved in the horrendous accident that ended not merely the German's title hopes but his life.

Von Trips was chasing Hill, but clinging to his coat-tails was Clark. Both Clark and von Trips were poised to overtake in the braking area as they approached the Parabolica. Instead they touched and whipped out of control. The Lotus went off the track but Clark was unhurt. The Ferrari, however, catapulted up a bank, smashed into a fence and overturned, killing von Trips and thirteen spectators.

Tim Parnell was making one of his two World Championship appearances that day: 'Taffy seemed to move out of the slip-stream of the other Ferrari, sideways into Jimmy's car. There were bits and pieces of car all over the track and the rest of us had to thread our way through.'

Despite Parnell's version of the collision, Clark had fingers of accusation pointed at him. As Italian anguish spilled over, a bewildered Clark was advised to get out of the country before he found himself in jail. He was smuggled away from the circuit and flown back to Britain by Jack Brabham in his light aeroplane. Hill won the race to become the first American Formula One World Champion, and Welshman Jack Lewis scored his only Championship points with fourth place, but this was no time for celebration.

Already, in his fledgling career, Clark had experienced moments of deep distress as well as high elation. He was driven on by familiar forces: a love of the sport, a will to compete and an ambition to win. Clark also had another force, called Colin Chapman. The year 1962, and the years beyond, held out great promise for Chapman, Lotus and Clark.

Lotus was not the only British team hopeful of eclipsing Ferrari. There was optimism, too, in the BRM camp. Their challenge would be led by a man who had worked with Chapman. Graham Hill was a late starter in motor racing but now, he believed, he was ready to graduate to the class of Grand Prix winners.

Hill, born in a Hampstead nursing home on 17 February 1929, gave the first indication of his path in life with his creations from a Meccano set. His father, who worked on the Stock Exchange, took the hint and, at the age of sixteen, Hill junior was sent to Smiths, the instrument makers, to serve a five-year apprenticeship. His courses at engineering college were to prove extremely valuable, though not in the manner he or his father anticipated.

The youthful Hill had no thoughts of becoming a racing driver. He never even drove a car until he was twenty-four. He did ride a motor-bike

Opposite page

Above: Jackie Stewart in a class of his own, Nurburgring, 1968

Below: Stewart the winner . . . this time at the Race of Champions, Brands Hatch, 1970

– with traumatic consequences. He ran into the back of a car which was parked with no lights on. He spent several months in hospital and the rest of his life limping on a bandy left leg half an inch shorter than the other.

National Service with the Navy gave him further engineering experience – and his first trip to Monaco. He wandered around like any visitor and won a few bob in the Casino. Little did he know he would become the master of the Monaco Grand Prix. Little did he know that they raced around these tight, twisting streets!

Hill was in the Navy when he met the young lady who was to become his wife. He had developed a keen interest in rowing and was at a Boxing Day regatta at the Auriol Rowing Club, Hammersmith. He wrote: 'When I was introduced to Bette I was told she'd been in the Wrens. This should have given us something in common right away but she told me some time afterwards that she wasn't impressed with me at all during that initial meeting.'

Bette Hill now says: 'I was there because I was going to be a bridesmaid to a girl who was engaged to one of Graham's crew members. I just went along because the engagement party was that evening. I met this petty officer and thought he was rather nice. He said why didn't I take up rowing, it was a good sport. I liked him and didn't want to go out with other fellas when he went back to his ship, so I joined the rowing club.'

Bette proved a very capable rower. Her team, coached by Graham, not only outpaced domestic opposition, they went on to earn several European titles as well.

Graham later recognised the connections between the sport of his early life and the sport that eventually dominated it: 'You can't play at rowing, you have to be dedicated. You've got to concentrate, too, and these and many other things which I learnt when I was rowing helped me when I became a racing driver.'

His late start in racing may explain why he was generally not credited with having great flair as a driver. Equally, though, it meant he had a great deal of fighting to do to catch up. That demanded determination, dedication and concentration. All those qualities he talked about in rowing. His achievements in motor racing were a triumph of application. He worked on a latent instinct, and drew from what was natural – guts, commitment and ambition. Eventually he saw no reason why he should not take on, and beat, the best.

His first road car, a Morris 8, was written off by a laundry van but that didn't put him off driving. He was back at Smiths when a colleague spotted an advertisement in a motoring magazine. Bette: 'Someone threw him an *Autosport* and said "here you are, Graham, this is what you should do". It said for five shillings you could do a lap of Brands Hatch. So he went down, did four laps for a pound and was totally smitten straight away. And he was good.'

Graham knew it was a turning-point: 'It was the most important pound I ever spent. The moment I did those four laps everything changed. The sensation of power and speed fascinated me, and so did the knowledge that if I wanted I could develop more and more power and still control it. After those laps my next thought was how to get back in the car again without paying.'

Opposite page

Above: Stewart's last British Grand Prix, 1973

Below: Still no British Grand Prix joy for Hill, Silverstone, 1973

Bette takes up the story: 'He gave up his job at Smiths, went on the dole [he collected 3s 6d a week] and worked on the cars at a racing school in return for the chance to drive them. He'd decided he wanted to be a racing driver and, by hook or by crook, he was going to get there.'

For three months he managed to keep his father in the dark about his new 'career'. He'd also done his best to fend off the Labour Exchange, who were having distinct problems finding him a job as a racing driver. It seems there were not too many openings! But he got what he wanted. The school entered him for his first race in April 1954. He had been driving only a year, had those four laps at Brands, yet here he was at the Kent track again – racing. It was only a modest contest, but he was highly delighted with his second place in his heat and fourth place in the final.

He had completed just one lap of another race at Brands when his engine broke and he was left to sit out the rest of the proceedings: 'While I was there I got talking to one or two people and as one of them had a transporter I asked him if he could give me a lift back to London. He said "yes, certainly," so I went back with him. His name was Colin Chapman.'

Ever the opportunist, Hill naturally asked for a job, too. And got one. He helped out at Chapman's base – then at Hornsey – for a pound a day.

Still impatient for regular racing, he linked up with Danny Margulies as his mechanic-cum-co-driver. Margulies had a C-type Jaguar, a car which opened up a whole new area of racing for the starry-eyed Hill. That world was not, as yet, willing to offer him a life of luxury and coming up was his wedding. 'I had precisely 1s 6d in the bank and £5 in my pocket. Bette provided £12 from her earnings as a secretary to pay for the reception and a friend lent me a twenty-year-old banger for our brief honeymoon.'

Bette: 'We got married on 13 August 1955, and stayed at the Frying Pan Hotel, near Goodwood – because he was first reserve to drive a Lotus for Colin in the nine-hour race there. That was our three-day honeymoon. We were all growing up and getting married at more or less the same time. Hazel and Colin, too. We were all of the same age and all had the same enthusiasm. We used to pile into anything available to get to a race track. Graham used to drive us there in the car he was going to race and we just prayed it didn't break down so we could get home again.'

Home in the early days was a tiny flat in London. They shared the bathroom with nine other people. Graham was on £9 a week as a full-time engineer at Lotus and the rent was five guineas a week: 'Bette had to go on working. We couldn't afford to start a family. Even clothes were a luxury.'

Chapman gave Hill the use of a car for the 1956 Autosport Championship and only a blown engine in the final event, at Oulton Park, cost him his chance of the title. It was, though, the break he had been seeking. The following year he was signed up as a Team Lotus driver and in 1958 he, and Lotus, arrived in Grand Prix motor racing at Monaco. It was to prove a significant venue throughout his World Championship career.

The Hills drove down to Monte Carlo in an Austin A35 and made good time. The transporter carrying his and team-mate Cliff Allison's cars didn't do so well. It broke down on the way and only just arrived in time for practice. The Lotus pair qualified for the last two places on the 16-car grid.

At three-quarter distance Hill was up to fourth: 'It all seemed too easy but then, as I went down to the sea-front and was turning right, the revs suddenly shot up and I spun round. I thought "bloody hell, it's jumped out of gear". I looked up and saw that my back wheel had fallen off. When I got out I fell over. I was suffering from heat exhaustion and didn't know it.'

The wheel kept running his way at the Casino that night, though. He had won £120 before he was finally dragged away. He was also earning money racing Formula Two and sportscars for Lotus, and amused himself racing his A35 and a mini in saloon car events.

Back in the Formula One arena he had another uncomfortable experience in the French Grand Prix at Rheims: 'I took one corner half standing in the cockpit. The crowd thought I had gone mad. But the gearbox had got so hot it melted the solder holding the oil-filler cap in place and boiling oil was splashing over my legs.'

The hopes and dreams of 1958 began to evaporate in 1959. Lotus and Hill had marched in step all the way to Formula One but now the routine was breaking up. A season of problems, frustrations and fruitless endeavour took its inevitable toll: 'I told Colin Chapman I was brassed-off and that I was going to join BRM in 1960. It was like jumping out of the frying pan into the fire because at the time BRM hadn't had any luck, either. Of course, directly I joined BRM, Lotus started winning. So there was a coincidence!'

Hill would have to wait another two seasons before he started winning Championship races. In 1960 he had four points to show for his labours, in 1961 a meagre three. The lessons of that period, however, were invaluable. And there were moments that assured him he had what was required for the job. He had the considerable satisfaction of qualifying on the front row for the first race of 1960, the Argentine Grand Prix; and he intelligently nursed his car to finish third, ahead of a charging Moss, in Holland.

He might have had his maiden success in the British Grand Prix at Silverstone that summer but, under pressure from Brabham, asked too much of his failing brakes and went off the road: 'I was approaching Copse Corner, where I came across two tail-enders in my path. I elected to go past them and, of course, the moment I arrived in the corner too fast the brakes didn't work and I spun off and ended up in the ditch. I had made the wrong decision and paid for it. But on occasions like this there's only one thing to do – put the experience gained into the bank, as it were, to draw on in future races.'

Hill picked up a point for sixth place in the 1961 French Grand Prix at Rheims and had to wait until the last race of the season to add two more. That was at the Glen, the final Grand Prix of Moss' career, the first and last won by Ireland. The advance of the Lotus was obvious but BRM, too, were confident of lengthening their stride. British forces – men and machines – were being mobilised for the great battle.

Another British driver about to make his presence felt was John Surtees. The title might still be beyond him in 1962, yet the jousting would stand him in good stead. After all, racing competition was not new to him. He had already enjoyed phenomenal success, though not on four wheels.

Surtees was brought up in the world of motor-bikes. Eventually he ruled it. The lead and inspiration came from his father. In 1949, at the age of fifteen, he began riding sidecar with his father. Their partnership ran through to 1952, by which time Surtees junior was ready for challenges new. That appetite for challenges was to take him through motor-cycling and into car racing like an unstoppable tidal wave. He washed away all before him in one of the most remarkable careers in sport.

The British Racing Hero

He won the first of his seven motor-bike World Championships – the 500cc title, riding an MV Agusta – in 1956 and carried on winning trophies in two-wheel competition while he was finding his way on four. The switch, in fact, appeared effortless. He was instantly quick, instantly assertive in his new world. He reached the Formula One pinnacle and remains the only man to have won world titles for both bikes and cars.

He took more than winning ways into car racing. He took a straight, nononsense attitude that was the norm among motor-cycling folk but something of a culture shock for certain four-wheel factions. He made no apologies then and makes none now. He despised some of what he found in Formula One, yet was not intimidated by any of it. That, too, was bound to antagonise those he had no time for.

Surtees' concern was the job. He simply wanted to get on with it. Those who shared that desire were drawn to him even before he had driven a racing car. He had been competing for barely a year when Enzo Ferrari was calling him. Surtees would not be rushed. He was astute enough – and bold enough – to decline. He reasoned that he was not ready. Everything had happened so quickly, so astonishingly quickly – and car racing had never figured in his schemes: 'When I was at my height on bikes I wasn't particularly thinking in terms of cars. It certainly wasn't an ambition of mine. In fact car racing hadn't occurred to me until, I suppose, Mike Hawthorn started talking to me about it at a Sportsmen of the Year function. At the same table were Reg Parnell and Tony Vandervell and they took a keen interest in the discussion. The only time I'd seen a racing car was at Monza. I'd been practising there just before the cars started practising for their Grand Prix.

'But they kept on about my trying cars and afterwards Reg Parnell called me and offered me a drive in an Aston Martin DBR1, which Stirling Moss had won with at the Nurburgring. So I went down to Goodwood, and though it felt a bit strange to start with I was quite happy with it by the end of the afternoon. They produced a contract but I said it was ridiculous, I was a cyclist, not a car man. They said I'd gone round quicker than anyone else had and asked me to go down again.

'A little later Tony came on the phone. He'd heard I'd driven Mr Parnell's car and said I should drive a real car. So I went down and drove the Vanwalls. He said that if I drove for him he'd build me a car and make a comeback. That was how he came to buy a Lotus and put one of his engines in as a test piece, and then build the Vanwall International rear-engined car. I raced it at Silverstone but the formula was then abandoned so it didn't run again. It was a great disappointment to Tony.

'Probably one of my greatest disappointments has been what I've seen going on around Tony's cars, the building of replicas, the juggling and the rather devious dealings. It's very sad for Britain that they have ended up as they have. I tried hard to get the rear-engined car because it was built specifically for me, but I came across the manoeuvrings that take place in the auction market.

'Anyway, back to the end of 1959. My contract with MV for the following season said I could only do Championship races so I thought as it said nothing about driving a car I'd do that. I told Tony and Reg I needed experience so I telephoned John Cooper and asked about buying a Formula Two Cooper Climax.

'I went to see John, and as it happened he'd arranged for Ken Tyrrell to be there. Ken said I needed to get my licence so why not drive a few races for him in a Formula Junior. So I arranged for the RAC to inspect me at Goodwood in 1960. It's now history that I had a dice with Jim Clark. He was in the Lotus. I was in the Cooper, and he just pipped me.'

The tidal wave was washing over the British car racing scene. He produced a series of impressive drives. His Goodwood effort was no flash in the pan. He was quick, consistently quick: 'I had no trouble producing the speed but I was a little unsafe because I'd never done it before. My apprenticeship and my start were coming together.

John Surtees . . . champion on two wheels and four wheels

'While Vandervell was building the rear-engined car, Colin Chapman came along talking about Formula One and offered me a drive at Silverstone. Innes Ireland was there and in those days Colin used to jump in the car and be as quick as anybody. It was the first time I'd sat in a Grand Prix car other than a front-engined Vanwall. I ended the day putting the nose in the bank but I was a bit quicker than Innes. Mind you, I think Colin was quicker than both of us! Anyway, Colin said to me "You're going to drive in the Monaco Grand Prix".

'This made Innes look pretty angry. "We haven't got enough cars for someone to go and shunt them" he said. But Colin gave me the car and I said it was fine by me. The race wasn't but I was in Formula One.'

He was also still in bike racing and it is a measure of the man's talent and aptitude that days later he was the master of the TT on his MV and the following month was back at the wheel of the Lotus Climax to take second place behind Jack Brabham in the British Grand Prix at Silverstone. It was only his second Formula One World Championship race.

For his third, the Portuguese, at Oporto, he outpaced Moss, Clark and Brabham and the rest to take pole position and might have had his first victory. He would go further: 'I *should* have had my first Grand Prix win. I had about a twenty-five second lead. It was a proper road circuit and the competitive edge got the better of wiser judgment and lack of experience. Stirling came out of the pits and he was in a Lotus as well so I thought I'd have a bit of a go. I tried to pass him but got stuck a bit in the tram-lines. Instead of just turning into them and running down the slip road I tried to make the corner, slid out, shunted the radiator in the kerb and that was it. That was my race. With such a good lead it was a silly mistake. At least I ended up with the fastest lap.

'I made a mess of the US Grand Prix at Riverside. I took out two of our cars. At the start I was too anxious to get to the front, went outside Jim, got on to the sand and lost it. Jim T-boned me and we were both out. It was my fault.

'When I think back to that year, 1960, the year I started, I had the most competitive car I had in my whole career, and that includes the Ferrari. The Ferrari lacked power. People talk about the power of the Ferraris but one of the reasons I joined them was that you could scratch round the corners and the cars would hold together. But we still lacked power.'

Surtees' Ferrari days were still ahead of him. For 1961 it seemed logical for him to stay at Lotus. Despite his mishaps in his first season he had shown his mettle. He was positive, competitive. Chapman liked what he'd seen. Surtees recalls: 'A number of things guided me, perhaps wrongly. Colin offered me the No. 1 spot and I went to New Zealand, where the car broke its steering on me about four times a day. When we got back there was a hell of a row with Innes Ireland. He'd supposedly been promised lots of things by Colin earlier in the year, before I came on to the scene. I'd come in for a bit of stick, being a motor cyclist. A few of the old stagers were very good but some, like the Jo Bonniers of this world, resented someone like me coming in and being so much quicker than they were. The last thing I wanted was stick. I wanted to enjoy it, so I didn't drive for Lotus. I told them I wasn't going to have any of the politics, the hassle and all the rest of it. Forget it.

'Breakages were another consideration, though. When I hadn't driven at Spa my car had been taken over by Alan Stacey and, of course, it broke. It was a bit of a worry. Mechanical failures causing serious accidents was something you never came across on bikes. A seizure or a lock-up possibly caused you worry.'

Re-enter Reg Parnell. 'He said they were going to run the works Cooper team, financed by Yeoman Credit. In fact they turned out to be production Coopers and it was a bit tiresome. But at the same time it was good experience. It was still early days for me. In terms of the competitiveness of the car it was a backward step but Cooper had a reputation and it appealed.'

It did not, however, make much of an impression on the Formula One World Championship. From top of the constructors' table, and first and second in the drivers' table (Brabham and McLaren), the name was reduced to more modest stature in 1961. Cooper tumbled beneath Ferrari, Lotus and Porsche, and Surtees could manage only four points. He was fifth in Belgium and again in Germany.

Backers Yeoman Credit became backers Bowmaker Hire Purchase in 1962 and Surtees, anxious to progress, instigated the production of a new Formula One car for the season, a Lola. Eric Broadley had established the company in 1956 and Surtees reckoned he was capable of stepping up to the Big League:

'During 1961 I thought that if we couldn't have a works car from Cooper why not build one. I thought it would also teach me a lot. So I went to see Eric Broadley, who lived just round the corner from me, and fixed up for him to build an F1 chassis.'

Broadley duly created a light, nimble car, fitted with the V8 Coventry-Climax engine, for the 1962 World Championship. Surtees would be joined by Roy Salvadori. Another all-British challenger was ready for the conflict.

5

British Rule

Tony Brooks had chosen to depart from the scene and, a month before the start of the 1962 World Championship, Stirling Moss was forced from it by his accident at Goodwood. Britain had lost two of the great racing drivers. Could their successors fill the void? The first race of the season, the Dutch Grand Prix at Zandvoort, would deliver an emphatic response.

Jim Clark had wintered well. He had four races in South Africa, winning three. The fourth was won by team-mate Trevor Taylor, the 'bloody good lad' from Sheffield who replaced Innes Ireland. For the 1962 Grand Prix programme Clark would have the Lotus 25, a model featuring the monocoque design which would become the norm in car construction.

The Easter Monday race that ended Moss' career provided Graham Hill with his first Formula One victory. He had another significant success in the International Trophy event at Silverstone. He had exhaust problems in the early part of the race, which stifled the potential of the BRM. However, as rain fell on the later stages he produced a charge and closed up on leader Clark, that day driving the Lotus 24. Through Woodcote for the final time Hill gambled and went wide on to the wet part of the road: 'It took me into a broadside which sent me over the finishing line sideways and I beat him by a gnat's whisker.' Hill, and BRM, were in good heart.

Eric Broadley, meanwhile, had been preparing two Lolas for John Surtees and Roy Salvadori. Surtees recalls: 'To start off with they were rather fragile cars. Like the Lotus, really. We had a number of breakages, which held up our progress somewhat. But we worked at it and by the end of the season it was fairly quick and competitive.'

Surtees did not exactly hang about when he introduced the Lola at Zandvoort. BRM and Lotus were, as they'd hoped, fast in practice, and Hill and Clark qualified for the front row of the grid. On pole, however, was the Lola Climax of Surtees. Lola's dreams lasted just nine laps of the race. A suspension failure sent Surtees sliding off the track and the team retired Salvadori's car.

Clark's Lotus 25 developed gearbox trouble early in the day and he had to withdraw from the front-line. Instead it was Hill's BRM marching through and by the end his closest challenger was Taylor. Hill maintained his form and had his first Championship race victory. Tony Rudd's team, under pressure to come up with the goods or else, had emphatically delivered.

Before the Monaco Grand Prix, Clark was on duty with the new Lotus 23 sportscar at the Nurburgring and led comfortably until fumes released by a broken exhaust manifold took hold of him and caused him to veer off the track. He set off for Monte Carlo in need of a change of fortune.

Practice suggested he might get it. He took pole with Hill and Bruce McLaren, in the Cooper Climax, alongside. The race started with mayhem and tragedy. A marshal was killed by Richie Ginther's BRM in a first corner pile-up. Hill went clear of McLaren and the debris, eventually to be pursued by Clark. The ferocity of the chase was to take its toll on both cars, opening the victory path for McLaren. It was to be a familiar Monaco story for Clark, but Hill would find ample consolation awaiting him here in future years. On this day he had to settle for sixth place, while Surtees emerged with fourth place and Lola's first points.

Hill was fastest in practice at Spa and though Taylor made the front row Clark was back on the fifth. If anyone thought the Scot was about to give in to the monster this time the evidence of the first lap indicated otherwise. Clark had advanced to fourth place. He took breath and went on the attack again, claiming the lead on the eighth lap. He won and, for good measure, had a lap record of 133.874 m.p.h. He had tamed the monster and, although he continued to despise it, he had it under his authority for the rest of his life.

Clark was in business. The poise and the seemingly effortless control were rewarded. He had his first Grand Prix win. Hill had to accept that this was not his race but had a valuable second place to add to his Championship account. Surtees, too, was on the score-sheet with fifth place. Clark and Hill set the pace before the race in France, but this time had nothing to show from the contest proper. Surtees, again, came in fifth.

The last British Grand Prix held at Aintree promised a home success and didn't disappoint the Liverpool crowd. Clark was the master that weekend. He took pole ahead of Surtees and Ireland, dominated the race and lapped all but three of the others. One local wag reckoned that if he stuck around he could win the Grand National, too. Second was the redoubtable Surtees, third McLaren and fourth Hill.

The heat was on. The Championship had begun well for Hill but, although he was scoring consistently, Clark was the man with the momentum. Then there was McLaren to keep an eye on – and there was Surtees. They were all men to be watched. They, in turn, were watching Dan Gurney's Porsche as the American claimed pride of place on the Nurburgring grid. Hill, Clark and Surtees were in close attendance. Clark stalled on the line and, despite a magnificent charge through the field, fourth place was his limit.

Surtees was the man with great expectations that day. He admits: 'A fumble on the last lap cost us the German Grand Prix. Just as I was getting up my speed for the sling-shot, I found a back-marker had taken the piece of road I was going for. It was the nearest I got to winning a Grand Prix that year.'

Instead it was another second place for Surtees and his Lola. Hill, equally determined to re-assert himself, had a crucial win and the fastest lap. He would later rate it among the most satisfying performances of his career. He said: 'The race was run in torrential rain with zero visibility from start to finish. My BRM went like a dream, hotly pursued by Dan Gurney's Porsche and John Surtees' Lola. We were never more than five seconds apart during the whole of the two and three-quarter hours. With that sort of pressure I had to concentrate like mad and by the time the race was over I was completely drained both mentally and physically.'

Clark beat Hill to pole in Italy but gearbox problems put the Lotus out of

Hill on course for his first Championship, 1962

the hunt in the race. Hill went on to collect his third victory of the season and Ginther completed a splendid one-two for BRM.

Hill was in sight of the Championship with two races remaining. If he won the United States Grand Prix the title would be his, regardless of the outcome in South Africa. It was all or nothing for Clark at Watkins Glen. He took all: pole, race, fastest lap. Hill was second in the race. Their duel had gone all the way to a last race decider.

Hill, with three firsts and two seconds, held the advantage, but Clark tilted the psychological advantage with devastating form in practice. The resolute Hill was second fastest. Both appeared to succumb to the tension at the start. Hill had massive wheel-spin and Clark was also jumped by an alert Ireland. Clark soon recovered, however, to take command of the race and therefore the Championship.

For three-quarters of the South African Grand Prix Hill could only track Clark in hope. Then, as Lotus were preparing their celebrations, the 25 began to spew oil. The tell-tale smoke left a trail of frustration as Clark headed for the pits. A wayward bolt had settled the issue. A despondent Clark was out. Hill had the race and the Championship. Hill recalled: 'It made me the first British driver to win the World Championship in an all-English car . . . the BRM. The Championship Cup itself wasn't all that imposing to look at, but it meant so much it didn't have to be.'

The final Championship standings were: Hill 42 points, Clark 30, McLaren 27, Surtees 19. BRM took the Constructors' title ahead of Lotus, Cooper and Lola. Porsche and Ferrari shared fifth place. Britain was the undisputed power-base of Formula One motor racing. Hill was only the second Briton to carry off the drivers' award but the third, and indeed the fourth, were not far behind him.

Hill and Ginther again carried the BRM challenge in 1963, and Lotus kept Clark and Taylor together in the belief that they had the wherewithal to relieve Tony Rudd's camp of their titles. Colin Chapman wasn't alone in his conviction that the Scot and his 25, given the reliability, would be unstoppable in the coming season.

Surtees was less assured about Lola's prospects. He had scored all their points in 1962 and was anxious to keep his four-wheel career on the ascendancy. Ferrari approached him again, and this time he was more interested in the prospect of a switch to Maranello: 'When I went to see them in 1961 I wasn't ready, but circumstances were different at the end of 1962. It was a whole new scene at Ferrari. A number of new engineers had come in, they were starting afresh. I decided this was the time to join them. We just got stuck in with both the sportscar and the V6. The big problem with the V6 was that it wasn't consistent on performance. It was affected drastically by changes in weather conditions. We worked at it and it started to come together and be competitive.'

Clark and Hill were competitive from the start of the 1963 season. They were again side by side at the first race, the Monaco Grand Prix, and, to the approval of the crowd, repeatedly exchanged the lead. Just when it seemed Clark had beaten off his old rival the gremlins attacked his gearbox. The Lotus was grounded and Hill flew on to register his first win in the Principality. Surtees had fourth place – and fastest lap – while Taylor was sixth.

In Belgium, pole was Hill's, the race Clark's. This time nothing would break the Scot's stride. In Holland his only problem was posed by the local police. Clark wandered out to a corner to watch the cars during practice and was challenged by two officers. He did not have a pass and the

A gift so rare . . .

policemen failed to recognise him. He protested, scuffled in defiance and was led away, only to be released after some convincing explanations had been delivered.

Back on the track, Clark was a law unto himself. He started from pole and lapped the entire field on his way to victory. Surtees, still diligently working at his Ferrari, was third, Ireland, now in a BRM, fourth. In France even an engine problem couldn't contain Clark and the Lotus. Hill was third, but already he knew he could say goodbye to his title.

Next was the British Grand Prix at Silverstone. Clark had another pole and, after some spirited opposition from the Brabham Climaxes of Jack Brabham and Dan Gurney, another race win. Surtees brought his Ferrari through for second place and Hill's BRM was third.

Clark was fastest in practice in Germany and went off into the Eifel Mountains to hunt his fifth successive victory. He came back with second place. Surtees hounded him, eventually took him and steered the Ferrari beyond the reach of the ailing Lotus. Surtees' strategy and commitment had paid their first dividends. Surtees says: 'The Ring was a place where rhythm was all important and we got the car to handle reasonably well. It was a turning point. It was my first Grand Prix win after a number of disappointments and it was Ferrari's first for a while. It was particularly important for the new team, perhaps justification for everything that had been done that year. We had begun to achieve what we set out to achieve.

'It was a good feeling and if you are having a successful run with an Italian team, with Ferrari, it is especially good. I like the Italian people. I like the way they express themselves and their outlook on things. They are not worried about showing their emotions. Yes, they can be devious, but then so can all other races. There's the politics and intrigue, but in Italy there's a feeling and an atmosphere I've always enjoyed.'

Surtees was entitled to enjoy his victory, not merely for the moment but for what it represented. Ferrari had broken from the lean spell and the Englishman, the man who made his name on bikes, was leading the team back to the forefront of Formula One.

Monza was already expectant before Surtees outpaced Hill to put the Ferrari on pole for the Italian Grand Prix. The place was humming when he led the early part of the race. He was on course for another win. This time, though, it was not to be. A dropped valve ended his hopes and left Clark and Gurney to slug it out. Clark's blows were decisive. He had victory, he had the Championship. In his hour of triumph Monza wouldn't let him forget the disaster of 1961. He left Italy a deeply distressed man.

Hill won at Watkins Glen but Clark finished the season with a flourish. He showed the rest the way round a new venue in Mexico City and wrapped up the year with another victory in South Africa.

It had been a stupendous Championship for Clark and Lotus. His record seven wins remained unchallenged until the modern era of sixteen race seasons. In 1963 there were only ten races. As if to underline Britain's domination, the others were won by Hill (two) and Surtees. Hill shared runner-up spot in the table with Ginther, Surtees was fourth.

The Bulldog Breed was intent on remaining mean with the spoils in 1964. Hill and Clark were still hungry and would no doubt be tugging at the title again. Surtees had tasted race victory and was ravenous for more.

He knew, though, that he would have to fight off his compatriots in order to sink his teeth into the Championship itself.

There was another obstacle. For all the optimism generated throughout the course of the previous season, the reality of early 1964 was less euphoric. He explains: 'At Ferrari in those days you started with a handicap. Until Le Mans was over you couldn't really do the work you wanted to do – and needed to do – in Formula One.

'I was always more concerned about what we might have been able to win or what we should have won rather than what we had won. But Mr Ferrari was always juggling and compromising to make ends meet. He didn't have the engineers because they were turned over to Le Mans and he didn't have the money.

'If you look at it, after 1963, when the team was still coming together, Ferrari should have won the Championship for years – 1964, 1965, 1966 and 1967. All the materials were there. They weren't beaten by the opposition, only by themselves. In a way they were their own worst enemies. We actually had engines back there that were far more competitive than the ones we were using. Instead of developing the flat 12, they kept the eight-cylinder and the six-cylinder going because they were committed to trying to sell the projects to Fiat. If Ferrari had had his way he wouldn't have bothered about building road cars, but the fact was he needed the money. There was no sponsorship then.

'So you had a situation where you didn't really have any progress through the winter months and still you were waiting until Le Mans was out of the way. I mean, I loved driving the sportscars, they were super cars. But . . . '

So it was that Ferrari made a less than awe-inspiring start to the 1964 Formula One World Championship. Clark carried on where he left off in 1963, earning pole position at Monaco. Again, though, these streets would not fall to his apparently all-conquering brilliance. He had a slight prang, called into the pits for repairs and could manage no better than fourth place. This was becoming the domain of Hill, and he won from BRM partner Ginther. A new name from the Lotus stable, Peter Arundell, was third on the board, and another two-wheel champion trying his luck on four, Mike Hailwood, picked up his first point.

Surtees, meanwhile, was hoping for a more satisfying trip to the seaside at Zandvoort. Second place from the Dutch Grand Prix was encouraging, but Clark's victory had an ominous ring to it. The alarm bells were ringing louder still in Belgium. Surtees led briefly, only for his challenge to disintegrate. Hill and Gurney ran out of fuel, and McLaren broke down. All of which gave Clark another Spa success. It seemed he simply couldn't fail here. Here, of all places!

Clark and Surtees made the front row at Rouen, France, but got nothing from the race. Hill, quietly picking up points as usual, was second behind Gurney.

The British Grand Prix this year was taken down to Brands Hatch, that dramatic, natural amphitheatre of a circuit in Kent. The occasion was recognised with the title *Grand Prix d'Europe*, though the Brits contrived to make it a domestic affair. Clark and Hill were first and second on the grid, first and second across the line. Surtees, no doubt feeling the benefit

The British Racing Hero

Winning combination . . . Clark, Chapman and Lotus, Brands Hatch, 1964

of a more concerted effort at Maranello, was third.

It was something, though scarcely enough to put Surtees in contention for the Championship. Clark was leading the way again and the consistent Hill was on his heels. Surtees sensed the makings of a strong finish but he couldn't afford to let the others get away. He needed points, big points. It was time to launch his attack.

The scene moved to the Nurburgring, where Surtees had scored his maiden Championship success the previous season. He instantly caught the mood. He beat Clark to pole and although the Lotus led for a while it was forced out by engine trouble. Gurney's Brabham also fell by the wayside, leaving the Ferrari to weave its red pattern of triumph across the stern mountains. Fastest lap completed the work. Hill, almost inevitably, followed Surtees in.

Ferrari were glowing, and Surtees joined Hill and Clark on the front row at Zeltweg, Austria. Here, however, they were all out of luck (Surtees was leading until a front suspension joint broke) and, for the first time in more than two years, a Formula One World Championship race was won by a non-British driver. The distinction went to Italian Lorenzo Bandini (the only Grand Prix victory of his career, incidentally), the consolation to Surtees. Bandini's car was a Ferrari. Top Brit that day was Bob Anderson in a Brabham.

It is worth pausing for just a moment to consider and put into context that run of success by Hill, Clark and Surtees. British motor racing turned into the 1990s seeking its first World Champion for fourteen years. During the 1980s only two Britons, John Watson and Nigel Mansell, won Formula One races. Watson had four of his five successes between 1981 and 1983. Mansell had fifteen victories between 1985 and 1989.

That 'failure' of Austria, in 1964, was swiftly avenged. Surtees was now ready to thrust for the title. At Monza he took pole, fastest lap and the race. Hill and Clark went home empty-handed. With two rounds of the Championship left, any one of the three could take the prize. Clark was fastest at Watkins Glen but a fuel injection problem ended his race. Victory went to Hill, second place to Surtees.

Formula One had another final race decider. The setting was Mexico City, the high-altitude circuit where Clark had won in 1963. He required nothing less than victory again this time and a blank for Hill to retain his crown.

This is how they stood at the start of the Grand Prix: 1st Hill, 39 points; 2nd Surtees, 34 points; 3rd Clark, 30 points.

Clark, his task clearly defined, was on the offensive from the start of proceedings. He was fastest in practice (while Surtees was on the second row, Hill on the third) and fastest from the line. Surtees was held up by an engine reluctant to rise to the occasion and Hill lost time fumbling with his goggles. After the first lap it was Clark in first position, Hill in tenth, Surtees in thirteenth. Surtees: 'We'd had a number of problems in practice. It's a difficult place to get things right, particularly with the direct injection. So they said Lorenzo could have the twelve and I'd stick to the safety of the eight. Initially it kept misfiring until it got stinking hot. Then it started to run all right and I was able to come through the pack.'

The situation was improving, too, for Hill. He advanced to third place behind Clark and Gurney, a position that would be good enough to give him the Championship. Surtees was up to fifth but still the outsider in the title stakes.

As they approached half-distance, though, Hill was put under severe pressure by Bandini, in his powerful if not necessarily reliable Ferrari. As the Italian tried to work out an opening, the Englishman was equally determined to defy him. Surtees had a perfect view of the increasingly desperate struggle.

Surtees recalls: 'I watched in wonder as Graham and Lorenzo fought it out, particularly through the hairpin, which you went into on the flat and came out of on a banked section. First one of them would dive up the inside, then the other would dive up the inside, everything locked.'

The almost inevitable coming-together sent both cars off the track. Bandini was soon back in the action – behind Surtees – but Hill's damaged BRM required repairs and he was left two laps adrift. All he could do was sit and hope.

Surtees has no doubt that Hill made an error of judgment: 'He'd left the door open the lap before and only just kept Bandini out. I think what worried him was seeing me in his mirrors. He was more concerned about me than about Bandini. I was just behind all this on the tow. It's all very well taking a tight line to block people out of the hairpin but that can mean you come out slower. I might have come along the outside and got a bigger shot out of the corner. Those were the things that could have been going through Graham's mind.

'Anyway he left the door open again and Lorenzo was actually through as Graham tried to go round and just ran out of space. There was a bank with a guardrail at the top and he crunched it.'

There was, naturally, a different version from the other camp. Bette Hill says: 'Bandini, a lovely, lovely person but Italian and very hot-headed, was going to get Graham out whatever. Surtees, after all, was his team-mate. He just kept charging Graham until eventually he hit him and pushed him into the Armco. One or two people wanted to go and punch Bandini on the nose, but Graham would have none of it. He wasn't going to show his disappointment like that.'

Another British driver would have to be disappointed before the day was out. But which one? Into the last lap of the race, the last lap of the season, it seemed that was Surtees' fate. He was back to fourth, Clark was still in the lead. The Lotus was leaking oil from a split pipe but he had a substantial advantage and could afford to cruise home. Surely the title was his for a second successive year.

Alas, no. It was one lap too many for the Lotus. The engine seized and it was Clark who had to face disappointment. Fifth place was no good to him. The race was Gurney's but second place would suffice for Surtees. Even if Bandini could have resisted his team-mate's final charge it would not have made sense. The title was there for the taking and Surtees took it. Surtees says: 'We didn't have any team rules then. Whether or not the team gave Bandini a signal I don't know. But the fact remains that he was losing oil pressure and couldn't have kept up the pace. It was not one of my most momentous races but one which had to be played very carefully according to requirements.'

That calm, measured approach left the World Championship table like this: 1st Surtees, 40 points; 2nd Hill, 39 points; 3rd Clark, 32 points.

Surtees had completed a unique sporting double. World motor cycle champion seven times between 1956 and 1960, he was the 1964 motor racing champion. A number of riders have made the switch, but none with anything like the same level of success. It remains a unique achievement.

The British Racing Hero

He was entitled to celebrate and then put his feet up for a while. He hardly had the time. Barely two months after the dramatic climax of Mexico, teams and drivers were assembling in South Africa for the start of the 1965 season. The race was scheduled for New Year's Day.

The new champion was again partnered by Bandini and they ought to have welcomed the early resumption of hostilities. They were the team on the up-and-up and here was the chance to maintain momentum. Life, of course, is not as simple as that, especially at Ferrari. For reasons Surtees has explained, they tended not to be at their most potent in the first half of the year.

Hill, champion in 1962, runner-up in 1963 and 1964, was as keen as ever to make his bid. BRM had a new team-mate for him, a twenty-five-year-old Scot called Jackie Stewart. Hill was aware, though, that to win the Championship he would have to beat that other Scot at Lotus. He was equally aware it would be no easy task. Clark had not had the best of fortune in 1964 and, given a reasonable roll of the dice, he anticipated more from 1965.

The opening skirmishes suggested the optimism in the Lotus camp was justified. Clark beat Surtees to pole and repeated the performance in the race. Hill was third. The familiar trio were up there still and, emphasising the depth of British talent, Mike Spence (Lotus Climax) was fourth, with Stewart, on his Grand Prix debut, sixth.

Next stop for the Formula One circus was Monaco, but not for Clark. His favourite circuit had consistently scorned him and this year the race clashed with the Indianapolis 500. The American classic and all its fancy dressing held nothing like the same appeal for Clark, but Chapman had committed the Lotus effort down that road and believed they would make it all the way this time. Besides, the chances were they would be unlucky yet again at Monte Carlo!

Clark had been second in the 1963 Indy and was leading in 1964 until he made a frightening exit through a tyre failure. This third trip, he decided, was not going to be wasted. He dominated the race and became the first British winner of the event, at an average speed of more than 150 m.p.h.

Opposite page

Above left: Graham Hill . . . the old master

Above right: Jackie Stewart . . . the tartan warrior

Below: Tony Brise, driving for Hill in the 1975 German Grand Prix

Back in Europe, Hill and the rest were similarly conscious that they could not afford to waste this rare opportunity. Clark's absence from the Monaco Grand Prix was the one break from what was likely to be a relentless Lotus onslaught. Hill seized the initiative in practice and the odds were he would not relinquish his hold during the race. He completed his hat-trick of wins, though not without incident. It all added up, in Hill's opinion, to one of the highlights of his career. He described it like this: 'The car was one of the nicest-looking BRMs ever built. It put up fastest time, I got off to a flier without any problems and continued to lead for the first twenty-four laps. Then I came across a back-marker as I came over

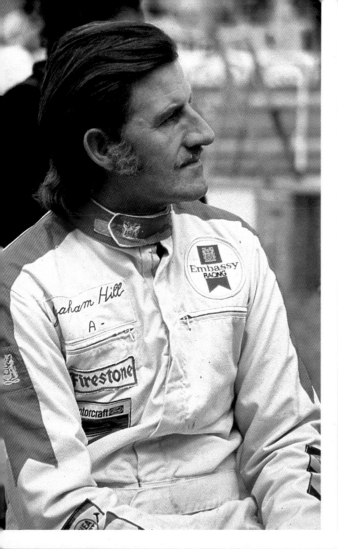

the brow of the hill towards the chicane. I was doing about 120 m.p.h. The other car was limping slowly towards the chicane with some sort of mechanical problem, and it was obvious he would be blocking the chicane at the precise moment I wanted to go through it.

'I couldn't get there first and I couldn't slow down in time to let him through ahead of me, so I braked as hard as I could and shot up the escape road. The engine stalled as I came to a halt, and I had to get out and push the car backwards on to the track. This lost me thirty seconds or so and dropped me back into fifth place. By now Lorenzo Bandini and John Surtees had their Ferraris in what seemed impregnable positions.

'I was pretty annoyed at this but there was still three-quarters of the race to go and I chased after them and gradually reduced their lead. I broke the lap record several times as I carved through the field and at about half distance I managed to take Surtees for second place. Only Bandini was ahead and as I gradually closed the gap I had several attempts at overtaking him. But the Italian was giving no quarter. This led to a terrific duel before I finally got by him and put the BRM back into the lead with thirty-three laps to run. The 2½-hour race ended at a new record average speed of 74.34 m.p.h.'

Bandini was second but Hill's partner Stewart, in only his second Championship race, came through to take third place ahead of Surtees. The Scot sustained his spectacular Formula One overture in the Belgian Grand Prix. He made the front row of the grid and was second in the race. Hill, starting from pole, had to be content with fifth. But Clark was back that day, and Clark was unstoppable.

'I reckon I've got the hang of this place.' Graham Hill at Monaco

Opposite page

Above: James Hunt . . . champion style

Below: Watson overtakes Arnoux and heads for victory at Silverstone, 1981

81

One great Scot following another

Much as he valued the win and the Championship points, he found it exasperating that while nothing would go right for him at Monaco, the race he desperately wanted, Spa was apparently destined to remain at his mercy. It was as if he had the monster under his spell.

The emerging star Stewart was Clark's closest challenger in practice and race at the French Grand Prix, this year switched to Clermont Ferrand. The BRM driver even had the audacity to take the lead until Clark resumed normal service and put him in his place. Clark was an inspiration and friend to Stewart. Eventually this bright newcomer would take over from his fellow Scot as the world's outstanding driver, but in 1965 Clark was, frankly, untouchable.

Hill took the BRM fight to Clark at Silverstone but again they could not lay a glove on the elusive Lotus. Even with an oil problem, Clark managed to duck the punches. Just as Monaco constantly evaded Clark's charms, so the British Grand Prix would not be seduced by Hill. Second place would remain his best result at home. That day Surtees had another third place, Spence was fourth and Stewart fifth. Yes, the first five men across the line were Britons.

Clark won from Stewart in Holland, where once more the police caused Lotus their main anxiety. Chapman was taken to jail, accused of assaulting an officer. The intervention of the British press corps helped secure his release. The German Grand Prix proved relatively free of incident, and Clark won from Hill.

Clark had not only a firm hold on his second World Championship but a record of six consecutive Grand Prix victories. His form was stunning.

Clark again . . . British Grand Prix, 1965

Triumphant Clark, flanked by Hill (left) *and Gurney, Nurburgring, 1965*

There seemed no reason why he shouldn't now go on to beat his 1963 total of seven wins. Curiously, though, his season tailed off. His sequence of success ended in Italy, where four British drivers produced a stirring spectacle. Hill, Surtees and Stewart all contested the lead with Clark. Gearbox trouble forced Surtees out of the scrap and Clark eventually gave in to a faulty fuel pump. Hill was in there fighting to the last, but Stewart kept his head and his lead to record his first Grand Prix win. Yet another Briton, Richard Attwood, had his first point driving a Lotus BRM.

Surtees had not been able to mount a genuine title challenge through 1965 and his season came to an abrupt and painful end. He was seriously injured in an accident during a sportscar race at Mosport, Canada. His concern now was to recover full fitness and then plan for 1966.

It was Hill's turn to fill in the register at Watkins Glen. He had a clean sweep of pole, fastest lap and race. Clark was on pole for the last race, in Mexico City, but his car was strangely uncompetitive in the race, which was won by Ginther in a Honda. Now there's a name to conjure with . . .

Despite the tepid finish, it had been a scorching year for Clark and Lotus, a fitting climax to the 1½-litre era. Hill was second for the third time in a row and Stewart, in his first World Championship season, was a splendid third. Surtees was fifth.

British drivers had taken the World Championship for four consecutive campaigns and showed every sign of retaining command. But would they? What effect would the introduction of 3-litre engines have? Chapman, for one, had to find a new supplier after the withdrawal of Coventry Climax. Now, perhaps, it might not be so straightforward for the Brits.

83

6

Line of Succession

Whatever the problems posed by the change in engine regulations for 1966, there were no concerns about the flow of British driving talent into the mainstream of Formula One. Britain still had the big fish – Graham Hill, John Surtees and the champion for a second time, Jim Clark. Now they were joined by the small, bouncy, self-assured Jackie Stewart, who was already becoming recognised as an important catch for any team.

He had won a Grand Prix in his first World Championship season and finished the campaign in third place behind Clark and Hill, a considerable achievement. Those two established drivers were to play valued roles in the development of young Stewart. Hill, his team-mate at BRM, was generous with his advice and encouragement, even though he must have seen a potential threat in Stewart. The pair were involved in a scrap for the Italian Grand Prix and there was some confusion over a skirmish that effectively gave it to Stewart. Hill, who had in fact made a slight mistake, had no complaints when many were ready to wag an admonishing finger at the rookie.

Clark, a fellow Scot, gave Stewart inspiration, guidance and companionship. For a time they even shared a flat in London. Clark had no hang-ups about an emerging compatriot and the gregarious Stewart was never going to be intimidated by the stature of a man who might have remained a distant idol. The young friend became the natural successor.

Stewart's confidence was evident in his youth but only after he had won his first significant contest. He admits: 'School was a misery for me. I had dyslexia and simply couldn't take in the information. I was regarded as stupid, a dummy. People didn't understand the problem then, I was forty-two before I discovered what it was. Even now, I could not recite the alphabet to save my life. I have to carry a dictionary around with me to help me with my letters and things.'

Anyone who has seen and heard Stewart holding court – and there cannot be many who have not – may find that astonishing. He had another, more obvious cause to be self-conscious. He was frail, his eyes were set unusually close together and he had a 'heavy' right eyelid. He was an easy target for insensitive school-mates. He says: 'Young boys can be cruel, of course. I had to get back at them and one way was playing football. I did well at that. Then when I started selling petrol at the age of fifteen I found I could do that quicker than the others and clean windows quicker than the others. It gave me a terrific feeling because until then all I had had was criticism. I began to feel much more self-confident, much more at ease. I had seen – and others had seen – what I could do and I realised I had nothing to fear.'

Jackie honed his wits at the family business, Dumbuck Garage, in Dumbarton, where he was taken on as an apprentice mechanic. The Stewarts were Jaguar dealers and had built up a reputation for quality and reliable service. They were comfortable and both Jackie and his brother Jimmy – eight years his senior – enjoyed privileges beyond the aspirations of many of their chums.

Jimmy was also a bit of a local celebrity. He had demonstrated a talent as a racing driver and made it to the World Championship stage, if only for one race. He drove an Ecurie Ecosse Cooper-Bristol in the 1953 British Grand Prix at Silverstone and, at the age of twenty-two, was the youngest in the field. He was running sixth when he went off in the wet at Copse.

The family environment inevitably influenced young Jackie. He says: 'I suppose I was bound to become interested in motor racing because my brother was keen, my father had the garage and we were surrounded by cars and motoring magazines. By the age of ten I'd started a scrap-book and then I went to the race tracks with my brother and collected autographs. I still have that autograph book, with names like Stirling Moss, Peter Collins, Mike Hawthorn, Duncan Hamilton and Tony Rolt.

Jackie Stewart . . . the natural successor

'I never had any hopes at that time of becoming a racing driver. I just followed around these heroes of mine. I followed Ascari around, I followed Fangio around. I remember looking at people like Harry Schell and thinking of him as the ultimate playboy character. Peter Collins was much the same. I followed them around for ages just to get their autographs.'

Despite all this interest and opportunity to mix with racing folk, Jackie didn't make an early entry as a competitor. Jimmy retired after an accident at Le Mans and Mrs Stewart could do without the anxiety of seeing another son venture on to the race track. Jackie, instead, took up shooting and was good – so good, in fact, that he blasted away virtually all opposition in clay pigeon competition and was certain he would make the British team for the 1960 Olympic Games. But he flopped miserably in the shoot-out. It was a salutory lesson: self-assurance is one thing, over-confidence quite another.

Jackie made the switch from guns to cars at the beginning of 1962. A racing enthusiast called Barry Filer, who happened to be a customer at Dumbuck Garage, offered Jackie the chance to test his cars down at Oulton Park Circuit, Cheshire. They took along an Aston Martin, an E-type Jaguar and a Marcos. They also took along big brother Jimmy to be the hare. They returned home in no doubt – young Jackie had got something.

Apart from talent, Jackie also had an incentive to make his way in motor racing. He had married his pretty childhood sweetheart Helen McGregor and was looking for a suitable income. An Ecurie Ecosse Cooper put him in the shop window and word filtered through to a certain Ken Tyrrell, of Surrey, that he should take a look.

Tyrrell was a far less likely candidate for the world of motor racing than Stewart. 'I knew nothing about it,' he says: 'I played football for the local village team and they got up a coach party to go to Silverstone. I sat in the Stowe Corner grandstand. In the supporting race were 500cc Coopers. One of the stars was Alan Brown and in the programme it said he lived in Guildford. As I also lived in Guildford I went and knocked on his door and asked if I could have a look at his car. He showed it to me and at the end of the season I bought it from him.

'So in 1952 I became a racing driver. Just like that. It was like that in

The way I see it, Ken. . . those days. There were no racing schools. I didn't know anything about over-steer or under-steer, or anything like that. The kids today know all about that sort of thing. When I started it was just a bit of fun. I never, in those days, contemplated running a team. Then I got to be not too bad. I was never a star. But I wasn't too bad, won a couple of races, then an international race and so moved up to Formula Two.

'I was now in a much higher class, of course, competing against people who could drive very much better, and I eventually found that a young chap called Michael Taylor could do so much better in my car than I could. I had found my niche, so to speak. I got more fun doing something properly for him than I did messing about finishing seventh or eighth myself.

'In 1960 I started to run my own team with Formula Junior cars and I was always looking for up-and-coming drivers. I used to have cars on loan from Cooper and engines on loan from BMC, so I had only the cost of preparing the cars and taking them to motor races. I didn't have to pay for shunts or engine blow-ups and things like that. It was the works Formula Junior team and my cars had the two white stripes down the front. John Surtees had his first race in a car for me.'

Tyrrell was on the look-out, as usual, for promising drivers to run in 1964 when he received a tip about a young man from Scotland: 'Robin McKay, who was the track manager at Goodwood, phoned me up and said "There's a bloke going round here in a sportscar which is a bit of a wreck, but he's quick. His name is Jackie Stewart." He also mentioned that his brother was Jimmy Stewart.

'I didn't know Jimmy very well but I knew about his racing so I called him and asked him if this younger brother of his really wanted to be a racing driver. He said he thought so and I asked him to get Jackie to come down and try a car at Goodwood. Jackie said he would come down.

'We were lucky. We got a nice spring day. Bruce McLaren [by then an experienced Formula One driver] had been doing all the testing for the new Cooper F3 car and in five laps Jackie was quicker. He'd never driven a single-seater car before. Bruce had another go, went quicker, but then Jackie went quicker still. You had to be an idiot not to see he was something special.'

Tyrrell was no idiot. He offered a Formula Three seat to Stewart, who in turn had been checking out Tyrrell's credentials. Tyrrell says: 'I only found out many years later that Jackie asked Jimmy Clark what he thought and Jimmy told him he wouldn't find a better place. He did me a big favour, which was very nice of him.'

Thus started a ten-year association that continued as it began. Stewart's first Formula Three victory was at Snetterton, the very circuit where twenty-five years later, his son Paul would have his maiden success at this level. Stewart won all but two of his events in that initial season with Tyrrell.

Eventually they would reach the summit of Formula One together. Then they would do it again – and again. Their double act was to rival the Chapman–Clark combination. But while Chapman remained very much Clark's mentor, Tyrrell and Stewart became more of a partnership. Stewart, determined and forthright, learned and grew up quickly;

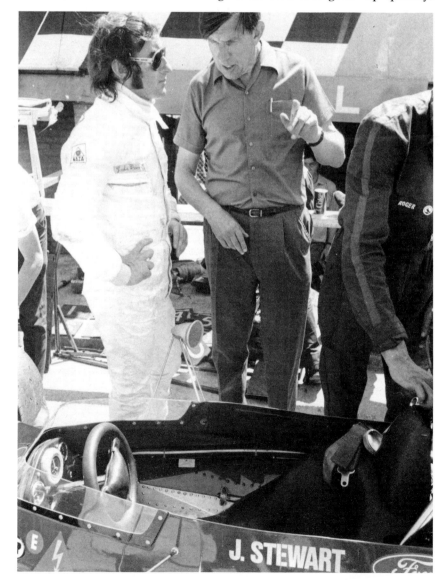

. . . but on the other hand, Jackie

Tyrrell, equally ambitious, was smart enough to let him have his say. They understood each other perfectly and worked together as near perfectly as could reasonably be hoped.

Stewart's rapid progress in that first season with Tyrrell's Formula Three operation naturally had the rest of motor racing sitting up. Soon he was having his first opportunities – and successes – in Formula Two and Formula One. He won an F2 race for Ron Harris at Snetterton and, as replacement for the injured Clark, the second heat of the Rand Grand Prix in a Lotus.

By then Stewart had committed himself to BRM for the 1965 Formula One World Championship. He considered Lotus but felt the Chapman–Clark bond might limit his scope. Cooper was another option but perhaps not, he suspected, a competitive one. BRM had a good car, a sound organisation, and offered the chance of substantial test work. It was the package that appealed to Stewart and he signed a £4,000 contract.

As we have seen, twenty-five-year-old Stewart immediately became acclimatised to the heady world of Grand Prix racing. On his debut, in South Africa, he scored his first Championship point. He followed up with third place at Monaco, second behind Clark in Belgium, second behind Clark in France, fifth behind Clark at Silverstone and second behind Clark in Holland. In Germany he retired but in Italy he stayed the course and was second to no-one. He had the first of what would be a record number of victories.

Stewart flexed his muscles for the 1966 World Championship by winning the 2½-litre Tasman Series. He had four wins, his BRM partner Hill had two, and Richard Attwood won the one race for which he replaced Hill. Clark had a solitary victory in a Lotus woefully down on power. It appeared that no-one was adequately prepared for the new 3-litre Grand Prix formula. It was a time for clever manipulation and compromises.

At Ferrari, Surtees was content with his fitness following his accident in Canada the previous autumn. As he prepared for the opening title race of 1966, the Monaco Grand Prix, he was less satisfied with his car: 'I had to drive the V12, whereas Bandini had the 2.4 which I had used as my convalescence car and was two seconds a lap quicker round Modena. It had about 240 b.h.p. but as it was 100 lb lighter than the 280 b.h.p. V12 it was considerably faster.'

For all that, Surtees led the first thirteen laps at Monte Carlo and looked capable of fending off Stewart's 2-litre BRM until the Ferrari's differential gave in. Stewart drove on to an accomplished victory. This year Hill had to settle for third place behind Bandini. This year, like every other year, Clark was out of luck. He had pole position but was left on the line, stuck in first gear. He made a spectacular surge up to second place, only for his rear suspension to break.

The 1966 calendar enabled Clark to take in Monaco as well as Indianapolis, and this time he had familiar company at the American Memorial race. Stewart, driving a Lola, led by almost a lap with eight laps to go but was let down by a scavenge pump. Hill went on to win, with Clark second, despite two high-speed spins. Even then, Chapman was not satisfied. He claimed there was a mix-up by the lap-scorers, a consequence of a big accident on the first lap. The officials were unmoved and confirmed Hill's Indy triumph.

Despite Stewart's misfortune at Indianapolis, his star was rising – inexorably, it seemed. He was driving magnificently and in this, only his second season at the highest level, he felt comfortable competing against the very best in the business. The Belgian Grand Prix at Spa, however, would interrupt his climb. More than that, it would prove a landmark for Stewart and for motor racing.

Changeable weather conditions have always been a notorious feature of this circuit and out at Malmedy a sudden cloud-burst trapped experienced and inexperienced drivers alike. A little further down the road Stewart, too, was caught out. Team-mate Hill said: 'I spun round like a top myself. When I came to a stop at the side of the road I saw Jackie's BRM in the ditch.

'He was in considerable pain, trapped by the side of the car, which had been pushed in. The petrol tanks had ruptured and he was covered with petrol. There was a big risk of fire and I turned off the fuel pump switches and then tried to lift him out. The steering wheel was jammed up against his leg and it was obvious that this would have to be removed before I could get him out.'

Stewart: 'I lay trapped in the car for twenty-five minutes, unable to be moved. Graham and Bob Bondurant [an American, also driving a BRM] got me out using the spanners from a spectator's tool kit. There were no doctors and there was nowhere to put me. They in fact put me in the back of a van.

'Eventually an ambulance took me to a first aid spot near the control tower and I was left on a stretcher, on the floor, surrounded by cigarette ends. I was put into an ambulance with a police escort and the police escort lost the ambulance, and the ambulance didn't know how to get to Liège. At the time they thought I had a spinal injury. As it turned out, I wasn't seriously injured, but they didn't know that.

'I realised that if this was the best we had there was something sadly wrong: things wrong with the race-track, the cars, the medical side, the fire-fighting and the emergency crews. There were also grass banks that were launch pads, things you went straight into, trees that were unprotected and so on. Young people today just wouldn't understand it. It was ridiculous.

'If I have any legacy to leave the sport I hope it will be seen to be in an area of safety because when I arrived in Grand Prix racing the so-called precautions and safety measures were diabolical.'

Stewart and Louis Stanley, a leading member of the BRM team, launched a dual campaign to improve safety standards and medical facilities. Stanley appealed inside and outside the sport for funds to finance his mobile medical unit. It was a noble gesture which unfortunately floundered, but thankfully modern Formula One is well organised in this area. Stewart, meanwhile, addressed himself to the wider aspects of safety and mobilised his fellow drivers to fight for improved standards. Much of what we see and take for granted today is a testimony to his triumph.

The triumph on the Spa track that day in 1966 belonged to Surtees. He drove superbly in the wet, pursuing and then overtaking Jochen Rindt's Cooper Maserati, in what was his last race for Ferrari. 'We got the power up to about 320 b.h.p. for the Belgian,' he says. 'That was much better and, of course, they continued to improve it after I left.'

Surtees' split with Ferrari came when he decided he no longer cared to put up with the politics and the intrigue that have always been essential ingredients of the Maranello soap opera. The final straw was a dispute over the pairings for Le Mans. Surtees, ever the honourable man, still declines to go into detail: 'Certainly politics were involved, certainly there were outside forces which brought pressure at Ferrari. But it was a series of things that came to a head. They were things very personal to me and to Mr Ferrari. He never discussed it and I never discussed it. But the break-up was stupid for him and it was stupid for me because we both lost the Championship. They made a big leap forward after Le Mans and one of the few times they had a specific power advantage was in the latter half of 1966, when I wasn't there. I still finished second in the Championship, but the fact is that Ferrari and I were both losers.'

The losers were not only Surtees and Ferrari. Britain lost its only realistic hope of the title that season. After four years of majestic, uninterrupted British rule, motor racing's greatest domain would fall into foreign hands.

Surtees would remain the closest challenger to Jack Brabham – driving the car of his own name – and, to his immense pleasure, he at least beat his new partner at the Cooper-Maserati team, the much-vaunted Austrian, Jochen Rindt.

The Englishman recalls: 'Certain people had criticised me because I sat behind Rindt for so long at Spa. They tried to make out that because of the accident Surtees was no longer the man he had been. How, they asked, could this man Rindt, in a Maserati-engined car, be in front of a Ferrari? One of my main satisfactions that year was that as soon as I joined the team I was faster than Rindt. That rather put one or two people in their places. Apart from a few little problems, we were normally faster than Ferrari.'

Another British driver, Mike Parkes, took over at Ferrari and made an impressive Grand Prix debut, taking second place behind Brabham in the French Grand Prix at Rheims. He was also second at Monza – after starting on pole – behind team-mate Ludovico Scarfiotti. And that was about all the rest of Ferrari's season amounted to.

Surtees: 'We had two or three possibilities to win with the Cooper-Maserati, including Monza, where a fuel tank split. But at least we had a satisfactory end to the season, winning in Mexico.'

The other British victory that season fell to Clark, at Watkins Glen. It was the only Grand Prix success for an H16 BRM-engined car. The unit was to power the challenges of BRM and Lotus that season, but it turned out to be too little, too late. It was largely a year of frustration for the Brits. Surtees finished the season with twenty-eight points, Hill (fifth) had seventeen, Clark (sixth) had sixteen, Stewart (seventh) had fourteen and Parkes (joint eighth) had twelve.

Stewart missed only one race, the French Grand Prix, following his accident and, if little else, was able to put some experience in the bank over the remaining course of the season. For 1967 he would be the team leader with a veritable backing group of British drivers – Mike Spence,

Surtees and Ferrari before the split, 1966

Piers Courage, Richard Attwood and Chris Irwin. He looked ahead to a change of fortune, particularly in the engine department.

Hill, on the other hand, had decided it was time to move on: 'I left BRM to rejoin Colin Chapman and Lotus. I'd been with BRM for seven years and I thought I'd better move in case they painted me over. People can get so used to you that they go deaf if you keep complaining about something. It was a difficult choice but we parted on the best of terms. I was very happy to join Jim Clark at Lotus.'

During the later stages of the 1966 season Surtees had talks with Honda. The motor cycling connection was obvious and yes, he was 'certainly interested'. Honda had been taking stock and there were doubts about their future in Formula One, but if Surtees agreed to join them they would continue. They would establish a base in England, though the budget would be tight. Surtees recognised that he would be putting his career at risk, and yet here was a new challenge. He'd rarely been able to resist a new challenge, and he couldn't resist this one.

For many of the Formula One fraternity, 1967 was a year of transition and further engine development programmes – euphemisms for problems and frustrations. Stewart wound up the season with only ten points, Hill with fifteen. In his book *Graham*, Hill dismisses the year like this: 'There were a lot of breakdowns during 1967, my first year with Lotus . . . ' With that he strides purposefully into 1968.

His new team-mate, Clark, had a more productive Championship, though only after a laboured start. Driving the H16 BRM-engined car, he was soon confronted with a losing battle against over-heating, and eventually a fuel pump failure terminated his South African Grand Prix. Surtees would have his moments this season, and he opened his Honda account with third place. The race winner was Mexican Pedro Rodriguez – in the Cooper-Maserati Surtees left behind.

Hill was, as usual, in the groove at Monaco, taking second place. Stewart was on form until a transmission failure on the fifteenth lap. Surtees was also in contention for more points until a piston went. Clark had an eventful day, spinning, breaking the lap record and spinning again, this time out of the race. He was unhurt but Surtees' former partner, Bandini, crashed his Ferrari chasing eventual winner Denny Hulme and died from his burns in hospital three days later. That tragedy and the death of Bob Anderson in testing at Silverstone three months later reinforced the campaign for improved safety standards.

At Zandvoort, a new chapter in the history of Formula One began. The Ford Cosworth V8 engine arrived, powering the Lotus 49 cars of Clark and Hill. Its impact was immediate and spectacular. Hill forced his way to pole position and led until he had to drop out with a camshaft failure. Clark's car had not gone so well in practice but he picked up the pace in the race and came through to give the engine a debut success. Mike Parkes was fifth, but no other British driver finished in the points.

Pat Mennem recalls Clark's first experience of the Cosworth: 'The power was such that they had to put a piece of wood behind the seat to brace his head when he put his foot down. They just weren't used to that sudden surge of power.'

Genuine 3-litre brawn carried Clark and Hill to the front row at Spa. Clark was the early race leader, opening up his new machine to reach speeds of more than 190 m.p.h. It did not last. A faulty plug sabotaged his plans. It was a fruitless exercise for Hill and for Surtees. Stewart had a more profitable day, coming in second behind American Dan Gurney, who registered the first and last victory for the Eagle Westlake.

Both Hill and Clark led in the French Grand Prix at Le Mans (held on the rather mundane Bugatti circuit as opposed to the longer, more formidable twenty-four-hour course) yet again they ran into trouble. Stewart had another useful day, picking up third place, while Irwin persisted with his BRM for fifth place. Clark and Hill were fastest at Silverstone and this time Clark, at least, kept going to win his home Grand Prix for the fifth time.

There were still disappointments to come for Clark and Hill, but they could console themselves with the certain knowledge that the new

John Surtees' victory for Honda in the 1967 Italian Grand Prix

Lotus–Ford combination had enormous potential. This Championship might be out of the question. The next one . . . now that would be a different matter.

The road ahead was less clear for Stewart and BRM, while Surtees knew it was time for positive action at Honda. Surtees toiled and suffered to coax his heavy car into fourth place at the Nurburgring and decided enough was enough. Surtees would miss the Canadian Grand Prix, but Monza was only five weeks away. Could they possibly build a new car in that time? With the help of his old friend Eric Broadley, they did. The lightweight Honda, albeit an interim version of what they really wanted, would make its debut in Italy.

It was an extraordinary occasion from start to finish. The cars were supposed to roll forward from a dummy grid but Jack Brabham misinterpreted the starter's signal and put his foot down. No-one stayed around to ask questions. The stampede was on. When the dust settled the men out front were Clark and Hulme. A puncture brought the Lotus into the pits and set up a familiar Clark charge. He advanced from fifteenth place to regain the lead – only to be denied by fuel problems. It was a race to the line for two men: Brabham and . . . Surtees. Amazingly, the Honda made it, by two-tenths of a second. The luckless Clark was third.

The race goes down as one of Clark's greatest, yet in the context of that season (and that five-week period!) it was a phenomenal achievement by Surtees and his workforce. The Italian fans – for whom Clark had never been a favourite – had no doubts about the hero of the hour. The echoes of 'Il Grande Gianni' still bring a smile to Surtees' face. 'It was very satisfying for me and for all the team,' he says: 'We had all put so much effort into it. And then, of course, the Italians gave me such a tremendous reception. They had accepted me as one of their own. They still go on about that day.'

The game also goes on, and the Lotus camp were not about to waste time dwelling on misfortune. Hill and Clark were fastest in practice at Watkins Glen and were so confident of dominating the race they spun a coin for the privilege of crossing the line first. Hill won but his car was a little off-colour on race day and Clark was obliged to assume command. Hill had the consolation of second place and Clark's sincere apologies.

Clark was on pole for the final race of the season in Mexico and, despite a messy start, came through to take the flag. It was the twenty-fourth win of his career and equalled Fangio's record. He finished third in the 1967 Championship behind the Brabham Repcos of Hulme and Brabham, but it was clear to all that the Lotus Ford would be the car to beat in 1968.

Surtees was fourth in Mexico City and, with twenty points, joint fourth in the final title table. Hill, on fifteen points, was joint sixth, Stewart ninth and Spence, fifth in that last race, completed the top ten.

We have established that Lotus were in 'good shape', as they say, and that Clark and Hill could look ahead with confidence. But what lay in store for the other British drivers? Surtees had pointed Honda in the right direction. He knew, though, that it was only the start. They needed the will and the funds to carry on down that road.

Of the Big Four, Stewart had endured the most tedious season. After that high-flying first year in Grand Prix racing he'd been brought down to earth with a resounding bump. It was patently time to move on, though in Stewart's case he didn't really have to move far. He'd stayed with Ken Tyrrell in the bread-and-butter racing and now they were ready to go off together in search of jam. Given their success in the following years, they were entitled to call it preserve.

Tyrrell reveals how the shrewd businessman in Stewart surfaced as they put their Formula One venture on the track: 'He was driving that awful sixteen-cylinder thing at BRM and we were running Matra cars in Formula Two. So I said to Jackie "How about if we get hold of that Ford engine and get Matra to build us a car?" He said it would cost me a lot of money to do that. I asked him how much he wanted and he said £20,000. Well, I didn't have 20,000 pennies, never mind £20,000. So I went to Walter Hayes, at Ford, and told him Jackie had an offer from Ferrari. [Stewart had, indeed, been involved in negotiations with Ferrari but eventually pulled out, saying he was not impressed with the way they conducted their business.]

'I said I thought Jackie would come with me and felt I could find the money to do it, but in order to get the thing on the move I needed £20,000. I asked him if he would guarantee me that amount whether or not I found it. Walter, who never misses a chance like that, said "You're on."

'I told Jackie I'd done the deal so we had to go and find the money. We went to Dunlop and we got £80,000 from them to run the team. Matra provided the chassis, I bought the engines and gearboxes and did all the race preparation. I called Walter, thanked him and explained we didn't need the money.

'That's how we did it. We did things together all the way through. When we needed money, we'd go out together to find some. That sort of thing is less likely to happen today, I suppose.'

Stewart knew and trusted Tyrrell, as a man and as a racing team manager. He was confident they could be effective in Formula One. He did not dare set his hopes too high, but after the traumas and setbacks of the previous eighteen months he felt there was, at any rate, some hope. Preparations were rushed through and, although the paint job left a little to be desired, Stewart's car was just about ready for the opening race of the 1968 World Championship, the South African Grand Prix, on 1 January.

Not surprisingly, Lotus approached the season in positive mood. Clark now seemed to be at his zenith, the 49 chassis and Ford engine appeared untouchable. Lotus arrived at Kyalami with familiar green and yellow livery, but sponsorship from Gold Leaf cigarettes was on the way. Chapman was a pioneer in all areas. The tobacco people soon had evidence that they were backing a winner. Clark and Hill were first and second on the grid, first and second across the finishing line.

Stewart lifted the spirits of the Tyrrell–Matra organisation by qualifying third and leading the first lap of the race. He had to give way to Clark, then Hill and eventually to engine damage. It had, however, been a hugely encouraging start.

For Lotus it was more than that. This, surely, was the beginning of an all-conquering season. Clark now had twenty-five Grand Prix wins, an outright record. There appeared no reason why he shouldn't take his total beyond the reach of generations to come.

The next Formula One World Championship race was not scheduled to take place until May. Clark went to the Tasman series and walked away with it. In March he was at Indianapolis testing the Lotus Turbine and then he travelled to Barcelona for a Formula Two event. It was the final warm-up race before the start of the F2 Championship at Hockenheim and Clark was none too pleased when Jacky Ickx shunted him off. The German race was, after all, only a week away.

Clark might have been at Brands Hatch that following Sunday, 7 April, driving a Ford in the BOAC 500, a round of the World Sportscar Championship. But he was contracted to Lotus, whose deal with Gold Leaf included Formula Two. Chapman was determined to give the F2 Championship his best shot and his best shot, of course, was Clark.

That weekend at Hockenheim, though, the signs were not good for Clark and Lotus. The weather conditions – cold and damp – were conspiring against them. Furthermore, Clark did not like the track. The car did not work well in practice, and the driver was uneasy.

In the same race, and staying at the same hotel, was Derek Bell. He recalls: 'Jimmy said to me "When you come up to lap me don't get too close." When I came up to lap him! If Stirling Moss was my hero, Jim Clark was my idol. He explained that he'd got a misfire. His mechanic had his car up and down the road outside the hotel at five or six o'clock in the morning, trying to sort out this misfire. I had breakfast with Jimmy and Graham and then drove to the track with them.'

Clark's mechanic was Dave Sims, now team manager of Tom's GB, who run the Toyotas in the World Sportscar Championship. He says: 'The problem was, it was so cold. It was freezing. There was a heavy frost. It was so cold it was affecting the metering units. Also, the drive belts were breaking. In the end I used boiling water. That cured it.

'I was the only mechanic on Jimmy's car. We were a bit stretched. But what happened had nothing to do with that. The car was running all right in the race. We started on wets, Firestones, and Jimmy wasn't happy with

Line of Succession

The last race . . . Dave Sims with Jim Clark at Hockenheim, 1968

95

them. Graham and Chris [Amon] weren't either. I was the last person to speak to Jimmy. He said he wasn't happy with the set-up, the handling, the grip, in the wet. He told me not to expect too much from him. He wasn't going to go off into the distance. He was just going to suss it out.

'He wasn't very confident, but I don't think he feared anything was going to happen to him. You can sense when drivers feel under pressure. But then he had a lot of other commitments. He had to get back for so many things. There was Formula One testing. It was all very hectic. In the early part of the race he was hanging back, just as he said he would.'

It was the first heat of the Deutschland Trophy. Clark was running a disconsolate eighth when he passed the pits, turned right and headed out into the woods for the fifth time. He never returned. A flag marshal posted where the fast road sweeps to the right said the Lotus twitched one way and then the other before spearing across the track, into a clump of saplings. The car was destroyed, Jim Clark was dead.

There are those who still regard the accident as a mystery. Hill wrote: 'Just what caused Jimmy's accident we'll never know. It certainly wasn't driver error. Nobody has satisfactorily explained why Stirling Moss went straight off the track at Goodwood and no-one is ever likely to come up with the answer to this one.'

There were many theories. One was that the engine cut out. Another, more extraordinary suggestion, was that children had run across the track. Chapman, on a family holiday in St. Moritz, was stunned by the news. He drove through the night to Hockenheim and instigated a full investigation.

The investigation eliminated structural failure and revealed that there was a cut in the right rear tyre. Chapman had no doubt that the cause of the accident was a puncture. When I asked Dave Sims for his opinion he was very precise, very definite in delivering his verdict: 'It was a right rear instant deflation.' He added: 'Jimmy was the perfect gentleman. He never lost his cool, never got out of control, never swore. I'm just proud to have known him and worked with him. I've never really talked to anyone about that day. Nobody asked me and I didn't want to, anyway. It was a bit personal, you know?'

Such was Jim Clark's greatness and popularity, everyone in Britain and motor racing felt a personal loss. And apart from the sadness and the tributes there were expressions of bewilderment. What, Jimmy? Surely not. Where did it happen? In what race? It seemed so incredible, so senseless. And from the drivers he left behind, there came another question: 'If Jimmy can be killed, how safe can we be?'

Trevor Taylor, friend and colleague, was at Brands Hatch the day Clark died. He says: 'Jimmy should have been with us instead of that silly tinpot race. I remember we were in the transporter when somebody came in and told us what had happened. I thought "you're joking". Everybody was numbed. But it didn't really sink in until that evening. Then you asked yourself "how can it be?".

'I had one or two accidents and eventually packed up when I realised I couldn't cope with age and the younger generation. People tell me I was unlucky in my career but I don't think so. I had some great times and I retired at the age of thirty-six with my limbs and my life. I think I've been

Opposite page

Above: The shy hero

Below: Watson's magnificent charge, Long Beach, 1983

lucky. Clark, Hawthorn, Collins . . . where are they?'

Jim Clark lived to the age of thirty-two. He died, as we are always reminded, doing what he wanted to do. He will be remembered as a supreme sportsman at the peak of his powers. He won two World Championships and twenty-five of his seventy-two races. Significantly, he finished second only once – behind Surtees. He had thirty-three pole positions (a record which stood for twenty-one years) and twenty-seven fastest laps.

But what of the man? Pat Mennem learned more than most about Clark while writing the driver's newspaper column. He says: 'It was very difficult to get to know Jimmy because of Colin Chapman's influence. Chapman had this Svengali effect on him. Jimmy kept to himself. While Graham enjoyed the adulation and playing the role of ambassador, Jimmy didn't. He was shy in a situation like that. He didn't like being accosted by people or slapped on the back. He was a reluctant hero. He absolutely detested Indianapolis. He couldn't stand all the razzmatazz.

'He was never able to relax. Often before a race he would bite his fingernails. I used to tell him to stop but he said "Look, you smoke, I bite my fingernails." With the mechanics and so on he would be all right but then, just before he got behind the wheel, he really used to get wound up.

'The only time he loosened up was when he went back up to Scotland. He was basically a gentleman, a Border farmer, and shy. I remember going up to the farm and then on in to town with him on market day. We went to lunch and met a lot of his farming friends. It was quite extraordinary. There he was, World Champion, and not one of them mentioned motor racing. They were chatting about sheep all the time. His achievements in racing didn't mean a thing to them.

'He was whisked out of his element and to some extent he couldn't cope. I don't think he was a desperately happy man. Eventually he had to go to France because of the tax situation. He was on the booze a bit, too, because he was getting so fed up. He once called me from Heathrow to go and join him for a drink. He was lonely and wanted some company. It didn't occur to him that it wasn't as easy as that. I would have had to go through Customs to meet him.'

One subject Clark kept to himself was his love life. He had a number of girlfriends, notably a model called Sally Stokes, but insisted he would not marry until he retired from racing. 'He told me that when he got married it would be to someone with a thousand acres in the Borders,' says Mennem.

Despite this rather sad portrait of Clark, he had a lighter side, too. Mennem points out: 'Occasionally he released the pressure and could be quite mischievous. He had this naughty schoolboy thing about him.'

Sims: 'Jimmy would start a bread-roll throwing free-for-all and then quietly slide away, leaving the rest to it. He'd stand watching from the side with that innocent "nothing to do with me" look on his face. One night in Rouen the Lotus mechanics and the Brabham mechanics were together and things got a bit out of control. There was a slight disturbance. The police weren't too impressed and locked us up for the night. Jimmy came round the following morning, sorted things out and we were released. He never told the Old Man. Jimmy saw the funny side of it. That's

The reluctant hero

Opposite page

Above: The breakthrough for Warwick and Toleman, Zandvoort, 1983

Below: Days of hope . . . Warwick and the Renault, 1984

Jim Clark . . . back in the environment he always missed

the sort of bloke he was.'

Clark's manner, as well as his ability, earned the respect of everyone around him. Taylor: 'He was a super team-mate, a genuine mate. It was no problem being No. 2 to Jimmy. He never talked about himself or his success. He was very modest.'

Bell takes a similar view: 'He was such a nice, polite bloke. He would talk to everybody. But because he was such an idol people didn't dare talk to him that much. They kept a respectful distance. I was amazed how easy-going he was.'

Sims describes another of Clark's abilities: 'He had this uncanny knack of knowing when something was wrong. If he said something was amiss you knew he was right. You had to take his word for it and start looking for the problem. Lots of drivers say this or that is wrong and often there's nothing wrong at all. With Jimmy, if he said something was wrong you KNEW there was.'

Above all, he was a quite brilliant driver. Perhaps the best? Such debates may well be dismissed as fatuous. It is, of course, difficult, if not impossible, to compare sportsmen of different eras. And yet the 'who-was-the-greatest?' arguments do go on, in motor racing as in all other sports. Leading the all-time, global contenders, would be men like Tazio Nuvolari and Fangio. Confine the discussion to British drivers and, with due deference to Stewart and the rest, it tends to come down to Moss versus Clark.

Tyrrell, Stewart's great accomplice, says: 'I think Jackie would tell you he would not have been World Champion if Jimmy had still been around. Jimmy was exceptional. I never try to say who was the best of all because I just don't know the answer. You have different times, different cars. I raced against Stirling in Formula Three and of course he won nearly every race he entered. I also have a very vivid F1 recollection of him, at Silverstone, coming through Woodcote in the wet when Woodcote was a very fast, open corner. He was lapping Jack Brabham and acknowledging the pit signals – driving one-handed in the rain! Now that's a touch of class. Showy, arrogant, maybe. But when you're that good, you can do it.'

Taylor: 'Jimmy was a natural. You get one in every sport, someone who is just born with it. Others have to work at it. Graham, for instance, worked and worked. Stirling learned like an engineer. Everything Jimmy did was natural. He was the finest I ever saw and superior, I felt, to Moss. I followed Jimmy at Oulton Park once and thought I'd try and stay with him, brake where he did and so on. I couldn't. You thought he was going to have an accident but of course he wasn't. I would have done if I'd tried to do the same thing. You know what you can do. Jimmy was just something else and you couldn't imitate him.'

Stewart: 'I don't know about Jimmy having more natural talent. Stirling had as much natural talent as there was. Jimmy had a unique style and skill of driving. Jimmy was also privileged and fortunate to have with him Colin Chapman, who to my mind will go down in history as the greatest designer of racing cars. That man broke boundaries wherever he went. I'm not suggesting it was purely Colin Chapman's achievement. Jim Clark was the greatest driver I ever raced against. It was the perfect marriage of the two ultimate skills. Together they were unbeatable.'

The 'Chapman factor' features in most of the evidence from the pro-Moss lobby. Tony Brooks: 'Jim was a great driver but he always had the fastest, or equal fastest car. You've a hell of a start in a situation like that. Stirling didn't often have the fastest car and the Vanwalls were quite difficult to drive. You could really see the difference between the drivers in Stirling's day and there were enough drivers for there to be really keen competition. I think that period showed up driver skills more than pre-War and more than the post-Moss eras.

'And Stirling drove everything. At one meeting he'd drive a 500, he'd get out of that and into a sportscar, then out of that and into a grand touring car, then out of that into a Grand Prix car. Now maybe Nuvolari and Clark could have done that, maybe Senna could. But Stirling *did* do that. If I had to pick one as the all-round best, the all-time great, I would go for Stirling.'

Innes Ireland: 'Stirling would have fitted in with today's racing. He was a very serious chap, very dedicated to racing. He applied himself and his intelligence to the cars and how to get the best out of them. He was very critical and rightly critical of many of the cars he drove, but he always made them better. Even Fangio would always pay attention to what Moss was doing when they were together at Mercedes. He would find out what Stirling was having done to his car and follow suit.

'I don't think you can really compare drivers of different eras. Stirling was certainly one of the greatest, though funnily enough I don't think he was a totally natural driver. Jimmy was a totally natural driver and so, I think, was Jackie. But then I think you have to say that Jimmy was in the right place at the right time. There have always been instances where somebody was in the right place at the right time, with the right car and everything else.'

Rob Walker: 'Jimmy was a natural. He was superb. But I don't think he was a Stirling because he had to have Colin Chapman. I truly believe Stirling was the greatest driver. I have a photograph of myself at the TT putting out a signal to Stirling: "122 seconds + Clark". Jimmy was driving an Aston Martin then. He didn't have Colin Chapman. And, as I've said before, Stirling used to drive anything, some of them terrible old bangers.'

Sims: 'It's fair to say that Moss, overall, didn't have such good machinery as Jimmy, but Clark also drove some beasts. Not all Chapman's cars were so good. Some were animals. The Lotus 30 and 40 sportscars, for instance. But Jimmy would still get in and drive at ten tenths. He could drive anything. Not every driver can go to Indianapolis and outdrive good, experienced guys on their own patch. Jimmy did.'

Bell: 'Stirling was more aggressive than Jimmy but then Jimmy, for some reason, didn't need the aggression. He always drove within himself. He was very calm and collected. He never looked as if he was stretched and I think he had it in him to go quicker. Yes, he had a wonderful rapport with Colin Chapman and I guess it must have been rather nice driving the Lotus Cosworth. I drove the Cooper–Maserati, which was like driving a tractor. But I think Jimmy was the ultimate driver. He didn't have to develop – he was that good all the way through.'

Mennem: 'Clark had fantastic balance. I think he was pretty fearless, as well. He took me round the Spa circuit in a Lotus Elan and never took his foot off the floor. He was explaining everything, driving with one hand and pointing with the other. Most people used to lift a little at the kink. Not Jimmy. He kept it flat. And, of course, he won Spa four times. Now that was really something. But then he was quite superb. The extraordinary thing about him was that he never seemed to make mistakes. He was impeccable.

'At Rouen he asked Patrick Lindsay if he could drive his ERA. He'd never sat upright in a single-seater in his life. It had the big steering wheel and everything. He climbed in, did one lap, and on the second lap he broke the record for vintage cars. Quite incredible. He did a bit of rallying. He went on the RAC. But he didn't have the time or the advantages to do as much as Stirling. Just think of him, though, in the Lotus Cortina on the track. He invented three-wheel driving in that.

'Stirling was a magnificent performer and he performed in everything. He really was very, very good. But in Grand Prix cars, I believe Jimmy just had the edge.'

What no-one disputes is that both Moss and Clark were stupendous drivers. Their legacy is a wealth of inspiring memories. It is generally regarded as a great pity that they never confronted each other in their pomp, with equal equipment, and similarly that Clark never met Stewart on equal terms.

But is it?

7

The Eternal Challenge

Graham Hill worked hard at everything. Now he had to make a huge effort to overcome the death of Jim Clark, his team-mate and friend, and carry on racing. He said: 'I was terribly upset but, as a racing driver, I couldn't allow my emotions to come through. If I did I would have been lost and unable to cope – and I'm sure all racing drivers feel the same. You may feel the loss deeply and grieve inwardly, but it must never be allowed to get on top of you.'

It was not easy and people could see it was not easy. He had the burden of lifting not only himself but an entire team. Colin Chapman and Lotus were devastated. Chapman even contemplated quitting motor racing. Yet no matter how onerous the task, how painful the process, Hill was determined to come through it. This year would test his resolve and his nerve like no other.

Little over a month after Clark's accident, Hill and Lotus prepared to face up once again to the business of World Championship motor racing. The first race of this strange new life without Jimmy was the Spanish Grand Prix at Jarama. The ordeal was unrelenting. News came through of another tragedy and the loss of another Briton – Mike Spence was killed in practice at Indianapolis. It seemed Chapman and Hill could not escape the gloom, and now a Grand Prix was upon them.

Mike Spence, killed at
Indianapolis

Hill assessed that the only antidote to this despair was victory. Apart from character and will-power he had, after all, the best car in Formula One. There would also be a significant absentee from the ranks of the opposition. Jackie Stewart had to pull out with a wrist injury – later revealed to be a broken scaphoid – sustained in practice for a Formula Two event at the same Spanish track. Stewart would also miss Monaco. The full significance of this enforced break would become apparent later in the year.

Hill was not the fastest in practice – Amon, Rodriguez and Hulme occupied the front row – but in the race things fell into place for the Englishman. Both Amon and Rodriguez led only to run out of luck. Hill, cagey and reliable as ever, ran out the winner, ahead of Hulme's McLaren Ford. Britain's Brian Redman, in only his second race, was third with the Cooper BRM. It was to remain his best result.

It was perfectly obvious to everyone that Hill would have a few more good results before the season was out. He was on pole at Monaco and, with a car now growing wings, claimed his fourth success at the Principality ahead of Richard Attwood's BRM. Hill's new partner, Jackie Oliver, had a bumpy ride and didn't stay the course.

Stewart could only look on in mounting frustration. He knew his car was competitive, perhaps even capable of putting the Lotus under pressure. But he had missed two races and Hill had taken full advantage. The

Scot was determined to be back for the Belgian Grand Prix, no matter what. He had his plaster cast replaced by a plastic sleeve and decided to give it a try in practice. He was universally certified as quite mad but second fastest qualifying time convinced him there was hope of regaining some Championship ground, if not necessarily his sanity.

The lead changed hands several times and Stewart confounded everybody by holding it for fifteen laps. The Matra spluttered to a halt on the last lap, however, and Stewart was classified fourth. Still, he felt the gamble had been justified and there was no doubt the car was making good progress. The wrist apart, he was in a healthy position, especially as Hill broke a drive-shaft and was not on the Spa score-sheet. Oliver was off the mark with fifth place.

Another leader that day was Surtees. He also set fastest lap – just under 150 m.p.h. – and thought his season was at last taking off. Instead a bolt parted company with the rest of the machine, the rear suspension was done and he added another 'should-have-been' episode to his hard luck story. The theme continued with an alternator failure in Holland.

The wet Zandvoort track trapped many but Stewart took the lead from Hill after three laps and protected it to the end. The slower pace of the race put less stress on the wrist and he was able to endure the full distance. Hill, like Surtees, had another blank.

Hill's barren spell persisted at Rouen, France, on a day when three other Britons were among the points. The promising Piers Courage was fifth, Stewart third and Surtees, relieved to be in business, finished second behind the Ferrari of Jacky Ickx. It was not, though, a joyous occasion for Surtees and Honda. Frenchman Jo Schlesser, driving an air-cooled Honda which Surtees considered 'unfit' to race, crashed and died.

Hill, aware of the emerging threat from Stewart, went to Brands Hatch intent on re-asserting himself. He should have known better. He had never won the British Grand Prix and there was to be no break with tradition. He led for twenty-three laps after taking over from Oliver, only for a universal joint to give in. His team-mate went on, local knowledge and his high-mounted aerofoil serving him well. Then he, too, was forced out by transmission trouble.

Surtees was looking strong – until his aerofoil fell off. It was all he could do to hold off Stewart for fifth place. It had not been the best of days for the home contingent.

When people talk about the great races they invariably talk about the 1968 German Grand Prix. That is, of course, a misnomer. It was not a race at all. It was one of the great *drives* – by Jackie Stewart. The rigours of Brands Hatch had drained him and waiting at the Nurburgring was torrential rain. Tyrrell was anxious to stay in contention for the Championship and Stewart agreed to go out.

As at Zandvoort, the conditions actually helped him. But while he confidently picked his way through the rivers of rain-water and the eerie low clouds, the rest were struggling in his wake. He went away and kept on going away. Stewart's performance was awe-inspiring. He won by almost seven miles. He was out of his car, sheltering from the rain and casually chatting when the next car, Hill's Lotus, arrived – 4 minutes and 3.2 seconds behind. Stewart recalls: 'It was very satisfying because I won

by such a big margin and because I was still troubled by my wrist. Had it been a dry race I don't know that I would have been able to go the distance. Because it was wet the steering was lighter. The conditions were so diabolical that the race would never be run today.'

All together . . . the start of the 1968 German Grand Prix

They came out of the darkness to Monza, five weeks later. Stewart's wrist was now healing fast and the Tyrrell camp were buoyant. Hill was in combative mood and so was Surtees. The British squad also included two ambitious rookies – David Hobbs in a Honda, and Derek Bell, in a Ferrari. It was Bell's first Formula One World Championship race. At one stage in the proceedings he decided it was his last.

Surtees started from pole but found himself contesting third place with Chris Amon's Ferrari: 'I was sitting on Amon's tail when his oil pump went and put oil all over the road, sending him off and me as well.'

Bell: 'My engine had stopped and I was walking back when Chris hit Surtees, and hit the guardrail backwards on the outside of the Lesmo, right in front of me. He went over the top and down into the trees. I

103

thought "that's it." Jimmy Clark and one or two other drivers had been killed that year and now I thought my team-mate had been killed. My confidence was shattered. Next thing I know Chris comes walking up on to the side of the track and says "hello".'

Amon had been left dangling by his belts from the car – which was wedged upside down in the trees! He was cut free, unhurt, by a marshal. Surtees, too, came out of the incident unharmed.

The British Racing Hero

Bell would have only a limited Formula One career. He appeared in nine races at this level, his last, ironically, in a Surtees Ford in 1974. His best result was sixth place in the 1970 United States Grand Prix. He was to enjoy enormous success, however, as a sportscar driver. He won Le Mans five times and the world title twice. He entered the 1990s still hungry for more.

At Monza Stewart broke down and Hill lost a wheel. It was still getting no easier. Courage was the best-placed British driver. He was fourth, as was Hill in Canada. Stewart got a point there after a lengthy pit stop, Surtees got nothing.

At Watkins Glen Stewart was beaten for pole by a Lotus Ford, driven not by Hill but by an American of Italian descent making his first appearance in Grand Prix racing. His name: Mario Andretti. Normality and British pride were restored in the race. It ended with Stewart first, Hill second and Surtees third.

The 1968 Championship had a last race decider. Surtees was not involved this time; Stewart and Hill were. Hill still had the edge, but Stewart had given himself a chance. So had Hulme, though he was the outsider. The scores were: Hill thirty-nine points, Stewart thirty-six, Hulme thirty-three.

Both British drivers felt the pressure during the countdown to the Mexican Grand Prix. The permutations pounded in their heads. Stewart knew that from his point of view it came down to this: he had to win or come well ahead of Hill's Lotus.

Hill admitted: 'As the two days of practice wore on I began to get more and more intense and withdrawn and became pretty anti-social. That's one of the reasons why Bette didn't come over. I knew I was going to be pretty mean and there was just the chance I might have taken it out on her. I don't like that kind of unpleasantness and prefer to be alone under such conditions.'

The early exchanges promised a classic. Stewart, Hill and Hulme were at the head of the field. Then Hulme's suspension failed and he went off. It was down to the Brits. Stewart feared the worst when the engine began to come and go. He was losing power and with it the Championship. He clung on in hope, but the Lotus maintained form and Hill was home. The Matra limped in seventh. The title was Hill's for a second time.

The final Championship standings were: Hill forty-eight points, Stewart thirty-six, Hulme thirty-three. Surtees, with twelve points, was joint seventh. Clark, with nine points from the last Grand Prix of his life, was listed eleventh.

Even given that the Lotus was a superb car and Stewart was distinctly handicapped by his broken wrist, this was a momentous triumph for Hill. He had displayed immense courage, dedication and loyalty. He gave the team strength – and eventually a smile again. Bette Hill's pride is enduring and justified: 'After Jimmy was killed Graham picked up that entire team and seven months later they were champions.'

The whole nation shared that pride. Stewart was already much admired but his time would come. In 1968 Hill was the man swimming with the tide of sentiment and popular support.

Surtees had been carried along on waves of promise only to come crashing down on the unforgiving rocks of reality: 'It was a year of ifs and buts and should-haves, but the fact is we didn't get the results. We should have won the Belgian Grand Prix, we were steaming away, and then that silly bolt fell out. We were going very well at Monza until that business with Amon. And so on.'

Honda decided this was not the time to pursue the challenge of Formula One. They would resume the course and follow it through with spectacular success a generation on. Surtees: 'The sad thing is that in 1968 it was coming right. A new engine was designed by Mr Kume, who is now the chief of Honda. The whole thing was laid out. Of course they had the air-cooled idea, which was very sad and totally wrong. Then the realities of commercial life hit hard. Financial forces told them they must concentrate on their business, so they went away and started the Civic programme which was, of course, the beginnings of what we see today. I was left to think "what do we do now?".'

Derek Bell found success in sportscar racing

He went to see BRM. 'They agreed to introduce a very down-to-earth programme. The thoughts of developing further the sixteen-cylinder would be forgotten and the programme with the twelve-cylinder would proceed. The twelve looked as if it had some promise so I joined them.'

New promise, new challenge: always an intoxicating cocktail for Surtees. He drank it . . . and got another hangover. He was fifth in the second race of the season, the Spanish Grand Prix, and third in the second last race, the United States Grand Prix. He emerged with a paltry six points: 'The twelve-cylinder would go quite well for a couple of laps and then lose power. This was finally traced to the cylinder head area. They improved this towards the end of the year and got it quite right during the winter. There were one or two good lads there with some good ideas but they couldn't follow them up. They didn't have much of a budget.

'By that time Tony Rudd had had enough of the politics, I think, and I'd certainly got sick of the political scene. You couldn't rely on anything that was said, you couldn't feel united in having a go at the opposition. I had to think of the future. It was the turning point. I'd unwittingly got involved in building some cars, the Formula 5000s, which were going rather well. I hadn't really intended getting involved but it took more and more time and distracted me from concentrating on being a driver.'

Another challenge was at his feet. A mighty challenge. It would take a lot of lifting to the level of his dreams but that – naturally – was not going to deter him. Surtees would run his own Grand Prix team, and his own cars. He drove a McLaren Ford during the early part of 1970 and introduced the Surtees Ford for the British Grand Prix at Brands Hatch.

Surtees' first points at the wheel of his own car came in their fifth race, the Canadian Grand Prix, where he finished fifth. Derek Bell brought in another for the team at the next race, at Watkins Glen. Surtees' cars scored eight points in 1971 and eighteen in 1972. They were fifth in the Constructors' Championship, behind Lotus, Tyrrell, McLaren and Ferrari, and ahead of March, BRM, Matra and Brabham. Surtees drove in only one race that year and decided to quit the cockpit to spend more time in the boss's hot seat.

The early years had encouraged him, but he was to get no nearer to his dream than he had in that 1972 season. His demands were high, as they had always been high. So, too, though, were the costs. The deeper he went into the jungle, the darker it became. He soldiered on until 1978 and could go no further. Surtees' cars had 117 starts in Grand Prix racing but no wins.

His recollections now are as clear as the day. The sun lights up a gentle, comforting scene, where the Surrey countryside rolls into Kent. Surtees' home is an imposing manor house. He sits quite still as he plays back his career: 'The biggest mistakes I made in my career were probably due to my getting a little bit carried away after my initial experience in car racing. I was swept along by enthusiasm and took on challenges which were, I suppose, dreams. I should possibly have put myself in the best car of the time rather than get all excited about a motor-cycle manufacturer coming in.

'I was convinced Honda would get it right and eventually they did. If they had put the resources into it then, they would not have had to wait all these years. My move to Honda was right by JS's thinking, but it wasn't right for JS as a driver. You don't have that many years and you should take what is capable of winning at that time rather than have these dreams.

'I think the most important thing to me is that in my mind – and of course people may dispute this – I was, over some years on bikes, the best. Similarly, I look back on those years when I honestly considered I was the fastest in cars. That's the biggest satisfaction I have. A lot of people tended to think they could turn from one sport to the other when they were over the hill in their own sport, whereas I was only twenty-five. I still had another ten years of motor cycling in me if I'd wanted it. I believed No. 1 in the team should be decided by whoever was the faster. That's the attitude I adopted all through my career.

'Obviously there are races I'd like to have won. I was leading Monte Carlo up to a couple of laps from the end and ran out of petrol. Another time something else happened. So I didn't win there. Same at Le Mans. A couple of times we might have won it when silly things happened. In motor racing the luck is either with you or it's not.

'The fact that I got a few things wrong, got side-tracked, is a little disappointing. But I suppose being the person I am I'd probably go back and make the same mistakes. It's sad that when I ran a team I couldn't be true to myself. I had to go along and compromise to a far greater extent than I had ever done. I had no alternative because I didn't have the money. I tried to be a Jack-of-all-trades and people said I did too much. I did, but then I had to. We couldn't afford to have other people do it.

'We put a Formula Two and a Formula One team on the grid with £23,000 worth of sponsorship in 1972 and we had cars which could run in the first six in Formula One and cars which won the Formula Two

Championship. We thought we had a major breakthrough when we got the offer of sponsorship from an electrical equipment company. The agreement was for more that £100,000.

'On the strength of it, we went for a new factory. We wanted to get the base camp right. It meant borrowing quite a bit of money. The only trouble was, the company didn't pay. So we were left carrying a big overdraft and in dire straits. We carried the burden as best we could but that was probably the beginning of the end.

'I came to a decision that no longer would I put people in cars because they could bring in a few pounds. I would either get a sponsor who would allow me to go out and do it the way I believed in, or not at all. At that time I had a recurrence of problems with my old injuries from the accident in Canada. I spent most of my time in hospital when I should have been trying to get sponsors. One thing after another built up the debit side which finally brought the whole thing to an end.'

The spirit, though, lives on: 'Our company is into all sorts of things, but mainly industrial construction. And I still like tinkering, particularly with bikes. I suppose I was always fonder of bikes. I ride bikes quite often in events. I don't do much car driving. I'm now looking at the remnants of the team. We've started to drag out the cars we have left, three of them, to put them together again.'

There is a glow in the face now. It is almost as if he has found a new challenge, a new dream . . .

Graham Hill – Graham Hill OBE, no less – would also take up the challenge of running his own racing operation, but at the beginning of 1969 he still had a number of driving landmarks ahead of him. Second place behind Jackie Stewart in the South African Grand Prix at Kyalami indicated a shift in the balance of power. When the Scot's Matra won again in Spain the take-over looked inevitable. Next, though, was Monaco, and here the old king was not ready to abdicate.

Stewart maintained his splendid early season form to take pole position, lead from the line and set the pace for the first twenty-two laps of the race. Then, suddenly, infuriatingly, a faulty universal coupling gave way, rendering the Matra impotent. All Stewart could do was tour down the hill to the harbour and retire – and guess who was there to take over. Hill, of course. He led for the rest of the race. Courage earned more rave notices with a stirring drive to second place and Attwood was fourth to complete what was, overall, a good day for British drivers.

Above all, though, it was Hill's day. He had won this classic for the fifth time, a staggering record. There was something about this up-and-down, round-the-houses circuit that brought the best out of him. It demanded – and still demands – precision driving and absolute physical and mental commitment. In modern racing Nigel Mansell describes it as the greatest challenge of all. Hill said: 'Drivers and cars take a terrific pounding at Monaco. To win any race you must have a car that's capable of finishing and the rest is up to you.'

Pat Mennem believes Hill's success rate at Monaco was no coincidence. He says: 'Graham was fantastic there. That circuit requires a drill and concentration. He was prepared to put everything he'd got into it. He was enormously disciplined. It was sheer determination, a determination to

The Princess, the Prince,
and the 'King' of Monaco

succeed. I think gutsiness has tended to be a strength of British drivers.'

That fifth victory at Monaco was the fourteenth and last of his Grand Prix career. It put him just three points behind Stewart in the World Championship and raised hopes that he might again make a play for the title. Instead the rest of the season became a catalogue of mishaps and misfortune. He had handling problems in Holland (no points) and France (one point). He ran out of fuel in the British Grand Prix (no points) and had gearbox problems in Germany (three points). In Italy a halfshaft broke (no points) and in Canada he had engine trouble (no points).

The Championship had long gone, the season had become a tedious grind. There were, thankfully, only two races remaining and Hill found an added incentive at Watkins Glen, scene of the United States Grand Prix: 'It's a terrific place for spectators and drivers, a real carnival occasion, and this year the organisers had raised the first prize to $50,000, making it the richest Grand Prix prize ever offered.'

He was, once more, unhappy with the handling, however, and running fifth when he had a spin. He climbed out, pushed the Lotus back to life and carried on, his belts unfastened, planning to change his badly worn tyres. He didn't get the chance.

'As I went along the straight the right-hand rear tyre collapsed and the car went out of control. It veered off the track, hit a bank, rolled over and shot me out while flying backwards, upside down, in the air. Apparently I was catapulted some distance through the air before I hit the ground and rolled twenty yards beyond the wreckage.

'The next thing that more or less came into focus was a siren, and I remember being in the ambulance. My team-mate, Jochen Rindt, went on to win and collect that lovely prize. I collected something different. When I got to the Arnott Ogden Memorial Hospital in Elmira a lot of my racing friends were around me. I was fairly well drugged but I could see my legs weren't too good. When I was thrown out of the car my lower legs had caught on the dashboard and the wrench had broken my right knee at the joint, and dislocated my left, and torn all the ligaments.'

The specialists told Hill it was unlikely he would be able to race again. His response was predictable: 'There was no question in my mind, this was just a temporary set-back and I would return to racing. While I was being treated I had to listen to their advice, of course, and go along with their recommendations.'

He was flown back to London and had surgery on his knee ligaments at University College Hospital: 'The surgeons hadn't been able to straighten my bandy left leg – it was even more bent. And the other one was bent, too. But I was grateful for all they had done. Not so grateful, though, when they told Bette I wouldn't be racing for another year. I told them that was no good and they complained bitterly to her about my refusing to listen to them. But I refused to believe it. If I want to do something and somebody tells me that I can't, there's an added challenge and it makes me more determined. I was aiming to get back into racing for the first Grand Prix of the new season, and that was the South African on 7 March, five months almost to the day from my shunt in America.'

He also made up his mind, typically, to enjoy himself in hospital. He let it be known that champagne would help the healing process and concerned friends faithfully came to his aid. He was also sent a brace of pheasants, which presented him with a problem. After they'd been hanging in his room for a couple of days noses were beginning to twitch, so he had to hang them out of the window.

He occupied himself tackling the mountains of mail. He also watched football on television with deep interest: 'I found myself watching the footballers' legs and knees. I spent hours watching how they worked, just to reassure myself that mine were going to work like that. I had to think positively and direct my efforts to getting better.'

He was permitted the occasional outing and equipped with a wheel-chair. He found a few back-ways to beat the 9 p.m. curfew but had some explaining to do when a night-watchman caught him being pushed by a friend through the boiler room at 2 a.m. His experience of being wheel-chair-bound gave him a greater awareness of the plight of the handicapped. He could now understand that what they wanted, more than anything, was to be treated as 'normal people'.

He was able to speed up his own recovery, meanwhile, on an exercise bike. Weekends at home aided the psychological battle. After a farewell party he was out of hospital for good. It was just before Christmas. The South African Grand Prix was two and a half months away. He began his own race with daily, three-hour therapy sessions at the Royal National Orthopaedic Hospital at Stanmore. He topped up the work-load by cycling the eight-mile round trip from his home at Mill Hill. He threw away the crutches for two sticks, then one.

Hill was lifted back into his racing car – now a Lotus entered by Rob Walker – for practice at Kyalami. Many doubted he would persist;

everyone questioned the wisdom of trying. Hill was defiant: 'They must have been out of their minds to think that I was going to stop once I'd got in the car. I was really enjoying it. I found myself easing my left foot across and tapping the brake pedals, just to check that the pressure was there. That was the only qualm I had.'

Hill would race. Of course he would. But even he could not be sure he would complete the distance on a hot day: 'My legs were still giving a lot of pain and you need strength to drive racing cars. Then I began to drive faster and faster – and I finished in sixth place, earning one Championship point. When I came into the pits it was fabulous to see the pleasure on everyone's faces. They all seemed to share the joy I felt that day. It was a great emotional experience. It was the hardest Championship point I'd ever won.'

He followed up with more points in Spain, where he was fourth, and Monaco, where he was fifth, to beat Fangio's World Championship points record. He added another point from the British Grand Prix at Brands Hatch. All of which, he felt, was justification for his perseverance against all medical advice and predictions: 'Rowing taught me never to give in. In motor racing, the determination has to come to terms with the desire for self-preservation, but always there must be this will to win.'

Hill and his colleagues once again had to come to terms with the perils of their trade that season. Bruce McLaren was killed testing his new CanAm sportscar at Goodwood and Piers Courage, one of Britain's bright hopes, died when his car, a de Tomaso entered by Frank Williams, flipped and caught fire in the Dutch Grand Prix. More tragedy was to beset the sport at Monza, where Hill's former team-mate Jochen Rindt lost his life during practice for the Italian Grand Prix. He was the first posthumous World Champion.

The year waned disappointingly for Hill. He had seven points and thirteenth place in the Championship. He then spent two years at Brabham but with still less success: a meagre six points in all.

Consolation came in his tenth attempt at the Le Mans 24-hour race in 1972. Partnering Frenchman Henri Pescarolo, he won the classic in a Matra-Simca. After his Championship and Indianapolis successes it completed a cherished triple crown. It was that Le Mans race, however, which claimed the life of Hill's friend and former BRM team-mate Jo Bonnier. The Swede, as president of the Grand Prix Drivers' Association, had been an early campaigner for better safety precautions at tracks.

At the end of 1972 Hill was ready for a new challenge and, like Surtees, he felt that meant setting up his own team. He found a sponsor – Embassy – and a workshop in Woking. He scheduled his arrival in the Shadow for the fourth race of the 1973 season, the Spanish Grand Prix.

It was not to be an ideal start and it was not to be an ideal season. A succession of problems left him scoreless: 'The fact that the car was new was the chief problem. It wasn't a car that had been tried and found true around the circuits for some time. A lot of engineering and adjusting still needed to be done to get it running properly.'

For 1974 Hill decided to switch from Shadow to Lola cars and moved his base to Feltham. The car finished races but scored only one point, the last of Hill's driving career, in Sweden. His last race was the 1975 Brazilian

Grand Prix. He wrote off his car during practice in South Africa and stood down in Spain. It became a tragic occasion. One of his cars, driven by the German, Rolf Stommelen, lost a rear aerofoil at 150 m.p.h., flew off the track and killed five people. Stommelen though, recovered from his injuries.

Hill had also run the British driver, Guy Edwards, and the Frenchman, François Migault. In Monaco, where the old master failed to qualify, he consoled himself with the capture of one of the most sought-after young drivers in motor racing, the Briton Tony Brise. He had made his debut driving a Williams Ford in Spain and impressed the Formula One fraternity in the Formula Three race at Monte Carlo.

Brise was of racing's modern generation. He started in karts at the age of eight and swept all before him at twelve. He was racing cars at eighteen and again despatched the opposition in Formula Ford. His rise to Formula One was rapid and inevitable. He made his first appearance for Hill in Belgium, where he had to drop out with engine trouble. At the next race, the Swedish Grand Prix, he stayed the course and collected his first Championship point with sixth place.

Hill wrote: 'Seeing him as a potential World Champion I was delighted to sign him up on a two-year contract. He was only twenty-three, which was half my age, and yet here he was in Grand Prix racing at an age before I'd even driven a car. His flair, competitive spirit, car control and maturity of driving belied his comparative youth. I think he is one of the most exciting drivers that Britain has seen for many years.'

Brise's arrival and the enormous demands of running a team confronted Hill with the dilemma of his own future as a driver. He knew he had to be honest with himself and his enthusiastic young team. He knew also he could reach only one verdict.

'One of the hardest decisions any Grand Prix driver has to make is when to retire. I've always found that one of the best places to make decisions is in the bath, and that's where I made up my mind to retire. It was after practice for the Belgian Grand Prix. I'd been tremendously impressed with Tony's performance that day and as I was running my team I felt I ought to be in the pits to back up my drivers and make sure that they and the new cars did well. If I continued to drive I wouldn't be able to do this and, although I was still enjoying being a racing driver, I would really only be indulging myself.'

He chose to make the announcement on the eve of the British Grand Prix at Silverstone and went on an emotional farewell lap of the circuit before the race: 'I had my helmet off and by the time I got to the first corner I had a lump in my throat because of the terrific reception from the crowd. I was so choked I couldn't see. When I watched Tony go out to the grid it was another bad moment – knowing I wouldn't ever be out there again.'

It was not the last bad moment of the day for Hill. As rain fell Brise slithered off the track into the catch-fencing. One of the wooden stakes tore off his helmet and knocked him out. He was taken to hospital but, to Hill's enormous relief, his injuries were not serious. He had heavy bruising and a cut over the left eye, which required seven stitches. Brise was one of many who went off that chaotic afternoon and the race was stopped after fifty-six of the scheduled sixty-seven laps.

Piers Courage . . . another devastating blow

The British Racing Hero

Australian Alan Jones drove the Hill Ford to fifth place in Germany, but Brise would not score again that season. He would surely have plenty of points to come in 1976 and the years beyond. Hill was content with the direction of his new career, and content with the one he'd left behind. Now, for a moment at least, he was entitled to reflect on a life that had taken in 176 Grands Prix – a record beaten only in 1989 by Riccardo Patrese – and so many other experiences:

'It was disappointing not to have won the British Grand Prix but that's the way the cookie crumbles. I came pretty close to it, but failures make you appreciate the successes more. Having won fourteen Grands Prix and 289 World Championship points I hadn't any cause for complaint.

'Looking back, the five races that stood out were the German race in the wet; the Monaco Grand Prix which I won after having to get out and push the car back into the race; the Indianapolis victory; coming sixth in the South African Grand Prix after my accident and all the work on that bicycle; and winning Le Mans, which gave me my "triple crown".'

There was, however, much more to Graham Hill's life and times. He was a great ambassador for sport and country. Moustachioed, pugnacious and proud, he was thoroughly British. His combative nature was an example to young and old, to those inside and outside motor racing. He was generous in his work for charity and a knock-out as an after-dinner speaker. His popularity was international. Pat Mennem recalls: 'He was racing in Spain, after his accident at Watkins Glen, and was limping quite badly. He hadn't been going too well and was towards the back of the grid. The drivers walked to their cars and as Graham limped all the way to his the crowd went absolutely mad. He was like the old wounded matador and the Spaniards loved him. And he, of course, absolutely adored it. I was in a fish restaurant when Graham and Bette walked in and the whole place rose and erupted in thunderous applause. And that at a time when he wasn't doing well! He always went up to the Tip Top after the Monaco Grand Prix and that pleased the British fans.'

By his own admission Hill had an occasionally explosive temper. He did not suffer fools gladly, particularly in the countdown to a race. Mennem says: 'He could be irritable, like a bear with a sore head.'

Derek Bell remembers the two faces of Hill. He says: 'I was doing the Tasman Series with him and ran into the back of Jochen Rindt on the grid. That night over a few drinks and dinner, Graham told me off for going before the bloke in front had gone. It was a very strong remark, but a valid one and I've never forgotten it. Graham was like that. He'd laugh and joke but if he had to be serious and make a point he would do, especially to a young driver.'

Bette Hill: 'I think most drivers wanted only their mechanics around before the race. I used to go up to Graham about an hour and a half before the start, just kiss him and say "keep safe" and then disappear. I'd be sitting up on my seat with my books and my watches, he'd look up and wink and then concentrate on his job. He didn't want to talk to anybody. A journalist went up to him once and asked him what was the most difficult time of a race. Graham told him "When an idiot like you comes up and asks me what's the most difficult time of a race".'

Graham was emphatic in his appreciation of Bette's part in his success.

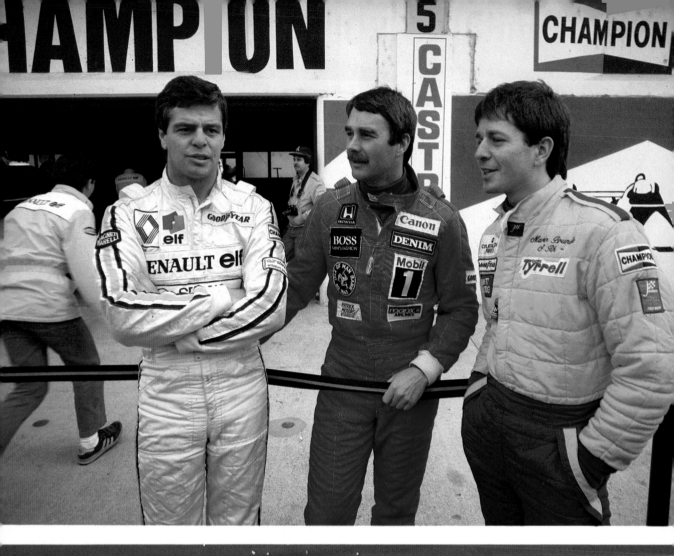

He said: 'I would never have won two World Championships if Bette had just tolerated the driving. She was *with* me all the way and never once suggested I should stop. The wives have a tough time because they must feel apprehensive about the dangers. In a way it's worse for them than us. But Bette never bothered me with any of her anxieties. She liked me to win and I think she was more disappointed than I was if I didn't.'

During practice Bette timed not only her husband's laps but also those of his opponents. They kept detailed information compiled at all the tracks and Graham devoured every new piece of data. Bette says: 'We had books, books, books. The records were meticulous. I'd note not only the times but the specific circumstances. If, for instance, he did a time with a tow I'd put that down. I was accepted by him and the rest of the team as part of the team. He could be hard on me if I made a mistake but he was even harder on himself. He was a perfectionist.

'It makes me cross when people say that Jimmy Clark was a natural and Graham had to work at it. They *all* had to work at it. All right, Jimmy was a natural but Graham had to work harder at it because his car wasn't so good. He made it good with the help of Tony Rudd and all those fantastic BRM mechanics.'

Throughout his career Hill declared himself an optimist, adding: 'You have to be in this business.' Despite the scares and the tragedies around him, he survived to quit driving for the safety of proprietorship. The 1975 season closed at Watkins Glen in October, and Hill and his team were soon down to work preparing for 1976. In late November they flew in Hill's plane to the South of France to test the new car at the Paul Ricard circuit. Graham planned to be back for lunch on Sunday the 30th, but sent Bette a message saying they'd be returning on Saturday night, instead.

Two of their children, Damon and Samantha, were watching television when the news was given. They ran into the kitchen. Damon, pale and distraught, said: 'Mummy, a plane has crashed in fog at Arkley Golf Club on the way from Marseilles to Elstree. They think it's Daddy.'

Police officers arrived and confirmed Graham was dead. So were Tony Brise, Andy Smallman, Terry Richards, Ray Brimble and Tony Alcock. Bette's other daughter, Brigitte, was brought back from a party. Together they would have to confront a new life. Bette see-sawed between near hysteria and hard pragmatism. 'We hugged each other a lot and cried a lot. I couldn't believe it. Graham had a charmed life. But I got the children back to school as soon as possible. We had to get our home in order.'

Graham's plane crashed in trees three miles from its Elstree destination. Bette felt a compulsion to visit the site and eventually did. Damon went with her. It helped. So did a further visit with Fay Coakley, Brigitte's Godmother. They planted daffodil bulbs: 'We were crying so much we couldn't tell which way up they were. I could imagine Graham saying "You twits, what ARE you doing?".'

Bette needed the support of friends like Fay Coakley. The crash had dire financial as well as emotional consequences. 'I had five lawsuits against me and I had three children to get through school. The house had to go, half the furniture went, the paintings all went. We had more than we could cope with really. That's what made me tough. I don't like being tough but you have to be to survive.'

Opposite page

Above: The Bulldog Breed . . . Warwick, Mansell and Brundle

Below: Sparking . . . Dumfries and the JPS Lotus, 1986

113

Even now, Bette is puzzled by the circumstances of the accident: 'Why Graham was over Arkley golf course I will never know. He'd never come in that way. And why he was that low I will never understand. There was never any question of bravado. He was such a perfectionist.'

Bette Hill now lives near Clapham Common. Damon is married, with a son, Oliver Graham. He is pursuing his own racing career and has advanced to Formula 3000, the modern second division. Brigitte has maintained links with the sport in a public relations capacity. Samantha has turned to the fashion world.

Bette spends much of her time working with an ever-imaginative ladies' charity organisation called the Doghouse Owners, and refining her golf game. She misses Graham and she misses motor racing. But she has her pictures, her books and her memories. There were the parties they threw and other drivers and their wives threw. There were the prize-giving ceremonies which drivers went to instead of hurrying away. And there was Monaco. When Graham reached the end of his driving career Prince Rainier told him: 'Now, dear Graham, we can grow old together.'

Bette says: 'Graham could mix and have fun with anybody. He even made a joke of his bad leg. When we started going out together I asked him why he was walking with one foot in the gutter. He said "You silly so-and-so, I've got one leg shorter than the other". Then when he had that terrible accident in America he sent a message, "Tell Bette I've now got a matching pair".

'He could play the clown and throw himself into anything. He loved being a showman, people expected it of him. But basically he was a very shy man. Before he went and did all those after-dinner speeches he was terribly nervous. He enjoyed winning and all that went with it but he was also a great loser and a great sportsman. I'm sure a lot of people learned from him. Ron Dennis was once his mechanic and look what he's done.

'Sometimes I miss Graham more than others. Sometimes I have a real downer. Yes, I still do, after all these years. I'll say "you old devil, I need you. Why the hell aren't you here?".'

Graham Hill was once asked if he believed in an after-life. He replied: 'I've always thought that if there is one, then it's a bit of a bonus, something I hadn't quite expected. If there is then cheers, I'm all for it. I've enjoyed this one so much, I wouldn't mind having another.'

Graham and the young Ron Dennis

8

Key to the Door

Jackie Stewart had learned much along the road to 1969. He arrived a more complete person and a more complete driver. He patently had outstanding ability. As Ken Tyrrell has said, you had to be an idiot not to recognise that. But by his fifth season in Formula One World Championship racing, Stewart had the capacity to take full advantage of his obvious gift. He had greater maturity, greater authority. Experience had taught him the procedure for winning races, how to prepare, how to stay calm and how to maintain control to the chequered flag. He had the key.

In later years Stewart would frequently talk about the key to motor racing success, the key to winning races and the key to winning Championships: 'Once you have that key and can unlock the door, the opportunities open up before you.'

Stewart had pushed Graham Hill to a last race decider in 1968 despite an unproductive start to the season and the lingering effects of his wrist injury. In 1969 he was intent on making his presence felt from the first race. He had recovered his fitness, he was tuned mentally. Tyrrell was equally determined to have his car thoroughly prepared. Test and development work was scheduled to give driver and team the best possible chance from day one.

Day one was March 1, the race the South African Grand Prix, the circuit Kyalami. Stewart used the new car in practice but teething problems left a question mark hanging over it. He wanted no questions, no doubts, no concerns. The old car would still be good for the job. Tried and trusted, Stewart would start from the second row. On the front row were Jack Brabham (Brabham Ford), Jochen Rindt (Lotus Ford) and Denny Hulme (McLaren Ford).

Stewart's personal preparations followed the set routine. He came to the grid free of tension yet fully conscious of the task in hand. The balance was just right. He was ready to turn the key and open the door.

He made an immaculate start, snaking through the front row and taking the Matra into the lead before the first corner. He kept it there for the rest of the eighty lap race. He had the pace to get away from the rest and give himself a cushion, then the self-confidence to relax on it while the others chased in vain. Here was instant evidence of the Scot's command. For every other driver in the pit-lane, it was an ominous display.

The top three at the end of 1968 were again the top three at the start of 1969, but this time the order was: first Stewart, second Hill, third Hulme.

Stewart had the initiative, just as he had wanted. The careful planning had paid off. This time the others had to do the chasing and he was determined to keep them chasing. The Tyrrell camp celebrated the win with champagne. They were to acquire a taste for the stuff in the months ahead.

In fact another two months had passed before the Formula One cast re-assembled on location, this time at the splendid setting of Montjuich Park, Barcelona. Rindt's Lotus was fastest round the tight, twisting circuit, with Chris Amon's Ferrari and Hill's Lotus completing the front row. Stewart's Matra was again on the second row.

This time, though, he did not make a good start. He was unusually sluggish from the grid and was swallowed by the pack. He was down in sixth place. Gradually, he made his way up the leader board, but not as a result of a superhuman effort on his part. The cars in front simply started falling away. Both Hill and Rindt crashed when their aerofoils broke.

Eventually the grateful Stewart found himself in the lead with nine points handed to him on a plate. It was not the most satisfying victory of his career, but somewhere along the way everyone needs a little luck and he knew he had had his quota that day. His rivals might well have sensed there and then that his name was on the Championship trophy.

Rindt was injured and missed the Monaco Grand Prix, but Stewart was convinced that he, and indeed Hill, would have paid a far greater price had the Montjuich track not been lined by barriers. Stewart and his colleagues in the Grand Prix Drivers' Association, who were campaigning for barriers round all circuits, together with other safety measures, believed they had been vindicated.

Hill came away from Spain virtually unscathed, eager to protect his beloved Monte Carlo. The authorities, meanwhile, decided that wings would not be allowed, a direct consequence of the accidents at Barcelona. Protests, meetings and political bargaining ensued. Many teams – including Tyrrell – were angry about being given such short notice, but in the end they were out-manoeuvred.

Out on the track it did not seem to matter too much to Stewart anyway. He set the pace with and without wings. Stewart was on pole, Amon alongside. Hill, on the second row, was aware that his fortress was under threat. Stewart's early domination spelled more than a threat – until that universal coupling let him down. Hill pounded on to his fifth Monaco win, while Stewart had nothing. What is more Hill was only three points behind him in the table.

The pressure for safety measures forced Spa off the 1969 calendar. The Belgian organisers rejected calls for flexibility over the starting time – a suggested means of beating the moody Ardennes weather – and lost their race. Next stop was Zandvoort, Holland.

Stewart's Matra Ford was sandwiched on the front row of the seaside circuit grid by the Lotus Fords of Rindt and Hill. The Lotus pair went clear; the Englishman led initially but then the daring Austrian got the better of the domestic squabble and took over. Stewart also had to fight his way past Hill, which gave Rindt the opportunity to open up a gap. Then Rindt's Lotus fell apart and Stewart had another open road to victory. He was followed in by Jo Siffert and Amon. Hill was seventh and failed to score.

Suddenly there was daylight between Stewart and the rest. The Championship looked like this: Stewart 27 points, Hill 15, Siffert 13, Hulme 11, McLaren 10. The luckless Rindt was still not in the hunt, but Stewart knew that he could yet prove a formidable obstacle. Jacky Ickx had only three points at that stage yet he, too, was capable of challenging. There was no danger of complacency in the Tyrrell camp.

They could be forgiven, though, for feeling smug after the French Grand Prix at Clermont Ferrand. Stewart was in a class of his own all weekend: through practice and through the race, from beginning to end. Here was a driver utterly in control, key in hand, opening the door and walking in without so much as a backward glance. No, the Championship certainly was not over yet. Yes, anything could really happen. The fact remained that Stewart would take an awful lot of shifting now.

The Tyrrell triumph was completed by Frenchman Jean-Pierre Beltoise, who beat Ickx in a thrilling contest to give Matra a one-two on home ground. Britain's Vic Elford, driving a McLaren, was fifth and Hill picked up a point to stay second in the title table – but all of twenty points adrift.

An expectant Silverstone crowd were ready to acclaim yet another British world champion. Hawthorn, Hill, Clark, Surtees . . . and now, surely, it was going to be Stewart. In practice the fans, and the hero, had a fright. He ran over a piece of concrete at Woodcote Corner, a tyre exploded and the Matra shot across the track into the sleepers at the other side. Stewart was unhurt but he had to take over his partner's car and settle for second place in the grid. Rindt had pole.

Stewart and Rindt, friends and travelling companions as well as rivals, turned the British Grand Prix into a stirring duel. Rindt would lead, Stewart would lead, then they would be side-by-side. The show, alas, ended when part of the rear aerofoil of the Lotus worked loose and Rindt had to pull into the pits for repairs. Stewart, despite a few minor concerns of his own, lapped the rest on his way to the chequered flag. Ickx was second, McLaren third and Rindt fourth. Courage was fifth and Vic Elford sixth.

Stewart had achieved an ambition shared by all British drivers – victory in the British Grand Prix. It had served also to bring him closer to the ultimate goal, the Championship. McLaren had moved into second place with seventeen points. Stewart had forty-five.

Stewart was edged out of pole position again at the Nurburgring, this time by Ickx. The Brabham Ford proved an effective machine on this daunting fourteen-mile circuit and the Belgian's knowledge of the Eifel Mountains was equally important. Rindt, on the other hand, was not able to function at his best and, although he made the front row, he was more than five seconds slower than the other two.

The men who contested pole went on to contest the main prize, and for almost half the race Stewart's Matra led the way. It was a lead he could not sustain. He was fighting a losing battle against his gearbox. For all his gentle coaxing, the mechanism became more and more erratic. He used his wit and guile to fend off the Brabham as long as he could but eventually had to accept second best. Ickx went by and won with ease. Stewart, in turn, was comfortably ahead of third man McLaren.

That win lifted Ickx to second place in the Championship, twenty-nine points behind Stewart. The title, however, was already out of the Brabham driver's reach. Under the points system he would have to drop one of his scores if he was placed in the remaining four races. McLaren, a point and a place behind Ickx, still had a mathematical chance.

In reality, most were already regarding Stewart as champion and expected to witness the completion of formalities at Monza. Ickx put himself out of contention for the Italian Grand Prix after an internal dispute. His car had problems in practice and he declined the offer of Brabham's. So he started from the back of the grid and left Stewart and Rindt to get on with it.

Stewart hit a hare in the early part of the race, yet still had another marvellous scrap with Rindt. But the arena was not entirely theirs. The maturing Courage had a spell in the lead as driver after driver exploited Monza's famous slip-streaming opportunities. According to official records, Stewart led for fifty-nine laps, Rindt for six, Hulme for one and Courage for two. Those figures relate to positions across the line and take no account of the place changes elsewhere on the circuit. The changes were frequent, the race close. It was like that to the end.

Stewart led across the start-finish line as they began the final lap. Into the Curva Grande, Rindt was in front. Stewart tracked him all the way to the Parabolica and regained the advantage only to find himself under attack from his team-mate Beltoise. On to the straight for the last time Stewart had to slip-stream the Frenchman and dive for the line. He managed it and Rindt used the tow to snatch second place. McLaren was a whisker behind Beltoise. The first four were covered by 0.19 seconds.

There was something else to talk about that September evening: John Young Stewart was World Champion.

Stewart was subjected to a little traditional Monza hysteria and finally escaped to celebrate. That bubbly stuff was flowing again – vast quantities of it – and gradually the achievement began to sink in. Back home the tributes, accolades and congratulations were endless. Most moving of all, he was presented with the Jim Clark Memorial Trophy – by Jimmy's father.

The rest of the season was something of an anti-climax for the new champion. Stewart was eager to add to his tally of wins and came through from the second row of the Mosport grid to lead the Canadian Grand Prix. Then, at a tricky corner, he was assaulted by an over-zealous Ickx. The Matra was shunted off the track and out of the race. The new champion was not a happy man. Ickx, who later apologised for his indiscretion, won from Brabham and Rindt.

From Canada the circus moved over the border for the United States Grand Prix at Watkins Glen, the race in which Hill had his big accident. Hill's team-mate Rindt renewed friendly hostilities with Stewart. Rindt, starting on pole, had the better of the early skirmishes. Stewart relieved him of control and held the lead for nine laps, until a niggling misfire became a serious handicap. Ultimately, Stewart had to drop out. The Austrian won from Courage and Surtees.

Rindt, so quick, so competitive, yet hitherto so unlucky, at last had his first Grand Prix victory. Stewart was genuinely pleased for him. They had come to know and respect each other in their Formula Two days and now seemed destined to be keen Formula One rivals for years to come.

They wrapped up the season in Mexico City, and although Stewart stayed the course he was far from content. He simply could not get the grip to sustain his early advantage, and he slipped down the leader board

to finish fourth. Hulme was first, Ickx second and Brabham third. Oliver, in a BRM, picked up his consolation point for the year.

The results of the 1969 Formula One Drivers' Championship were:

1st, J. Stewart (GB), 63 points; 2nd, J. Ickx (Bel), 37 points; 3rd, B. McLaren (NZ), 26 points; 4th, J. Rindt (Austria), 22 points; 5th, J-P. Beltoise (Fra), 21 points; 6th, D. Hulme (NZ), 20 points; 7th, G. Hill (GB), 19 points; 8th, P. Courage (GB), 16 points.

The results of the 1969 Formula One Constructors' Championship were:

1st, Matra, 66 points; 2nd, Brabham, 51 points; 3rd, Lotus, 47 points; 4th, McLaren, 40 points; 5th, Ferrari and BRM, 7 points.

The conclusion of racing meant the resumption of the tributes, the accolades and the congratulations. There were interviews, receptions and meetings. Stewart was a worthy champion. He had brought to his obvious and considerable talent a smooth, efficient style. He had the experience, the control, the key. He would say later: 'Experience and the knowledge gained from experience are vital. It took me five seasons to win my first Championship and it's not surprising that it has taken other

Champion elect . . . Stewart on his way to victory in the 1969 British Grand Prix

119

drivers that long to win their first Championships. No matter how good you are, you need time.'

In recent times, both Alain Prost and Ayrton Senna won their first titles after five seasons in Formula One.

If it was a great triumph for the garage boy from Dumbarton, it was no less a success for the village team footballer from Surrey. Tyrrell's rise had been meteoric and, in its way, as controlled as Stewart's. Now he, too, was savouring the supreme moment. He says: 'We had many memorable times but winning that title for the first time was very special.'

Enough of the back-slapping. Motor racing is a fast-moving game every day, not just race day. The strength of the Stewart–Tyrrell campaign in 1969 had lain in their preparation. Mid-way through the year they were already looking ahead to 1970 and already they realised it might not be so straightforward the next time. The Matra–Ford combination was excellent, but would the French continue with the association? It became clear that Matra wanted to use their own engine.

Stewart and Tyrrell were apprehensive. They wanted to stick with Ford-Cosworth, with engines they knew and trusted. They started looking round for a new chassis. Brabham was a natural consideration, as were BRM and Lola. Stewart, now a driver in some demand, had talks with McLaren. The talks and the meetings went on and on. The talks and meetings that proved decisive were with March, an organisation headed by Robin Herd. The deal was done: Tyrrell bought cars from March.

The 1970 Championship would begin in South Africa on 7 March. It was the second half of February when Stewart had his first test drive in the March Ford. There were bound to be teething problems and Stewart was patient. He soon realised, however, that his car was not up to the standard of the Matra. Tyrrell realised it, too, and decided he should look even further ahead. He was becoming more and more convinced he should build his own car.

In the meantime, they had to make the best of what they had. They might not have the best car, but they could try to make sure it was reliable. Despite the misgivings, Stewart and Chris Amon, in another March, were fastest in qualifying. Yet Stewart was still not convinced and in the race the car was a handful. Stewart led for nineteen laps but finished third, behind Brabham and Hulme.

Stewart was on the front row again in Spain and, much to his astonishment, led from start to finish. He refused to be taken in. So many other cars had dropped out that he simply did not have any competition. Not real competition, anyway. The preparations might not have been what Tyrrell and Stewart wanted, but it appeared they were still better than some of their opponents had managed. These were early days, though. The others had time.

Stewart's time beat the rest in qualifying for the Monaco Grand Prix. For twenty-seven splendid laps he also led the race. He appeared to be in control, he seemed to have the key. Had he been sand-bagging? In the event, the engine began to play up and he finally had to give up. A blunder by Jack Brabham at the last corner gave the victory to Rindt. Third was Henri Pescarolo – in a Matra.

Spa was back on the calendar for 1970 but Stewart made no bones about it. He still did not like it, he still felt it was too dangerous and he still wanted it stopped. He was also still a professional racing driver and who do you think was on pole for the Belgian Grand Prix? Yes, of course – he was.

To Stewart's immense relief, it was not raining. He took Amon for the lead but soon lost it again. More engine problems hindered his progress and eventually blew him off the track. So much for reliability.

On to Zandvoort. Rindt brandished the new Lotus 72, a formidable weapon. In practice Rindt was fastest, Stewart second, Ickx third. In the race the order was the same. But places and Championship points were forgotten that evening. Piers Courage, driving Frank Williams' de Tomaso, had crashed and died. Another friend, another Briton.

Stewart and the rest went back to work in France. He was among those who hit trouble at Clermont Ferrand; Rindt was not. The Austrian's luck was changing. Brands Hatch: more misery for Stewart, and another win for Rindt. Hockenheim: yet more misery for Stewart, yet another win for Rindt. Zeltweg: still more misery for Stewart, and some for Rindt too.

It was a disappointing outcome for the Austrian in his home Grand Prix, but in the context of the season it seemed scarcely to matter. He was in command of the Championship. Even throughout 1969, there had been much debate about the relative skills of Stewart and Rindt. Now he was proving his class. He headed for Monza meaning to underline it.

Jochen Rindt did not race in the Italian Grand Prix. During practice he crashed as he braked for the Parabolica and died. Now Stewart had lost not only another colleague, another friend; he had lost his best friend on the circuit.

Many years later, at Monza, Stewart said: 'We lost so many friends, so many good friends. But drivers are somewhat peculiar in their mentality. You get so much pleasure from what you are doing, so much fulfilment, that you do go on. What makes this a peculiar challenge is the life and death aspect, the risk of pain and injury. But man chooses to expose himself to these risks. I'm sure there's a loneliness on the mountains and the other activities where man faces the ultimate penalty.

'It was a terrible weekend here when Jochen was killed. He and Nina and Helen and I were very close. We spent a lot of time together. And there had been so many tragedies in such a short time: Jimmy, Piers, and many, many more. And then Jochen.'

Stewart had lost a friend, motor racing had lost one of its brightest stars. Pat Mennem: 'Jochen never got the opportunity to explore fully his talents. I think he could have been one of the all-time greats. He was a fantastic racer.'

The 'peculiar mentality' took Stewart back on to the track that tragic day and he went round Monza faster than he had ever done previously. In the race, twenty-four hours later, he led for fifteen laps and finished second.

Stewart had raced the new Tyrrell Ford in the Oulton Park Gold Cup and tried it out in practice at Monza, but problems forced him to revert to the March. In Canada they were ready to take the Grand Prix plunge. It was a tense situation for everyone, but especially for Tyrrell. This car would determine his immediate future. It could also determine whether Stewart would stay with the team. Through days of testing and practice,

121

there still seemed a long way to go. Then, towards the end of qualifying, Stewart settled into his rhythm – and posted fastest time. The Tyrrell Ford would make its entry from pole position.

For 31 glorious laps the Tyrrell Ford also led the Canadian Grand Prix. Stewart, smooth, assured, was in control again, holding the key again. A debut victory? It was not to be. Axle damage crippled the car and Stewart ushered it back to the pits. In the United States Grand Prix he led by more than a minute when he started to lose oil. He carried on for as long as he could, and then the car simply stopped.

The potential was there. A finish, in Mexico City, would set them up for 1971. Down Mexico way, though, Stewart and his colleagues had another concern. Spectators had spilled over the fences and were sitting at the side of the circuit. When police tried to force them back they hurled bottles on to the track. Stewart warned the organisers there could be carnage. He was told 'Don't worry, you're insured.'

There really was no answer to that.

When the organisers also pointed out that unless the race went ahead there would be a riot, the drivers were left with no alternative, either. The spectators moved back for the start, then gradually crept forward again. Stewart was anxiously monitoring their progress when a dog ran on to the track and he collected it. Somehow he managed to keep his broken, wayward car out of the crowd. It was not quite the sign-off he had been looking for.

For Stewart the most consoling thought at the end of the 1970 season was that no-one had taken his friend's Championship. The final standings were:

1st, Rindt, 45 points; 2nd, Ickx, 40 points; 3rd, Regazzoni, 33 points; 4th, Hulme, 27 points; 5th, Brabham and Stewart, 25 points.

It was time to look ahead, hopefully to happier times, perhaps to a more successful season. Stewart would be staying with Tyrrell and together they would take on the world again.

During the winter they worked on Derek Gardner's creation, refining it, almost manicuring it. Another important part of the package was tyres. They had switched to Goodyear. Ken Tyrrell's team were ready. Jackie Stewart was ready – key in hand.

The 1971 trail began at Kyalami with the South African Grand Prix, and Stewart was first to show taking pole. He was second in the race, behind Mario Andretti's Ferrari, but that was not a role he had in mind for the rest of the year. In Spain he saved his best for the race, taking the 003 to its first win ahead of Ickx's Ferrari. In Monaco he was the absolute master. His pole time was 1.2 seconds better than Ickx. The race, too, was a one-man show. Stewart calmly went away and stayed in the distance. He did not add to his score in Holland but in France he was in charge again – pole and first throughout the Grand Prix. Team-mate Francois Cevert, on home ground, made it a Tyrrell one-two.

Silverstone prepared to push Stewart along to his second title. Clay Regazzoni, in the Ferrari, was equal to Stewart in qualifying and led the first three laps of the British Grand Prix. Stewart, totally unruffled, relieved the Swiss of the burden and accepted the responsibility for the rest of the race. His pace and his line were consistent. Regazzoni went but in truth he was never going to pose a threat. Nobody could threaten Stewart in this form. He won from the Swede, Ronnie Peterson, in a March Ford, and Brazilian Emerson Fittipaldi's Lotus Ford. No other car finished on the same lap.

The opposition had been flattened. Stewart and Tyrrell were turning the Formula One World Championship into a travelling exhibition. The only question to be answered was: how many wins would he wind up with? He had four from the first six races and five remained. In Germany he had his fifth win, with Cevert second.

He closed the season with, for him, a relatively modest sequence of results. He went off in Austria, led briefly then ran into problems in Italy, won in Canada and came fifth after leading in the United States. At the end of the trail he had six wins, sixty-two points and his second title. His closest 'challengers' were Peterson, on thirty-three points, and his Tyrrell partner Cevert, on twenty-six. Tyrrell topped the Constructors' Championship with seventy-three points, more than twice as many as the second-placed team, BRM.

Much as Britain was able to wallow in Stewart's success, a glance at the drivers' table that year indicates a general shift in power. The new generation of contenders were from Europe and beyond. For so long the old country had been able to boast not only the best but strength in depth. Not now. The second highest Briton in the 1971 rankings was Peter Gethin. He was one of the five drivers who shared ninth place with nine points. His nine points came from one drive, a win in Italy. He scored only two other points in his career. A one-hit wonder, yes. But what a hit!

Gethin drove for McLaren in 1970 and through much of the 1971 season, until he knew it was time to move on: 'I didn't figure in Teddy Mayer's plans and there was no point waiting around to be sacked. I'd been talking to BRM about the following year so in the circumstances I thought to myself "why delay? If you are going to do it you might as well do it now."'

Gethin made his first appearance for BRM in Austria. His second was at Monza, and there was no particular reason to suspect he might disturb the likes of Stewart and Peterson. In fact it was Regazzoni who led the opening laps, much to the approval of the Ferrari faithful. But not for long. Next up was Peterson, followed by a group that included Stewart . . . and Gethin. He recalls: 'I was quite well placed at that stage but I began to lose touch with the leaders and by half distance I was quite well down. I had to drive flat out every second to make up the difference.'

Up ahead the lead was changing hands as drivers employed the familiar slip-streaming tactics. Stewart was in front for a spell, so was another British driver, Mike Hailwood, seeking to emulate Surtees' successful switch from two wheels to four. Stewart went, as Ickx and Regazzoni went. Hailwood was still there, with Peterson and Cevert. Then Amon came through, only to lose ground again fiddling with his visor. The five at the front were Peterson, Hailwood, Cevert, Gethin and the New Zealander, Howden Ganley, driving a BRM.

Gethin recalls: 'The leaders had been so occupied watching each other it enabled me to catch up. I got to the point where the tow started working and it pulled me up to them. I'd worked so hard to get back I thought

"You've done this much so you might as well go and win it now". About twelve laps from the end I was quite sure I could win it.

'It was pretty clear that the race was going to go all the way, and I had a good idea when and how to go for it. I felt that if I could be first or second out of the Parabolica I'd do it. I think Ronnie and Cevert thought it was between the two of them and they were busy looking at each other, which suited me.'

It came down to a desperate last-corner dice. Cevert got it slightly wrong, Peterson came out wide. Gethin says: 'I was sideways but OK. I felt if I kept my foot hard in it I'd make it.' He did. Just. Peterson recovered sufficiently to shade second. Hailwood was fourth behind Cevert. The first four were covered by 0.18 seconds, the first five by 0.61. Their times were:

1. P. Gethin (GB) BRM, 1:18, 12.60.
2. R. Peterson (Sweden) March Ford, 1:18, 12.61.
3. F. Cevert (France) Tyrrell Ford, 1:18, 12.69.
4. M. Hailwood (GB) Surtees Ford, 1:18, 12.78.
5. H. Ganley (NZ) BRM, 1:18, 13.21.

It amounted to the closest Grand Prix finish of all time. Gethin's margin of victory – 0.01 seconds – is officially the smallest, too, though it is not known whether it beats the Ayrton Senna–Nigel Mansell finish in Spain, in 1986, which was recorded to thousands of a second: 0.014. Gethin's average speed – 150.75 m.p.h. – established another record. He says: 'It wasn't luck. I'd worked it out over the previous few laps and it went as I'd hoped. After that we thought we were on our way. The trouble was that BRM felt a barrage of cars would win everything. Instead it diluted resources. It just didn't work out as they'd figured.'

That day at Monza marked the beginning of Hailwood's second attempt at Formula One. His first, ill-starred stint, had been in the mid-1960s. He made his debut in a Lotus Climax at the 1963 British Grand Prix and raced most of the following season in a Lotus BRM. But he turned his back on the car game in 1965, frustrated and disillusioned. That period yielded just one point, from the 1964 Monaco Grand Prix.

In motor cycling he was a champion and a star, but in car racing he felt he had the equipment and treatment of a nobody. At that stage he was competing in both sports. He was fêted one week, ignored the next. He probably took on too much, and probably also underestimated the challenge of cars. He felt ill at ease and unaccepted in Formula One. He found Graham Hill helpful, but not many others.

He took as much as he could and then reached the conclusion that he had made the biggest mistake of his life. His inferiority complex may have blinkered him. He admitted he had the wrong approach, but he was getting out. Riding was what he did best. He completed his cycling career with nine world titles.

Six years on, he was prepared to explore the alien world of Formula One again. This time he had a guiding hand, a confidant, and more experience. He had teamed up with John Surtees and worked his way up the scale. In 1972 he scored thirteen points to finish eighth in the Championship. His best result was a second – at Monza. But then, as we have

seen, the Surtees operation ran into financial difficulties.

Surtees: 'Mike was a good friend and probably the most genuine person we had in the team. He was a good, forceful driver. He perhaps didn't have that touch of brilliance that someone like Carlos Pace had, but he was good all right. He was a bit frightened by the car world, rather like I was. He was a little uneasy about it and I could understand. There was less deviousness in the bike world. People called a spade a spade. You knew where you stood. He felt a lot more at ease, I believe, because he was with me and he knew I'd experienced the same problems. I made sure there were people around him who gave him the comfort he needed.

'When I first took on Mike people said I was mad, but he immediately got into our 5000 and went quick. He was consistent and he didn't crash it. He won the Formula Two Championship and went quick in Formula One. He did a good job for us and I would have loved him to continue with us, but we had to part because of the sponsorship situation. The company involved wanted Jochen Mass, a German. As it turned out, the whole thing was a disaster.'

Hailwood was awarded the George Medal for bravery after hauling Regazzoni from his blazing car in the 1973 South African Grand Prix. The following season, his first with McLaren, he crashed during the German Grand Prix at the Nurburgring. It was the end of his car racing career, though he did have a final fling on bikes. Mennem: 'When Hailwood came along he didn't bring with him a bag of gold or anything that appealed to the sponsors, so he found himself in a hopeless situation. I remember him at Monaco, pushing round that thing as best he could. He was a very warm and likeable chap, good fun to be with.'

Mike Hailwood was the victim of yet another tragic irony. Having survived careers and scares in two forms of motor sport, he was killed near Birmingham, driving daughter Michelle and son David to a fish-and-chip shop in 1981. Their Rover collided with a lorry which was heading for a gap in the dual carriageway. Nine-year-old Michelle died instantly, her father two days later.

Hailwood was the second highest-placed British driver in 1972. The leading Brit, for a fourth successive year, was Stewart. The garage boy from Dumbarton was also in great demand: to make personal appearances, to make business deals, to be interviewed, to be Jackie Stewart. Most of the time, he loved it. He made no pretence about it – he liked money. But perhaps even more he liked the lifestyle, the fame, the attention, the constant buzz. He appeared to thrive on it.

But the hectic schedules, and the pressures on and off the track were taking their toll. He developed an ulcer, missed a race and lost ground in the 1972 Championship. His form at the end of the season served to underline his earlier folly.

Stewart began the defence of his second title in impressive form, too. He made the front row in Argentina, set fastest lap and won the race. He had pole in South Africa and led more than half the race before running into problems. He led in Spain, then went off. In a wet, processional Monaco Grand Prix, he had to be content with fourth place.

Stewart had a fight on his hands. It was apparent that his title was under threat from two men: the wily old New Zealander Hulme, and the bright young Brazilian Fittipaldi. Stewart's absence was fully exploited by Fittipaldi in the Belgian Grand Prix, held now at Nivelles rather than the dreaded Spa. Stewart coaxed the 003 to its eighth victory in France – an all-time record for a chassis – but Fittipaldi turned the tables in the British Grand Prix at Brands Hatch. The Scot's bold late assault was to no avail. The Lotus 72 was a little too good.

'We could do no more with that chassis,' says Stewart. 'By the middle of that year we were simply unable to hold up against Emerson in that Lotus.'

The 003 had an ignominious end. It was punted into the barrier by Regazzoni's Ferrari during the German Grand Prix at the Ring. The famous car was later presented by Tyrrell to Stewart, who then passed it on to his sons, Paul and Mark. The car, and its dignity, have now been fully restored.

Ickx won the German race but successes in Austria and Italy made Fittipaldi, at the age of twenty-five, the youngest-ever World Champion. Stewart and Tyrrell were already looking ahead to 1973, introducing a second

Mike Hailwood . . .
untapped talent

126

Partners . . . Surtees (in car) and Hailwood, Monza, 1971

generation of their cars to the world of racing. Victories in the last two Grands Prix of the season – the Canadian and United States – suggested they were growing up quickly.

The top of the 1972 drivers' table read: Fittipaldi first with sixty-one points, Stewart second with forty-five, and Hulme third with thirty-nine. Lotus won the Constructors' Championship, ahead of Tyrrell and McLaren.

The Stewart–Fittipaldi and Tyrrell–Lotus duels would continue into and through the 1973 season. Emerson, hungry again after the break, helped himself to the Argentine Grand Prix and his home race, at Interlagos. Stewart had to make do with third and second places. The South African Grand Prix went to Stewart, the Spanish to Fittipaldi.

Three of the first four races had gone to the champion combination. Ominous indeed. Stewart knew he had to hit back hard and hit back immediately. He delivered a solid blow in the Belgian Grand Prix – this time at Zolder – and followed up with another at Monaco. Stewart had pole on a slightly revised and slower Monte Carlo circuit, took charge of the race on the eighth lap after Cevert, Peterson and Regazzoni had all come unstuck, and held off Fittipaldi's snarling JPS Lotus to win by 1.3 seconds.

There were other interested parties, though. Hulme (McLaren) won in Sweden, with Peterson (Lotus) second and Cevert (Tyrrell) third. Stewart was fifth, Fittipaldi shunted. In France, Peterson won from Cevert, with Stewart fourth and Fittipaldi again on the accident list.

Stewart flew past Peterson on the first lap of the British Grand Prix but a raw South African, Jody Scheckter, caused pandemonium at Woodcote. The race had to be stopped and that dramatic corner would have to be changed. Gearbox trouble scuppered the Tyrrell after the re-start and Peterson had to give way to the McLaren driven by American Peter Revson. Third was Hulme and fourth a young Englishman called James Hunt, driving Lord Hesketh's March Ford. Again, there was nothing for Fittipaldi.

The title was slipping away from the Brazilian, and Stewart was determined none of these upstarts would claim it. Victory in Holland made the point. It also took him past Jim Clark's all-time record total of twenty-five wins. Scotland's second champion driver had his twenty-seventh win at the Nurburgring. He was in mean, decisive mood. And yet there remained a fitting, final flourish to his season – and to his career.

After taking second place in Austria behind Peterson he went into the Italian Grand Prix at Monza needing fourth place to secure the Championship. On the face of it, a modest task. It became, in reality, a near impossible one. Early in the race he had a puncture and made his sorry way into the pits. Lightning wheel changes were still a thing of the future and Stewart could only sit, watching the field and the race go by. Reflecting, again at Monza, he said: 'Everyone went through, into the distance and out of sight. When I got out again I was all on my own.'

Not for very long. It was an opportunity to display the best of Jackie Stewart and that is what an enraptured gallery saw. It was not a desperate, hairy charge, but a smooth, controlled, almost clinical performance. He had company again, and he was overtaking: 'I remember taking Mike Hailwood and of course when I got up to Francois he knew the situation and wasn't going to be a problem.'

It was as far as he could go. Time was up. Ahead of him still were Peterson, Fittipaldi and Revson, but fourth was enough to give him his third title. Tyrrell says: 'It was one of the highlights of our years together. It was a really tremendous drive. He'd been complaining about the car all weekend, saying what a heap it was. Then he has a flat and has to come in. After that . . . fantastic. Another ten laps and he would have won it.'

Stewart: 'The Nurburgring win in the wet was obviously very satisfying but this was probably a better drive in a technical sense. Monza was an easy circuit and it's more difficult to take advantage of the field on an easy circuit. It had to be a very precise, calculated drive. I couldn't afford to over-drive.'

Beneath the cool, technical satisfaction, emotions were stirring, too. He had not just won the Championship, or even just his third Championship. He had won his last Championship. It was the climax of his career. For months he, Tyrrell and Walter Hayes of Ford had kept the secret that Stewart would retire at the end of the season. Even Helen wasn't told because Jackie wanted to spare her the ordeal of the countdown. He

The British Racing Hero

Opposite page

Above left: Before the trials of Formula One . . . Julian Bailey savours Formula 3000 victory at Brands Hatch, 1987

Above right: Mansell's triumphant debut for Ferrari, Brazil, 1989

Below: Old adversaries . . . Senna and Mansell on the Silverstone podium, 1988

would bow out after Watkins Glen, his hundredth Grand Prix. 'That's why it was so special, why I so wanted to get that fourth place. I still wasn't sure I had it when I came in but the organisers assured me: I had got fourth place and I had got the Championship.'

Stewart's ninety-ninth race was in Canada. He led briefly but in a topsy-turvy race finished fifth. He did not complete his century. Cevert, about to be named Tyrrell's new No. 1, was killed when he lost control and crashed during practice for the United States Grand Prix. Stewart withdrew from the race and then announced his retirement. The 'peculiar mentality' would no doubt have enabled him to go on, as it had always enabled him to go on, but the decision was made and the decision was irreversible. Many tried, over a considerable period, to lure him back. All of them failed.

Stewart quit at the age of thirty-four. His nine-year, ninety-nine race Formula One career had yielded twenty-seven victories, a record beaten by Alain Prost fourteen years later, and three World Championships. Only one man, Fangio, has won more, and only four others, Brabham, Lauda, Piquet and Prost, have won as many.

Tyrrell saw the greatness in those wins and those Championships, and in so many other ways besides. He says: 'Jackie would go like hell on the first lap. He had the ability to get away from the grid and immediately produce a quick lap. He took his second lap with much more caution – because he didn't know whether there was any debris or whether anything had been dumped by the other cars first time round.

'He was going round Brands Hatch once and as he entered Clearways he backed off. He smelt new-mown grass and to him that was a warning. He was asking himself "What is new-mown grass doing anywhere near the track?" He knew that something had happened. Sure enough, someone had spun off and come back on again, bringing grass with him. That was typical of Jackie.

'We used to do hundreds of miles of testing at Kyalami and one day Jackie stopped because he said he could hear a funny noise and didn't know what it was. It took us some time to find there was a fastener securing a hose just touching another piece of metal when the engine was at a certain vibration. He always noticed things like that. He would pick up minuscule details. The number of times at Kyalami he would say "There's someone out there in a red shirt who keeps moving. I wish he'd stand still because I'm picking my corner by him".'

Both men were money-wise. Ken recalls: 'At Monza, before they put in the chicanes, slip-streaming was the big thing and we took advantage of it to get as much prize money as we could. Remember you get prize money for leading at quarter, half and three-quarter distance as well as winning and when Jackie approached the appropriate pay point in the race I gave him the lap countdown and he would make sure he got in front at just the right time. It was like ringing up the cash till.

'It was a phenomenal period with Jackie. Ten fabulous years. Continuity was probably the strength of it. Even in the early days, he never felt there was anything he couldn't reach for.'

It was one of sport's greatest liaisons. Mennem says: 'Jackie was lucky in that he and Ken just happened to come together at the right time. But

Opposite page

Above: Calm before the storm . . . Mansell at the 1989 Portuguese Grand Prix

Below: Palmer in the Tyrrell at the 1989 Mexican Grand Prix

then given that situation he applied himself with enormous ferocity.'

Stewart recalls: 'What he had was like a family. It was a sort of marriage, almost. Ken came for me when I needed him most and perhaps I came for Ken when he needed me most. For me they were immensely satisfying years and for Ken they were his years of greatness, his years of hunger, of achieving the kind of things boys only dream of.'

Stewart's eye and ear for detail were essential to the years of greatness: 'I always wanted everything to be right and eventually I was able to identify what needed to be done to achieve a particular aim. In the early days I didn't know what I was doing so much but as I matured everything was done consciously to achieve the ultimate goal, which was to win.'

That ability to concentrate the mind and sort out what was needed defied his dyslexia. His mastery of the forbidding Nurburgring is a case in point. Few drivers could memorise in sequence half the reputed 187 corners of the 14.189 mile circuit. Stewart could take you through the lot. 'I had to know it all,' he says. 'Seat of the pants driving is still what a lot of people do. They don't develop their mental application until a lot of their flair has gone and it's too late. If you can find that intelligence and use it early enough, the difference is considerable.

'We've said it before – you need experience. I don't think bravery has a place in all this [echoes of Moss]. Sometimes there is courage, which I think in some respects is controlled fear. But bravery is when someone does something spontaneously. That can be very dangerous. The ultimate fulfilment for any racing driver is to be able to drive a car to its absolute limits and match that with the limit of his own ability. Maybe very few men arrive at that point, in any sport or sphere of life.'

Stewart, of course, was aware of dangers as he was aware of all those minuscule details. His success on the safety campaign trail is as tangible as the race wins and the Championships. The demise of the original Spa circuit is a prime example, as Mennem relates: 'Drivers always had complaints about the place but they never thought to ban it because they thought this circuit sorted the men from the boys. It was the boys led by Jackie who got rid of the old Spa. What we have now are circuits that are safer and cars that are safer.'

Such a legacy of success and safety might send a man into quiet, contented retirement. But then achievers do not retire. The Dumbarton garage boy who had to work at the world is a restless, almost obsessive achiever still. He now lives in Switzerland. Be it business, television commentary, driving instruction, organising charity clay-pigeon shoots, or master-minding son Paul's racing team, activity is Stewart's lifeblood. He remains attentive to detail and boundlessly enthusiastic. He says: 'A lot of people retire from sport with the impression that the world owes them a living. They have been spoiled, pampered, treated like gods. They can't understand when all that is over. It's no good being bitter. You have to use what you have, work at it, put in the effort. Good PR is understanding and believing in what you have to offer, not just bull.

'I am enormously stimulated by all my activities and I can't remember the last time I was bored or depressed. My life is a kaleidoscope. There is still so much I want to do.'

No doubt he'll do it, whatever it is, and do it well. He has the key.

9

Game, Set and Match

Jackie Stewart's retirement left a gaping hole in British motor racing. For the first time since the early fifties, the nation that staged the inaugural World Championship Grand Prix had no driver with obvious title credentials. Certainly there seemed no realistic contender for 1974.

Already one young driver had been lost. The aggressive, gritty Roger Williamson was killed driving a March in the 1973 Dutch Grand Prix at Zandvoort. He was twenty-five and it was his second race.

Two other drivers who had shown promise were James Hunt and John Watson. But how much promise? No-one could be sure, of course. Watson had only two outings in a Brabham Ford. He made his debut – along with Williamson – in the British Grand Prix at Silverstone and then raced in the United States. He had not inconvenienced the headline writers, and he slipped quietly into the winter.

Hunt had rather more of a first season and made good use of it. He arrived at Monaco with the Hesketh March and competed in seven races. He earned his first point in France and gave that audacious display at Silverstone. He followed up the fourth place in the British with a third in Holland and completed the year with second in America. Stewart had departed with the crown and Britain was seeking a successor. So what about this chap Hunt?

All right, so caution would have to prevail. Fourteen points from his first seven races was not bad, but it was far from conclusive evidence of a major find. And besides, this Hesketh lot, could they really be taken seriously? It was all a trifle improbable for the Establishment. But others, less blinkered, were at least prepared to recognise the potential of this tall, fair-haired Englishman.

Hunt's rise in Grand Prix motor racing would be spectacular, the stuff of childhood dreams – except that Master James never had the vaguest desire to become a racing driver.

James Simon Wallis Hunt was born in a nursing home in Sutton, Surrey, on 29 August 1947, the second of six children. At the age of eight he went to Westerleigh boarding preparatory school and at thirteen to his father's old school, Wellington College, Berkshire. Mr Wallis Hunt, a stockbroker, and the school were intent on steering James along a professional course. James now says: 'I was destined for medicine purely by a process of elimination because it was the least of the evils in the unimaginative list of careers you were given at school. The careers master's job was in its infancy, which was patently obvious to me. I didn't really have any choice. I was going to be a doctor.'

That was until his eighteenth birthday, when James, an able all-round sportsman and particularly enthusiastic tennis player, accepted that he would never be a Wimbledon champion – and when he suddenly became hooked on motor racing: 'It happened to me in an instant. At eighteen I ceased to be a junior tennis player and I wasn't good enough to be a senior. Anyway, my doubles partner took me to watch his elder brother racing in the August Bank Holiday meeting at Silverstone. He was driving a Mini he'd built himself. It was only a club race but I thought "this is pretty bloody good" and decided that was what I was going to do. It was as simple as that. I started in a Mini.'

The British Racing Hero

His course determined, Hunt was equally positive about his destination: 'I am a competitor, I am ambitious and I always tried to be the best in whatever sport I took on, so Formula One had to be the target right from the start of my racing career.'

Each step along the way was deliberate. He left behind his Mini and the nursery for Formula Ford. Once he had got the hang of preparing his Alexis he learned how to win. In 1969 he went on to Formula Three and by the end of the year, driving a two-year-old Brabham with a three-year-old engine, he was making an impact. So much so that he received a Grovewood Award. The awards scheme was devised to recognise, encourage and reward promising young drivers, and Hunt now slotted into that category.

Any financial assistance was gratefully accepted. This brave adventure might well lead to Formula One, fame and fortune, but that scenario was still a fantasy. In the meantime, there was reality to face and there were bills to pay. He worked at what he could, when he could: 'My first job was as a van driver for a printing firm. I worked for the Medical Research Council for a while driving their cars around, which was a wonderful job. I had the run of the Government cars for probably six or seven of the eight hours I was supposed to be working and as there was nothing to do I could go and get parts for my Mini and generally get on with building it. The research place was at the Royal Marsden Hospital in Belmont and when I'd finished I used to do night cleaning at the Royal Marsden.'

He didn't get all the jobs he wanted, though: 'I was turned down as a bus conductor because I was too tall. They said why not be a driver but then they found I was too young.'

In 1970 Hunt was ready to spread his wings. Armed with some sponsorship and a Lotus 59, he joined the wandering tribe of drivers scouring the Continent for more competition and more recognition. He had his first international win at Rouen and was consistent enough to survive when the sponsorship money ran out. He had a factory-backed March for 1971 and now the ride became bumpy. He had a number of offs and mishaps, notably at Zandvoort, where his car slid upside down for 100 yards. He was fortunate to emerge unhurt. 'Hunt the shunt' was getting a reputation he didn't want, but remained philosophical. He now says: 'It didn't bother me because I told myself it was a natural rhyme and not necessarily an aspersion, so I could ease the pain. I never thought it revealed a flaw in my make-up because my shunting was always through getting involved in multiples. I was never a shunter of cars on my own. It was all brought on by not really having a competitive car. I had to stick my neck out more than most. You have to try and make up for the deficiencies of your car. It was probably over-eagerness and inexperience. As experience came I learned to avoid those situations.'

He also learned a few harsh facts of racing life that year: 'I'd cobbled a deal together with March. I brought a little bit of sponsorship and managed a free engine. But we were under-financed and it was a disaster. We were just uncompetitive. The chassis wasn't good and by Monaco the following year, Ford Germany had approached them with a bag of gold to put Jochen Mass in the car, so they fired me and snatched it.'

It was from this low in Hunt's career that he was picked up by the Hesketh team. Together they would write one of the most unlikely – and romantic – chapters in motor racing.

'My career had really stagnated badly and it was time to do something different. At that moment, fortunately for me, Hesketh Racing decided to come and talk to me. They had already approached me in the winter without actually revealing who they were because they were a new team. They were also having a bit of a disaster. The next race was at Chimay, in Belgium, and somebody had just lent me a car to drive there. I decided that as I'd got nothing else I'd go and talk to this Hesketh team.'

Lord Alexander Hesketh, a large man with a large estate near Towcester and a still larger appetite for life, had set up a team with Anthony 'Bubbles' Horsley and soon they were planning to run a second car. Hesketh and Horsley also decided it was time they and Hunt had a proper talk. 'Bubbles and I bumped into each other in the middle of this field in Belgium,' recollects Hunt. 'We'd each set off to see the other at the same moment. That was the start of it.'

It was still not the end, though, of a wretched Formula Three season. The Hesketh Dastle was out of its depth and when both Hunt and Horsley crashed at Brands Hatch their Formula Three venture was laid to rest. As Hunt recalls, their Formula Two bid revived optimism all round: 'In cancellation of my deal with March I blagued out of them a Formula Two chassis. It was the previous year's but, armed with that, I told Hesketh that if they bought the engine I'd do the rest. We painted 'Hesketh' on the car, went off and did fantastically well. I actually caused March great embarrassment by blowing their works cars into the weeds at Oulton Park – with Peterson and Lauda driving them. That was in their old car with an 1800 engine, while they had new cars with two-litre engines. That, and another couple of good results, rekindled Hesketh's interest. He came back from shooting in Scotland and we were off and running again.'

'Off and running' meant rather more than simply racing. Hesketh, as was his wont, ensured that the off-the-track activities were just as stimulating. Their camp would be an oasis of joviality in the desert of stony-faced professionalism, and yet when it came to the business, they were as thorough and conscientious as the rest. Hunt: 'Alexander would bring his mates and they'd have a huge party, but behind the smokescreen – because it was very difficult to see through it – the team were very serious and professional. The combination of the fun and the seriousness suited me. When I was concentrating on the race it didn't interfere or bother me having all that fun around. They were a jolly nice crowd and after the race, when it was time to stop work, I was able to enjoy the party.'

The environment accommodated Hunt perfectly. A gangling, un-gainly-looking figure, he did not fit the contemporary image of a racing driver. He was never going to go through life playing a straight bat. Intelligent, articulate and forthright, sometimes unconventional in manner and dress, he was not going to be everybody's cup of tea. But for the Hesketh set, he was tailor-made. He says: 'I wouldn't call it a non-conformist attitude, I think it's a practical one. I am anti-humbug and bull. That is just part of my philosophy of life. I suppose one goes through phases. I went through my hippy phase when I was driving. I am still a bit of a hippy at heart but just a bit too old to be practising.'

The British Racing Hero

With momentum regained and Hesketh's interest rekindled, the team now had Formula One in their sights. The plan for 1973 was to ease into the big league while continuing in Formula Two, but Hesketh reappraised the situation and decided to go for broke. Formula One it would be. They hired a Surtees to give Hunt a run in the non-Championship event, the Race of Champions, at Brands Hatch. Third place provided the confidence-booster they sought. Hesketh would give Hunt his World Championship debut in a March at the Monaco Grand Prix on 3 June 1973.

It was an appropriate curtain-raiser for the Hesketh extravaganza. The fun-loving aristocrat instantly made himself at home – and noticed – among the boats and champagne set. Conspicuous, too, was the efficiency of the racing team operation under Horsley's management and the performance of their English driver. Hunt put the March on the ninth row and was heading for sixth place in the race when his engine gave up.

That first point arrived in France and at the end of the season – which in Hunt's case was only seven races, remember – he had fourteen points and eighth place in the Championship. It was time for Formula One to take seriously the arrival of Hesketh Racing and the one-time tennis hopeful.

While the young Hunt had dreamt of Wimbledon, all Master Watson's boyhood schemes had led to the great race tracks of the world. His father raced in Northern Ireland in the post-war years and young John eventually followed him on to the club scene. 'I went to the races with my father and then, when I started racing, the roles were reversed,' he says. 'I decided from an early age, eight or nine, that I wanted to be a Formula One driver. I became a great follower of Porsche. And I had my British heroes, of course: Moss, Hawthorn, Collins and Clark. Jim Clark's career, I suspect, was the last I looked on as being ideal. I remember the very minute, the very second on that fateful day when I heard of his death. The fact that somebody as outstanding as Jim Clark could be killed in a racing car altered my perspective a little bit. It didn't put me off but it made me realise that as human beings in racing cars we are fallible.

'The trouble for me as a young driver was that there was no obvious, well-trodden path to follow from Ireland to Formula One. I should have set out on an international career at twenty-one instead of waiting until I was twenty-three or twenty-four. I should have had more inherent confidence.'

That admission is pertinent. Watson, a gifted driver, would produce some quite brilliant and aggressive performances in his long career. And yet he remained an essentially quiet, unassuming man. Had he imposed himself on the sport more forcefully, more consistently, there is no telling what more he might have achieved. He goes on: 'I just enjoyed cars and racing but I suppose I also saw racing as a way of establishing my identity as a man, if you like. That, for me, was a very important part of it. The other factor is that racing is a means of seeking your own limits. You push yourself as close to the limit as you can.'

When Watson finally generated sufficient self-confidence to tread his own path, he made his way with considerable style and purpose. Fifteen months older than Hunt, he had his World Championship debut in the 1973 British Grand Prix at the age of twenty-seven. Typically, he came into Formula One almost unnoticed. In 1974, however, he had a regular Brabham Ford drive and the opportunity to draw a little more attention to himself.

These were still early Formula One days for both Watson and Hunt. Watson was learning the hard way. That 1974 season yielded six points. He was sixth in Monaco, fourth in Austria and fifth in the United States. The 1975 season, spent mainly at the wheel of a Surtees, proved an enormous test of his character and resolve. He had absolutely nothing to show for his efforts. The path seemed to be leading nowhere.

The going was difficult for Hunt during the early part of 1974. He had two races in the March before designer Harvey Postlethwaite was ready to introduce the first Hesketh. A maiden Formula One victory in the non-Championship International Trophy race at Silverstone brought some relief and provided a good excuse for a party, but the team had no illusions. Making an impression in Grand Prix racing was one thing, winning was quite another. Third place in Sweden, and again in Austria, were rare moments of encouragement through tedious summer months. The suggestion of a breakthrough came at the end of the year – fourth place in Canada followed by a front row grid position and third place in the United States.

Hunt completed the season with fifteen points, just one more than he had from his seven races in 1973. He was again eighth in the Championship. But this time he was the top British driver. The names above him were: Fittipaldi, Regazzoni, Scheckter, Lauda, Peterson, Reutemann and Hulme. Mike Hailwood, with twelve points, was tenth, Watson joint fourteenth and Graham Hill was one of three drivers with a solitary point. Another was Tom Pryce, a modest Welshman who had made his debut that season. He brought home his Shadow Ford in sixth place at the Nurburgring.

Pryce scored eight points in 1975. At the British Grand Prix he earned the distinction of being the first driver through Silverstone's Woodcote chicane and then claimed pole position. But Hunt confirmed his status as top Brit.

The Hesketh was a more consistent and reliable car, Hunt was becoming a more consistent and reliable driver. The Hesketh team were growing up together. They opened the season with second place and fastest lap in Argentina. It was an indication of the possibilities. The proof came in Holland. Hunt demonstrated great skill and judgment to hold off eventual champion Niki Lauda for his first Grand Prix victory.

Hunt recalls: 'It was both exciting and important for me. It rounded off my education. On three occasions before then I'd seen the chance to win a Grand Prix and panicked, got over-excited and made a mistake. The problem was that, unlike most other drivers, I'd not done all that much

135

winning in my career. I hadn't the experience of leading races. Suddenly finding myself leading a Grand Prix with somebody snapping at my heels was too much for me. It was too unnerving an experience. At Zandvoort I laid to rest the ghost completely because I couldn't have had greater pressure than I had in that race.

'It was a wet-dry race and I made my stop for dry tyres early. Lauda and Jarier came out of the pits ahead of me after they changed to dry tyres but I had already been out a few laps and sussed the circuit. I had quite a manoeuvre to get past them because I had to do it on the wet part with slicks. It was dry only on the line. Off-line it was very wet. I was on the inside so I had a dry patch to hit as I slithered across their bows. Luckily the car gripped on the dry patch.

'Then I built up a ten-second lead very quickly while they were still getting their tyres warmed up, but by half-distance they'd caught me up again. From then on I had to keep them at bay. Remember that Lauda's Ferrari had a big power advantage over the Fords that year.'

Eventually it was Hunt versus Lauda, a trailer for an epic to come. The Englishman's nerve and concentration stayed the distance and he took the chequered flat 1.06 seconds ahead of the Austrian. The Hesketh pit exploded in jubilation.

Hunt: 'It was good to win like that, with that sort of pressure, and from Lauda particularly. I had commanded a race from the front. I'd had no experience of that before. But after sixty-odd laps like that at Zandvoort I was very experienced. It was my coming of age.

'My education in racing owed a lot to Bubbles Horsley. He took a close interest in me and my approach, and certainly helped me mature. He rounded me off. He taught me how to deliver of my best all the time instead of some of the time. He taught me how to prepare mentally, to spot when I wasn't properly motivated. He also taught me how to eke out the points when the circumstances weren't exactly perfect for me, how to soldier on in a bad car.

'All of which meant that by the time I got to McLaren I was complete. This was just as well because at McLaren I really needed to be in charge. I was in charge of myself and also paid a contribution towards getting the team together.'

Hunt went on delivering during that 1975 season and although a second win eluded him he built up a total of thirty-three points to finish fourth in the World Championship – behind Lauda, Fittipaldi and Reutemann. The Hesketh fairytale, however, was coming to an unhappy end. Financial pressures had begun to weigh too heavily and although Horsley soldiered on under the Hesketh Racing banner, the old days had gone, his Lordship had gone, and Hunt had gone.

Hunt says: 'Hesketh had put in no money at all during 1975. We raced the whole season off income, our earnings on the track and a bit of ducking and weaving by Bubbles. Hesketh kept saying he'd get sponsorship. He'd set it up and then torpedo it just as it was about to happen. He'd get cold feet. He didn't really want to give it away. So in the end there was no sponsor and no money. I stuck it out until the November and luckily a top drive became available at that rather strange time of the year.

'Lotus had approached me but I wasn't about to drive for them. Suffice

136

to say, I think, that Colin Chapman and I would not have got on. But then along came McLaren. Luckily, because Fittipaldi went off to Copersucar to drive his Brazilian car. The deal was done and dusted in no time at all.

'The deal was done with Teddy Mayer, the McLaren team manager, and John Hogan, the Marlboro man responsible for that company's racing involvement. Hunt insisted they delete from the contract one clause – that stipulating the wearing of the team uniform. Hunt and Mayer would not always be in harmony, but the driver's assessment of the team's potential was well founded. Watson, now driving a Penske, was also hopeful of making progress in 1976. Progress for Hunt meant challenging for the Championship, yet before he could do that he had to establish himself within the team: 'McLaren was a bigger team than Hesketh, a bigger operation with more personnel. It was also a two-car team and I'd just come from a one-car team. But Hesketh's team had management, whereas McLaren didn't have any direction. It was a rudderless ship. Luckily Alistair Caldwell, who wasn't officially team manager, took on that role at the track and was very good. He was very much responsible for getting the car turned out and getting the team run properly.

'With relatively little experience I had to establish myself in the team as the senior Championship contender and luckily that happened very emphatically at the first race of the season. It might have destroyed any relationship I could have had with Mayer but it put the team 100 per cent behind me.'

Hunt in the Hesketh 308, at the 1975 German Grand Prix

That first race was at Interlagos, Brazil, and circumstances conspired to make his plan more complicated than he had anticipated. For a start he was too big to fit comfortably into the M23 and an engine blow-up also cost him valuable practice time. All of this when he was trying to out-manoeuvre his equally ambitious team-mate Jochen Mass. 'I had to have a shouting match with Mayer about how the car was set up because I was going out with twenty minutes left on a five-mile track. You don't get many laps in that time. I was guessing the settings and he said "You can't do that." But I said *I* was driving the thing. I wasn't going to be pushed around when I knew what I wanted. I insisted. This was in the garage, in front of all the mechanics. I went out and on my first flying lap I got the first pole of my career. That impressed the boys, of course. They like chargers and they'd seen me stand up to Mayer. After that I was very much No. 1.'

A break-down in the race, however, did nothing for his status. Defending champion Lauda cruised on to a comfortable victory. The gauntlet had been thrown down. Pryce was third, Mass sixth.

Hunt again beat Lauda to pole in South Africa but from the line the Ferrari was ahead. The pattern for the season had already been established. A tyre problem slowed the Austrian in the later stages and Hunt charged. To no avail. Lauda won by 1.3 seconds. Mass was third, Watson fifth.

Few now doubted Hunt was a man to be taken seriously in the Championship contest, but he couldn't afford to let Lauda pile up the wins. In Long Beach, the street setting for the United States West Grand Prix, the situation did not improve for the Englishman. He was barged into the wall by Patrick Depailler's Tyrrell. He was left at the side of the track, brandishing his fist in anger, and later, at a press conference, he launched a verbal assault on the Frenchman. Lauda, meanwhile, had finished second behind Ferrari team-mate Regazzoni, and Mass was fifth.

On to Jarama, Spain, and a third pole from four to Hunt. For the third time, too, Lauda – fortunate to be suffering only the pain of broken ribs after falling from a tractor at his home in Austria – was alongside. Not so usual was the appearance of the car behind Hunt – a six-wheeled Tyrrell, driven by Depailler. Hunt again lost the advantage at the start but was in the lead by half-distance, the champion clearly in discomfort. Mass took second place only to blow up. Hunt came first, Lauda second. The McLaren man was in business.

Or was he? Stewards measured the winning car and found it to be, according to revised regulations, too wide – by 1.8 centimetres – across the rear wheels. Hunt was disqualified. McLaren lodged an appeal and would continue their fight for weeks to come. For now victory, and another nine points, were Lauda's. The Austrian's total went up to thirty-three points, Hunt's down to six.

The McLaren's width was adjusted for Belgium and, between practice sessions on the first day, the position of the oil coolers was altered. It was like Samson having his hair cropped. The car, handling wickedly, was powerless in the race and eventually capitulated with a transmission failure. Lauda was first again, Mass sixth.

At Monaco an engine blow-up ended Hunt's race. Lauda collected yet another win, Mass another two points with fifth place. Hunt was stuck on six points, while Lauda was up to fifty-one. To make matters worse for the Englishman, Mass was up to ten. In Hunt's mind he was the team's No. 1 but the mathematics might swing the McLaren effort behind the German.

Hunt continued to struggle in practice in Sweden, where the Tyrrell six-wheelers emerged triumphant. Scheckter was first, Depailler second. Lauda was immediately behind the Tyrrell pair, with Hunt fifth. Lauda had stretched his lead over Hunt to forty-seven points. McLaren were in despair, the Championship was a lost cause. They had banged their heads against brick walls in their endeavours to make the car work. All they got were headaches.

Coming up was the French Grand Prix, which would complete the first half of the sixteen-race season. The team were testing at the Paul Ricard circuit ahead of the Grand Prix and, having tried all else, moved back the oil coolers. Samson had his hair again. The position had been changed by less than half an inch but the effect on the balance was enormous.

It did not, however, alter the Championship table and Hunt gave scant consideration to it. He says: 'By that time the Championship was so far out of reach there was no point worrying or even thinking about it. There was absolutely no pressure on me at all. Then I won two Grands Prix in two days . . .'

Order was restored in practice for the French: Hunt fastest, Lauda second fastest. Lauda went away – naturally – but not for long. Hunt: 'Luckily for us both Ferraris blew their engines. Ricard being a power circuit, we couldn't match them for speed, but they self-destructed.' Hunt picked up the nine points and this time no-one took them away. Watson was third – but was then disqualified because his rear wing was too high. Another appeal had to be heard.

Hunt and Mayer went straight on to Paris for their Spanish Grand Prix hearing and successfully argued that the punishment of nine points did not fit the crime. Instead the team were fined $3,000. Hunt had his second 'win' in two days. Lauda was back to second place in the Spanish Grand Prix, his total therefore trimmed by three points. Events in France left Lauda on fifty-two points and Hunt on twenty-six with half the season to go.

Despite the sudden change in Hunt's fortunes, Lauda remained very much in control, very much the favourite. It seemed to Hunt that it was down to Lauda – he could win it or he could throw it away. 'All I could do was keep winning,' says Hunt. 'There was still no real pressure on me.'

There was, though, expectancy among the home fans. Next stop was Brands Hatch for the British Grand Prix, otherwise billed as the Hunt–Lauda showdown. First blow went to Lauda. He edged out Hunt for pole and elected to start from the higher, left side of the track to give himself a better line into Paddock Hill Bend. Behind Hunt was Lauda's team-mate Regazzoni. Hunt, not for the first time, was sluggish from the line but it didn't matter. The race was stopped almost before it started. Hunt: 'I think I'd managed to get as far as Druids when the flags came out. Regazzoni had a serious attack of brain-fade into Paddock and assaulted his own team-mate. The shunt was right in front of me and I had nowhere to go at all. They were sideways-on.'

Regazzoni's Ferrari tipped the McLaren on to its side and although it came back down on to four wheels it was damaged and in no condition to contest a Grand Prix. McLaren mechanics wheeled out the spare for the re-start – and officials brought out the rule-books.

It became apparent there was some dispute as to whether Hunt would be permitted to race because he had not completed the first lap. Then, with the crowd growing hostile, they decided that the cars still running when the original race was stopped would line up for the re-start. Drivers were not allowed to change cars. Hunt's McLaren, though crippled, was still hobbling along when the flags came out. Ferrari did not see it that way and would protest.

Hunt's hastily repaired car was back on the grid and chased after Lauda's Ferrari. As the fuel load went down and the handling of the McLaren improved, so Hunt mounted his challenge. Both men broke the lap record as their battle raged across the fields of Kent. Hunt drew ever-closer and, on the forty-fifth lap, dived inside the Ferrari at Druids. The great bowl of Brands erupted in appreciation and cheered Britain's new hero all the way home. Motor racing's courts would have the final say as far as the result was concerned, but Hunt had an experience nothing could erase: 'It was certainly my most emotional race. Brands is such an intimate circuit, anyway. You feel the crowd more than you do anywhere else. And, from the crowd's point of view, I had the perfect race. I had a long struggle to get past Lauda. That was the problem. I was always going to be a lot quicker once I had.

'I wasn't particularly aware of being any sort of hero to the British fans because I was living in Spain at the time. I wasn't spending much time in England. That season I'd obviously become bigger news but I wasn't really aware of it. Being British and having all that support and emotion was terrific. There was no way I was going to miss that race. The organisers had decided that even if I might later be disqualified, they were going to start me.'

Rain clouds hung menacingly over the Nurburgring as Hunt and Lauda took up their positions on the front row of the grid for the German Grand Prix. Both opted for wet tyres. Mass gambled on dry tyres. It paid off. At the end of the first lap – all 14.189 miles of it, remember – Hunt, Lauda and most of the others headed for the pits to change tyres. Next time round Mass, the German, had a half-minute advantage over his partner. Just then his March, and the race, were stopped. There was an accident out at Bergwerk.

Inexplicably Lauda, who had, ironically, called for a boycott of the track, had shot off exiting an insignificant left-hander. The Ferrari cannoned back off the barrier in flames. Two other cars were unable to avoid hitting the blazing wreckage. Four drivers – Briton Guy Edwards, Italian Arturo Merzario, Austrian Harald Ertl and American Brett Lunger – pulled Lauda from the inferno.

He was taken to hospital in a critical condition. He had severe burns and had inhaled flames and smoke. His lungs were badly damaged. He was given the last rites. Amazingly, he was racing again six weeks later. Hunt: 'I was ahead of the accident and by the time I'd gone round again Niki had been taken away. It didn't really affect me and that is the way it should be because a driver ought to know the risks and consequences before he goes motor racing. If you don't understand the risks you are a mug. Well, I did understand the risks, so it didn't change anything, except on a personal level because that was a friend of mine being badly hurt.

'As it turned out, the story had a happy ending. Niki not only returned to racing, he came out of it a stronger, happier and better person. He would be the first to tell you that. It changed his life absolutely for the better.'

In Lauda's absence they regrouped on the Nurburgring grid and Hunt won comfortably from Scheckter and Mass. Lauda's Championship lead was down to fourteen points and next was the Austrian Grand Prix, his home race. With Lauda in hospital and Hunt on a charge, Enzo Ferrari chose the moment to announce his team's withdrawal from Formula One until the authorities sorted out their rules and regulations. He claimed he had been cheated out of wins in Spain and Britain. Then came a call for the Austrian race to be cancelled.

The race, in fact, went ahead and Lauda watched from his hospital bed as Hunt struggled with a car unsettled by a damaged wing to finish a modest fourth. Victory went to another British driver, the hirsute John Watson. It was the first Grand Prix win of the Ulsterman's career and he honoured pre-race bets by shaving off his beard. Watson displayed his control and growing confidence to bring in his Penske Ford ten seconds ahead of Frenchman Jacques Laffite's Ligier Matra.

In Holland Hunt celebrated his twenty-ninth birthday by taking charge again. Twelve months earlier he had his maiden success at Zandvoort; now he was an assured, accomplished Championship contender. Not that it was an easy day's work. During the early laps he watched as

Watson, on the ascendancy, scrapped over the lead with Peterson. Soon he manoeuvred his McLaren past Watson, then got past Peterson without really trying at all, and the Swede dropped out of the chase. Hunt led the final sixty-four laps but only by defying Watson's retaliation and a late assault by Regazzoni, back after all in the Ferrari. Watson retired with transmission trouble. Pryce stayed the course to take fourth place.

Hunt enjoyed his birthday to the full. His car had been below par, yet he'd conjured a crucial victory. Now the Championship was on. The top of the table read: Lauda fifty-eight points, Hunt fifty-six.

Hunt had been in regular telephone contact with his great rival and knew he was anxious to get back. Hunt, also, was willing the Austrian to return: 'I wanted Niki to be well and racing again. I didn't want to beat him while he was lying in a hospital bed.'

Their joint wish was granted at Monza. The extent of Lauda's head and facial burns now apparent, the world marvelled at the man's courage in stepping into the open again, let alone climbing into a racing car.

The political talking point that weekend concerned fuel regulations and, more especially, the octane level of McLaren's petrol. McLaren – and Penske – were duly declared to be running on illegal fuel, had their Saturday times scrubbed and found themselves at the back of the grid. Hunt had nothing to gain by holding back and nothing to lose by having a go.

Initially his rampaging strategy carried him through the field, but progress inevitably became harder. He still figured that he had nothing to lose and took one risk too many. Much to the delight of the sneering Italians, he was out of the race. Lauda, astonishingly, took fourth place. With three races remaining it was: Lauda sixty-one, Hunt fifty-six.

Hunt was playing squash in Canada when word filtered through that he had been stripped of his British Grand Prix victory. His anger was compounded by further reports that Lauda had declared the decision good for the sport. The press gratefully pounced on the opportunity to build up the rivalry between them but in truth Hunt was more concerned about the gap between them. It was now seventeen points.

Lauda, sixth fastest in practice, was never in contention during the race at Mosport. Hunt took pole and then the lead from Peterson. The serious opposition came from Depailler, who pressed and threatened for most of the race, only to drop back towards the end. That was explained when he clambered from the car and flopped like a rag doll. He had been overcome by fumes from a ruptured fuel line in the cockpit.

The title rivals were now eight points apart. Two races were left. The odds were still very much with Lauda. Before they moved on to the United States they made a point of telling the media there was no animosity between them, and that both had been misquoted in recent days. So what was their relationship *really* like? Hunt now says: 'I got on very well with Niki and always had done. We first met and raced together in Formula Three in early 1970. By the end of that year we were good friends because we'd been travelling together, camping and gypsying around Europe with our Formula Three cars on our trailers. We teamed up as mates, not just casual acquaintances. He moved into Formula Two and Formula One much faster than I did but we still saw a fair bit of each other. We stayed friends.

'When we were driving together in Formula One we teamed up again as mates, and that lasted all the way through, thick and thin, the 1976 season except for just twenty-four hours in Canada. After they announced the results there the press were winding us up badly and we got a bit irritated. We had a good relationship right through.

'For example, at Watkins Glen, the race after Canada. We had adjoining rooms with a connecting door and in the evenings we had our door open and we socialised together. I'll never forget Niki's attempt to psyche me on race day. I always got up at eight o'clock on race days to be at the circuit at nine. Knowing full well what time I had my call booked for he barged into my room at seven o'clock. He was fully bedecked in his overalls and stood to attention as he said "Today I vin ze championship!" With that he marched out again. I thought it was hilarious.'

So much for the simmering feud . . .

Hunt had his eighth pole position of the season for the United States East Grand Prix. He was again beaten from the grid, though, this time by Scheckter. Hunt had seen it all before and patiently went about retrieving the advantage. That much he achieved, but Scheckter would not be shaken off and when Hunt's rhythm was upset by a back-marker the South African seized his chance. Hunt had to do it all again. He had nine hard-earned points. Lauda had his own fight to keep third place.

There was one race left. The scores: Lauda sixty-eight, Hunt sixty-five.

They would complete their global duel in Japan, under the gaze of Mount Fuji. Lauda still had the upper hand, but this was a Lauda finding his way again – perhaps a new way. The cool, fearless Austrian had been close to death. Perhaps this 'better person' was not so cool and fearless any more. The permutations were various but Hunt knew that victory would give him the title even if Lauda came second. Going into the Japanese Grand Prix the Englishman had six wins, Lauda five. That tally could prove a crucial factor. On the day, there was another crucial factor. Rain.

Officials and drivers debated the issue: should they race or shouldn't they? Some young lions were all for getting out there, Pryce among them. Hunt would race if he had to, but he favoured a delay. He says: 'Niki and I were on the safety committee and we were both against racing that day because of the conditions. We thought it should be held over until the next day. The track was flooded.'

The stewards decided the race would go ahead that day, but would be delayed. Hunt: 'They were lucky because, unexpectedly, it stopped raining. It hardly rained at all during the race. In fact the sun came out and that really was a problem because it was so low. You couldn't see a thing.'

Lauda had seen enough after two laps. While Hunt had, for once, rocketed from his front row position into the lead, Lauda, starting from third place on the grid, had been lost in the spray and confusion behind. His vision was further affected because he still couldn't blink his eyes. To Niki Lauda, life itself now seemed a bigger prize than a second Championship. He pulled into the pits and retired. There were those, in Italy, who branded Lauda a coward. He would give his response in his own good time.

As the weather improved and the track dried, tyre conservation became vital. Worse still for Hunt, he had a deflating left rear. Depailler was catching fast. Fourth place was now enough to give Hunt the title, but could he afford to stop for a tyre change? Could he afford not to? The team were not prepared to make the decision. Depailler went past, only to be slowed by a puncture and Andretti, in the Lotus, took over.

Then Hunt's left front tyre shredded, fortunately for him as he came out of the last corner, and he dived into the pits. He went back out prepared to charge, anger and frustration firing his final attack. His pit signal told him he was sixth. After taking Regazzoni and Alan Jones, in the Surtees, the signal was P3. So where *was* he? He crossed the line in the tracks of Andretti and Depailler, though the American was a lap ahead.

Hunt did not know that. He was not sure of anything, least of all the outcome of the Championship: 'It was the sort of confusion we'd had all year. It was quite clear from the pit signals that the McLaren lap chart was scrambled. They were all over the place and didn't know where I was. That was down to Teddy. He was supposed to be running the thing. That's probably why I tried to strangle him when I got out of the car!'

Mayer and dozens of others gave three-fingered gestures of triumph to Hunt, indicating his position. But he was not convinced: 'I wasn't prepared to believe I'd got it. The point at which I believed that I had definitely won the Championship was when I came out of the press room and everybody had gone. The place was deserted. I reckoned that even if anyone wanted to do anything about taking the title from me they couldn't be bothered. Everyone had had enough. I decided to accept it. I must be World Champion.'

Game, Set and Match

Tom Pryce at the German Grand Prix, 1975

The British Racing Hero

That other decision, eleven years earlier, when he laid down his tennis racket and picked up a helmet, had been justified and rewarded. He had proved himself competitive, a winner, a champion. Game, set and match to Hunt.

There are those who will say – and have said – that he was lucky, that but for the accident Lauda would have been champion again. Hunt says he recalls Watson making such a statement: 'I got my office to go through the season's breakdowns and missed races and it worked out that I had more trouble than Niki that year.'

Watson now says: 'Had it not been for the accident I'm sure Niki would have won it. In the end he lost it by pulling out in Japan. But James deserved it for what he did in the second half of the season. He did what he had to do and he did it impressively. I have certainly never underestimated what he did.'

Hunt says: 'I am very proud of that Championship. I had great sympathy for Niki, as others had, but I don't think that situation detracted from what I did. I think people in Britain still wanted me to win. The McLaren chassis was as good as the Ferrari, it may have been marginally better at times. But we were definitely down on power.'

Their final scores were: Hunt, sixty-nine points, Lauda sixty-eight. Watson was joint seventh with twenty points, Pryce joint eleventh with ten.

It was time to pay the piper. The sponsors would keep Hunt busy for several weeks on a promotional tour. Then it was back to training, and then it was January and back to the Championship racing: 'Driving and racing again was like finding an oasis in the desert, so there was no problem of motivation. The other thing you have to understand on the motivation level is that winning is like a drug. It certainly had that effect on me. I wanted more. It was addictive. I'd done very little winning before and this seemed like a reward for all the hard work.'

Rewards in 1977 proved even harder to come by. Hunt started the season in the old car. The M26 was still undergoing development work back at the factory. Following the withdrawal of Penske, Watson was in a Martini-backed Brabham Alfa. Pryce was still in a Shadow.

Hunt began the first race, in Argentina, on pole with Watson alongside. Hunt was then beaten from the grid by Watson and Lauda. Nothing had changed. Hunt, patient, confident, took Lauda and then Watson – only for a rear suspension failure to send him into the catch-fencing. It was also a pointless exercise for Watson and Lauda. The Austrian's luck would change, taking him to his second World Championship. For the British pair there would be many more might-have-beens.

Pryce set off in hope that season, but the South African Grand Prix was his last race. Pryce's team-mate, Italian Renzo Zorzi, stopped when fuel from a broken pipe caught fire. Two marshals ran from the opposite side of the track to tend to the Shadow as Pryce and the German, Hans Stuck, came over the brow of the hill. One marshal managed to get across, the other, nineteen-year-old Jansen van Vauren, ran into the path of Pryce's car and was killed instantly. The Welsh man was killed, too, as the marshal's fire extinguisher smashed into his face. With the accelerator on full throttle, the car continued down to Crowthorne Corner at 160 m.p.h.,

144

collecting Laffite's Ligier as it went off. The Frenchman was unhurt, but Pryce was found to be dead.

A catalogue of mishaps could not detract from the performances of Hunt and Watson that season. In France Hunt led briefly and then Watson took charge for seventy-five laps before he spluttered, low on fuel, a few hundred yards short of the line and came second. The Irishman shared the front row of the grid with Hunt's M26 for the British Grand Prix at Silverstone and led until more fuel trouble put him out of his stride again. It was Hunt's race and this time it was not taken away from him.

Hunt also won the United States East and Japanese Grands Prix to finish the season with forty points and fifth place in the Championship. He says: 'We just had a very bad run of luck and, for the most part, a lousy car. I was driving even better than in 1976, obviously with more confidence. I won three races in that car and broke down three times in sight of victory. Niki won the Championship with only three wins.'

Watson had only nine points and thirteenth place in return for his contribution. In 1978 his score went up to twenty-five and his placing to sixth, making him top Brit. More victories, however, eluded him until he got a second wind, in the early 1980s.

Hunt could manage just eight points and joint thirteenth place in 1978. He moved to the Wolf team in 1979 but it was the beginning of the end of his Formula One career. Already disenchanted with a sport taken over by ground-effect cars, he found no consolation driving the Wolf. He brought down the curtain mid-season, at Monaco, the very stage where he had made his debut with the Hesketh company. His ninety-two races had brought him ten wins and one World Championship. 'I'd decided at the beginning of the season it was going to be my last. I was keen to do it and keen to win the Championship. I was fired to do that, but as it turned out the cars were so hopelessly uncompetitive there seemed no point carrying on. I'd done six seasons in Formula One and I thought that was enough for anybody. I reckoned I'd had a fair crack of the whip. The main thing was self-preservation. I didn't want to end up in a box or permanently injured.

'I'd given them that long to get the car right but they couldn't and they refused to build a new one. Even Keke Rosberg struggled to qualify it. There's slightly more of a risk in the middle of the pack than at the front, so going out there without a hope in hell of winning seemed a totally pointless exercise.'

A sympathetic Pat Mennem says: 'I can remember James running around like somebody demented at Monaco. The car was unsafe and it really worried him there more than at any other circuit. It was interesting watching James. He was a very intelligent, hightly-strung chap. Motor racing put the fear of God into him but he went out and did it. I think he had a lot of courage. He was often ill before and after races. In Japan, when he won the Championship and wouldn't believe it, I told him he had and got him a beer. He drank it and was immediately ill.'

Hunt: 'The times when I was actually sick before getting into a car were more in my Formula Three days. That was just the tension and nerves. I was permanently under tremendous pressure because if anything happened to the car I had to pay for it. And I never had enough money with

Opposite page

Above: Flying colours . . . Herbert's dream debut, Brazil, 1989

Below: Master and pupil . . . Ken Tyrrell and Johnny Herbert

James Hunt – anxious
moments before the race

which to do that.'

He may not have made it to the Centre Court, but he has made his home at Wimbledon, just round the corner from the All England Club. He has a keen and unlikely interest in budgerigars. Less surprising are his strident views from the BBC commentary box.

'My involvement in Formula One these days gives me a different enjoyment. I've been working with Murray Walker for more than ten years. He's such fun and such an enthusiast. I try not to make a strong comment unless I'm certain I'm right. I think, by and large, that I am and the people who are having the finger pointed at them by me are happy to take it because they know I am right. When I have been wrong I have been at pains to rectify it.

'I misjudged the Senna–Mansell incident at Spa in 1987. I blamed Senna, an assessment based on a quick glimpse. I did not have the benefit of action replay. When I got home and looked at it on tape I could see that I had been wrong. So I sought out Senna when I got to the next race, told him that I'd wronged him, and that I would not only apologise to him personally but also put the record straight on air, which I did.

'That, I think, has been the only time when I've really misjudged a situation and criticised someone unfairly. I stand by what I said about Senna in his incident with Mansell at Portugal in 1989. Senna did a spectacularly stupid thing there. He needed to be in that race to win the Championship, Mansell was inside him, he knew he was there, but he just drove into him. And at those speeds it was a dangerous thing to do.

'Senna didn't actually come and say anything to me about my comments on either incident. The only person who has ever said anything to me is Piquet, and that was just Piquet being childish about my calling him childish. One would expect it.'

Just as one would expect James to be James.

10

Where There's a Will . . .

When James Hunt switched to Wolf for the 1979 World Championship season, John Watson moved to McLaren. That year he distinguished himself not so much as the leading British driver on the scoreboard as the only British driver on the scoreboard. He totted up fifteen points and was ninth in the standings. The following year he maintained his domestic status with an even less spectacular score, six points. He shared tenth place with, among others, the Republic of Ireland's Derek Daly. The nation that had won ten drivers' titles in the first three decades of the Championship was at its lowest ebb as it confronted the 1980s.

Watson would soldier on, but he needed support, and British motor racing needed fresh faces. At the beginning of 1981 there was a hint that help was on the way. Toleman, flushed with Formula Two success, breezed into Formula One full of optimism. They were equipped for the new era with a Hart turbo and lined up with two British drivers, Brian Henton, an East Midlander who was never backward at coming forward, and Derek Warwick, a rugged, jovial Hampshire man. Henton had actually made his debut in a Lotus at the 1975 British Grand Prix but his experience since had been minimal.

Warwick was totally new to this level. Born on 27 August 1954, he nurtured his racing instincts in go-karts and stock cars. He won English, British and world Super-stocks championships before moving on to Formula Ford. Armed with a European Championship and second place in the British Championship he then took on Formula Three. He came first in the Vandervell Championship (ahead of Nelson Piquet) and second in the British Championship (behind Piquet). Two seasons in Formula Two culminated with runner-up spot in the European Championship and graduation to Formula One.

Another British driver was embarking upon his first full season of Formula One with a rather more established team. That team was Lotus, the driver Nigel Mansell. He had his baptism the previous August, in Austria, where Lotus entered a third car. The regular drivers were Mario Andretti and the gifted young Italian, Elio de Angelis. Late into practice Andretti and de Angelis had safely qualified, but Mansell's car was proving less co-operative. He was put in de Angelis' car and sneaked on to the back of the grid.

Mansell's first race lasted forty laps, a blown engine forcing his retirement. He was not too dismayed. Petrol had spilt into his seat while the tank was being topped up. By that stage of the afternoon his backside was burnt and he was suffering considerable discomfort. 'I had difficulty just walking back to the pits,' he said.

Discomfort and difficulties were no strangers to Mansell. Even to get that far his will-power and self-belief had been stretched to their limits.

The British Racing Hero

His struggle against adversity would go on. He cleared the financial barrier only to face a wall of prejudiced and jaundiced opinion.

Nigel Ernest James Mansell came into the world on 8 August 1953, above his parents' tea-room near Upton-on-Severn, Worcestershire. The seeds of his motor racing career were sown in a field at a schoolfriend's farm. Together they thrashed through the long grass in an old Austin Seven. Nigel was ten and soon looking to extend himself. The path was karts. Modest to start with, like the practice 'track' round the allotments. As he made his way into competition, the machinery, and the driving, improved. He was seven times Midland champion, Welsh champion, Northern champion and short circuit British champion. He also had the occasional mishap. He was badly injured at Morecambe and came round to find a priest at his hospital bedside intent on giving him the last rites.

The momentum inevitably carried him into car racing. In 1977 he won the Formula Ford Championship despite breaking his neck in an accident at Brands Hatch and being told he might never race again. He had to get pole and fastest lap as well as victory from the last race to clinch the title. He pulled off all three.

Formula Three was not only painful. It almost destroyed him as well. Mansell, a trained engineer, gave up the security of his job to throw himself into racing. He had a number of part-time jobs, including window cleaning, to keep body and soul together but he and his wife Rosanne had to make the ultimate sacrifice of selling their apartment. They sold other possessions and raised his racing budget. For £8,000 he got five races and at the end of it – nothing.

A sponsorship deal gave him a new lease of life the following year, 1979. In September, however, he broke his back at Oulton Park. Barely a

Brian Henton and the wreckage of his Toleman, Silverstone 1981

month later, as he was still recovering, he was offered a test drive with Lotus. He stuffed himself with painkillers and joined the other candidates at the Paul Ricard Circuit in the South of France. The pay-off was a test contract and three races in 1980.

Two weeks after that hot reception in Austria he qualified a creditable 16th in Holland, only for his brakes to fail and send him off after 15 laps. In Italy he didn't qualify, but he had done enough to impress Colin Chapman. When Andretti moved on, Mansell was given the drive for '81.

Mansell would not have to wait too long to score his first points. As for Henton and Warwick, they had to wait what seemed an eternity just to get into a race. Henton eventually made it into the Italian Grand Prix in September, while Warwick's frustration extended to the final race of the season in Las Vegas.

Warwick now says: 'You couldn't have dreamt it was so bad. Our designer, Rory Byrne, is one of the cleverest guys I've worked with and his F2 car was great. But the F1 car – just dreadful. Rory had simply got it wrong. The engine was bad, too. Those were very much character-building days.'

None of the British drivers was quickly into his stride, but Mansell began to show in Belgium. He was third behind Reutemann and Laffite, his satisfaction swelled by beating the dazzling Gilles Villeneuve into fourth place. He followed up by qualifying third in Monaco. He was the up-and-coming man. Chapman certainly believed so. He gave his latest protégé a lucrative new contract.

John Watson . . . 'I wish I'd had more arrogance'

Mansell was sixth in the Spanish Grand Prix, but this was where Watson began to get up a head of steam. He was third carriage in the famous train pulled by Villeneuve. The Ulsterman continued to gather pace. On to France, and he was second in. Next stop Silverstone, Britain. Could he complete the 3-2-1 run?

Watson was back in the role of the sole British hope for the home race. The Toleman-Hart was still giving Henton and Warwick a hard time and Mansell failed to qualify after his car was hastily modified to comply with regulations. Watson's carbon fibre McLaren proved far more co-operative and gave him fifth place on the grid. He was still not confident, though, pointing out that pole man Rene Arnoux, in the Renault turbo, was 1.7 seconds quicker.

Watson made a cautious start, managed to avoid an accident started by Villeneuve and then advanced – calmly, skilfully, surely. When Alain Prost's Renault blew only Arnoux remained ahead of him and he hacked at the Frenchman's twenty-five second lead. The Renault was in trouble: turbo. Eight laps from the end Watson was in the lead and Silverstone roared its approval. Watson had the second win of his Formula One career – five years after his first.

It was all too much for the quiet, low-profile man: 'I just couldn't understand what I was experiencing or believe what I was seeing that day. This enormous crowd, reacting in such a way – for me. Why? I was embarrassed by it all. I tend to understate any achievement, but that's me. I had no idea what it was like, winning your home Grand Prix. Obviously I'd seen James winning it, but you have no idea what it's like until it happens to you.

'It seemed to me totally uncharacteristic for a British crowd to respond as they did. British crowds are knowledgeable and very appreciative but reserved, supposedly. And yet look at them at Wimbledon when Virginia Wade won the title. And we've seen it since at Brands Hatch and Silverstone for Nigel. We pride ourselves on being unemotional but in fact when we are 'pricked' the abandon that I experienced is there. I just hope we can show that appreciation for more British successes.

'Looking back now, it has to be the greatest memory of my career. It was just a remarkable, special day, and I know I will never experience the like of it again. If I am remembered at all, I think I would like to be remembered for winning the British Grand Prix, because I can now understand that I gave something to a lot of people that day and there's never going to be an opportunity for me to do it again.'

A second place in Canada helped Watson to a score of twenty-seven points and a final position of sixth in the Championship. Mansell signed off with an encouraging fourth in Las Vegas. His eight points made him fourteenth overall.

Having made the breakthrough as a qualifier, the next task for Warwick was to steer the 'Flying Pig' to the line and score. Points, however, would elude Toleman and the game Warwick throughout 1982. Henton had a race with Arrows and most of the season with Tyrrell, but with no joy. He left the scene at the end of the year.

Mansell was still in tandem with de Angelis, but Watson had a new partner – N. Lauda, of Austria. The man who simply walked away from the sport in 1979, 'bored with going round in circles,' had been lured back by the re-shaping Marlboro McLaren organisation. Lauda's impact was immediate. He was a leading activist in the drivers' strike over super-licences at Kyalami. When they got down to racing Lauda was fourth, Watson sixth. Disqualifications for Piquet and Rosberg lifted Watson and Mansell to second and third places respectively in Brazil.

It was not, though, to be a productive year for Mansell. His only other score was at Monaco, where he finished fourth. A wrist injury effectively punched a hole in the middle of his season and by the end the JPS Lotus Ford was powerless against the growing might of the turbos.

Watson took up the flag again. He was sixth at Long Beach and then demonstrated considerable race-craft to win the Belgian Grand Prix at Zolder. It was, however, a sad weekend for Watson and all motor racing. During the second qualifying session Villeneuve, the French Canadian who had become something of a folk hero, ran into the back of Jochen Mass' March and was thrown from his No. 27 Ferrari. He died that evening. Watson: 'From the driving point of view it was satisfying but this was not a win I could enjoy.'

Tragedy stalked Formula One that year. Ricardo Paletti, an Italian starting only his second race, ran into the back of Didier Pironi's stalled Ferrari on the Montreal grid and was killed. Pironi himself was seriously injured in a crash during a wet practice session at Hockenheim and never raced in Formula One again. He died in a powerboat accident in 1987. In December 1982 Colin Chapman, the sport's great innovator, died of a heart attack. Mansell was devastated.

Pironi had been on course for the Championship. Suddenly it was open to a bunch of drivers – including Watson. The Ulsterman's superb street circuit technique brought him through to victory in Detroit and he was third in Canada. Then he had a barren spell and the consistent Rosberg poached a crucial win in the Swiss Grand Prix (at Dijon). Watson's fourth place in Italy sent him to the last race, in Caesar's Palace parking lot, Las Vegas, with his hopes still alive. Just. He had to attack; Rosberg could bide his time.

Watson guided his McLaren to second place, but Michele Alboreto maintained a safe distance in his Tyrrell to win. Rosberg, one of the great chargers, needed no heroics. He sealed his title success with fifth place. The Finn was the last champion in a normally aspirated car before the turbos were outlawed. Rosberg had forty-four points, Watson and Pironi thirty-nine, Prost thirty-four, Lauda thirty. Mansell's seven points left him in fourteenth place.

In 1983 the cars were stripped of side-skirts, had flat bottoms and were refuelled mid-race; the fast ones had turbo engines. But on the street circuits power was not of the essence, as Watson and his McLaren Ford illustrated in Long Beach. With one of the outstanding drives, he threaded his way from twenty-second place on the grid to register what proved to be his last Formula One victory. Team-mate Lauda, who started from twenty-third, tagged on to take second place.

Rosberg's Williams Ford won in Monaco and downtown Detroit was the appropriate location for the Ford Cosworth's last stand. Alboreto (Tyrrell Ford) was first, Rosberg second and Watson (McLaren Ford) third. Mansell (Lotus Ford) was sixth.

The Championship contenders, however, had turbo-charged engines. Lotus were already running one car powered by a Renault turbo, for de Angelis. But it was not a good car and in five weeks they produced new models – designed by Frenchman Gerard Ducarouge – for both the Italian and Mansell to race in the British Grand Prix at Silverstone. Problems hampered Mansell in practice but in the race his new car responded and he came a fine fourth.

Watson was fifth in Germany, Mansell fifth in Austria, Watson third in Holland, Warwick fourth in Holland . . . 'Wait a minute,' I hear you say, 'Warwick, fourth?' Yes, Warwick fourth. The diligence of team and driver were finally rewarded on an emotional afternoon at Zandvoort. More than two-and-a-half years into their Formula One venture, they had their first points.

Warwick: 'There are moments in your life you always want to re-live and for me that finish was one. When I got out of the car everyone was crying. It didn't just affect me, it affected the whole of the pit road. It showed the feeling everybody had for us. It had started to come together and I was the only driver to finish in the points in the last four races.'

The high-point for Mansell came in the penultimate race, the Grand Prix of Europe at Brands Hatch. He recorded the fastest lap and finished third behind the main Championship contenders, Piquet and Prost. It was a performance which ensured his seat for 1984.

Piquet, in the Brabham BMW turbo, took the title, with Watson joint sixth (twenty-two points), Mansell joint twelfth (ten points) and Warwick fourteenth (nine points).

The failure of Prost and Renault to clinch a Championship that had looked as if it was theirs led to national inquests and internal disputes, and driver and team parted company. McLaren, unable to agree terms with Watson, scooped up the little Frenchman and left the Irishman in the wilderness. Watson made a final appearance in a McLaren in the 1985 Grand Prix of Europe at Brands, but by then the fire had been doused. He made 152 Grand Prix appearances, winning five times.

Watson, still quiet and self-effacing – and no less endearing for that – reflects: 'I think I had lots of ability but not enough self-belief. I wish I'd had more arrogance. Maybe I wasn't demanding and forceful enough in certain situations with the team. In 1982, for instance, there were various reasons why I failed to win the Championship. I have to accept responsibility in part and so do the team. But one of the factors was my not seizing the opportunity and going to the team and saying "Forget about Niki Lauda, I'm the person who's going to win the Championship, concentrate on me". Had I done that it could have changed the team's attitude to their two drivers. They may still have decided to give us equal opportunities, I don't know. But I should have been more emphatic.

'I think as a nation we are too understated, but on the other hand we have that bulldog mentality and we seem to need adversity to excel. It almost seems as if we need a World War II situation to bring out the best of British. I'm sure many of our sportsmen and women have not fulfilled their potential because of this.'

Warwick's persistence and eventual mastery of the 'Flying Pig' had earned him quite a reputation and when Renault, the turbo pioneers, offered him a drive he viewed it as a major advance in his career. Watson's involuntary exile left Warwick and Mansell, still at Lotus, to pick up the flag.

There were, though, two British newcomers for 1984. Jonathan Palmer, who gave up a medical career to go into full-time racing, made his debut in a Williams at the 1983 Grand Prix of Europe. The former British Formula Three and European Formula Two champion now embarked upon his first full season with the RAM Hart turbo.

The other rookie was a twenty-four-year-old from King's Lynn, Norfolk, called Martin Brundle. He had emerged from an excellent Formula Three season, beating the highly-rated Austrian Gerhard Berger in his own backyard, and then pushing the even more acclaimed Brazilian, Ayrton Senna da Silva, to a last race decider in the British Championship. The title eluded him at Thruxton, but the call from Tyrrell was ample consolation.

Brundle made a splendid start, finishing fifth in the Brazilian Grand Prix at Jacarepagua, near Rio. The authorities would strip him of those two points – and others – later in the year, but on 25 March the world of Formula One looked a wonderful place.

Warwick might have been on top of that world. He led for twelve laps of his debut with Renault, only to drop out smelling victory: 'In the early stages Lauda came by me, pulled straight over and his rear wheel just touched my front left. With ten laps to go I was leading comfortably and as I braked for the hairpin the front wheel just collapsed. We thought it was down to that little ding with Lauda.'

Undeterred by the early setback, Warwick began to pile up the results and the points. He was third in South Africa, second in Belgium and fourth in the San Marino Grand Prix at Imola. Mansell made his mark with third place in France and second place on the Monaco grid. Soon he was in the lead and going away in the wet. Then he slid, hit the barrier and his race was over.

There was more drama for Mansell, and Brundle, in America. A start-line pile-up at Detroit forced the race to be stopped and FISA later adjudged Mansell the culprit, fining him $6,000. When they got the show on the road it was Brundle who threatened to steal it, dashing into second place behind a watchful Piquet. The young Englishman was, however, disqualified because of fuel irregularities and an FIA Appeal Court scrubbed all the Tyrrell team's points. Officially then, Brundle did not score on his Formula One debut. Try telling him that.

Worse still was awaiting Brundle in Dallas, the first and so far the only time Formula One has stopped by these parts. He crashed in practice, shattering his feet, and missed not only the race but the rest of the season. Mansell's weekend started much better. He claimed the first pole position of his career and for more than half the race stayed in front. Warwick went off trying to overtake, one of many caught out by the crumbling track. Mansell eventually lost the lead to Rosberg, clipped a wall and tried to push his crippled car over the line. He collapsed from exhaustion, but came round to be told he was classified sixth.

Gearbox trouble put paid to Mansell's British Grand Prix. Warwick had a more satisfying afternoon, taking second place behind Lauda's formidable McLaren TAG Turbo. He concluded business by agreeing a new contract with Renault for 1985. He had enhanced his reputation while Mansell's fortunes had see-sawed. Now Warwick was widely regarded as the coming man. Comparisons between the two men vying for the position of top Brit were inevitable and rivalries always make good newspaper copy. Warwick smiles: 'I tell you, there was no rivalry between us. Nothing. I remember there was a Renault press conference. Nigel and I were there and the people were trying to put us against each other. We just made a big joke of it. I've always got on well with Nigel.'

Despite a fourth place in Germany, Mansell was not getting on well with Lotus chief Peter Warr and a parting of the ways was inevitable. Lotus announced, on the weekend of the Dutch Grand Prix, that Senna would be joining them. Mansell had already set up a move to Williams and had the last word at Zandvoort with third place in the race.

He almost had a decisive say in the Championship. In the final race, at Estoril, Portugal, Mansell was running second, behind Prost and immediately ahead of Lauda. If it stayed that way the title would be Prost's. Alas for the Frenchman, Mansell's brakes gave up the cause and the Austrian had his third title – by half a point. Warwick had twenty-three points and seventh place, Mansell thirteen points and joint ninth – with Senna.

The 1985 season would be a watershed for both Warwick and Mansell. Unfortunately for Warwick, Renault were on the way out. He wound up the year with five points and a pile of broken plans, fifth place at Silverstone providing a rare moment of consolation. Brundle was back, using the Ford engine in the first half of the season, the Renault turbo in the second. It made no difference to the results. He still had nothing to celebrate. Palmer switched to the German Zakspeed team and endured endless frustrations.

But what of Mansell? Little, frankly, was expected of him. He had had four years in Formula One and his critics had decided he would never be a winner. Even Frank Williams, the man who had just hired him, believed he was getting no more than a 'journeyman', a solid No. 2 who would pick up points. Williams' No. 1, Rosberg, made no secret of the fact that he did not welcome Mansell on board. By the end of 1985 Rosberg, Williams and those critics were all changing their minds about Mansell.

The will-power and self-conviction that sustained Mansell through the early days of hardship had fortified him through the past two years at Lotus. He said: 'Although I hadn't won a race I still believed in myself. I felt that given the car, the team and the backing I could win races. I needed a chance. I needed a fresh start.'

He sensed, also, that he was joining the right team at the right time. Williams provided Championship-winning cars for Alan Jones in 1980 and for Rosberg in 1982. The tie-up with Honda promised the muscle to go with their undoubted expertise. 'They had started again and so had I,' said Mansell. 'It would be like a breath of fresh air.'

There were still a few ill winds blowing during the early part of the season. Williams and Honda had to work on their marriage and Mansell's results were modest. He had a rousing drive from the pit-lane to fifth in the wet in Estoril, another fifth at Imola and sixth at Montreal. The breakthrough was forced by Rosberg with victory in Detroit.

During practice for the French Grand Prix at the Paul Ricard circuit Mansell was approaching the end of the Mistral Straight at 200 m.p.h. when his left rear tyre exploded. The Williams ploughed into the catch-fencing and Mansell was carried from the wreckage unconscious. He missed that race but was back for the British, at Silverstone, a fortnight later. He qualified fifth but was not distressed about retiring with clutch trouble.

When the show moved into Belgium three-quarters of the season had gone and Mansell had seven points. But here, at the new Spa circuit – shorter and safer than the old one yet still a daunting challenge – the pieces began to fall into place. He took second place in a wet-dry race, the best result of his career to date. That, and a productive test session, sent him to Brands Hatch for the *Grand Prix d'Europe* in good heart.

He qualified third, behind Senna and Piquet, but ran fourth in the early stages, Rosberg having split the Brazilians. Then Piquet was caught in Rosberg's spin and the Brabham was out. Rosberg limped in with a puncture and roared back out just as Senna and Mansell were coming round again. Senna found the Finn in his path, checked, probed, and, to his dismay, saw Mansell go the other way into the open road.

The British driver led and the British crowd rose as one. This, though, was only lap nine. It was a seventy-five-lap race, so it was much too early to celebrate. Mansell knew that better than anyone. He went about the job of building his lead, then consolidating. As the prospect of success grew, so did the tension. The fans gave him the count-down signals: five laps to go . . . four . . . three . . . two . . . one. He made it. Now they could celebrate.

It was Mansell's first Grand Prix victory in seventy-two attempts and the first by any British driver since Watson's drive through Long Beach two-and-a-half years before. Mansell recalls: 'I stood on top of the podium for the first time and tried to take it all in. I'd gone through the barrier, I'd arrived. That one achievement had made it all worthwhile. All the effort, the setbacks and the knocks. This was the great satisfaction, the realisation that it had been worth it.'

There was another triumph that clear, warm autumn day. Prost's fourth place was enough to give him the Championship, his mission accomplished. Mansell's mission was only just beginning. Assured and purposeful, he went to South Africa determined to make more progress. He took pole and then the race, keeping his head and position despite coming under attack from Rosberg.

Mansell's season ended in early retirement at Adelaide and Rosberg departed the Williams camp with a win. He also went with a different opinion of the Englishman: 'Nigel is one of the three best team-mates I've had. I was wrong about him, I admit it.'

Mansell's season had produced thirty-one points and sixth place in the Championship standings. More significantly, the final quarter had yielded twenty-four points. He flew back to the Isle of Man a contented man, yet an even more ambitious man. The 1986 season could not come soon enough.

For Warwick the year ahead promised absolutely nothing. He had planned to join Lotus and Lotus had planned to sign him – until Senna, now the team's No. 1, objected on the grounds that they had not the resources to satisfy the demands of the two front-line drivers. Lotus gave in to the Brazilian and Warwick's world caved in on him. 'I'd put all my eggs in the Lotus basket and when they were smashed by Senna I was very angry. I felt a lot of malice towards Ayrton. I had nowhere to go by that time. Later on I suppose I saw his point and even developed some admiration for him. He took a lot of stick but stuck to his guns because he believed he was right. Maybe that's what makes him special. He is so single-minded and doesn't give a damn what anyone else says or thinks.'

Warwick returned to Formula One the following June in circumstances every driver dreads. He was called up by Brabham after Elio de Angelis was killed testing at Paul Ricard. He was twenty-eight.

Lotus – with Senna's approval – took on another Briton, the Earl of Dumfries, or just plain Johnny Dumfries as he preferred to be called. He had succeeded Senna as British Formula Three champion, but the Brazilian clearly felt he represented no threat. Dumfries would score three points that season and not be retained. A more rewarding experience would be his part in Jaguar's sportscar triumph at Le Mans in 1988.

Palmer's fruitless endeavours with the Zakspeed would continue through 1986 but Brundle was to pick up eight points along the way. British hopes of success, though, rested on the shoulders of Mansell. He had proved himself capable of winning races and the Canon Williams Honda was ready to take on the Marlboro McLaren TAG.

Johnny Dumfries . . . brief encounter

155

The favourite for the title, however, had to be his new team-mate Piquet. He had proved himself capable not only of winning races but also of winning Championships. He was signed as No. 1 before Mansell had broken his duck, and anticipated no serious competition from the Englishman. It was a gross miscalculation by Piquet and, in fairness, by many others too.

The entire Williams team were buoyant as the season approached, but the mood changed as final preparations were completed at Ricard. Leaving the circuit, Frank Williams crashed his hire car and was critically injured. He would eventually return to lead his team, but would be confined to a wheel-chair. They would have to go to Brazil, and launch their bid for the World Championship, without him.

In Rio the launch was successful and Piquet was the man at the controls. The calculations looked to be accurate. Mansell tangled with Senna on the first lap and was out of the race. The wounded beast in Mansell was ready to bite back. He lunged at Senna on the line in the Spanish Grand Prix at Jerez and fell short by ninety-three centimetres, or 0.014 seconds. It may have been closer than the Gethin–Peterson finish at Monza in 1971. No-one will ever know.

Engine trouble chained him down in the San Marino Grand Prix, where victory went to Prost, and second place to Piquet. Mansell managed fourth in Monaco but Prost won again. Rosberg, now with McLaren, was second and Senna third. After four races, a quarter of the season, the top of the Championship table looked like this: 1st, Prost, 22 points; 2nd, Senna, 19 points; 3rd, Piquet, 15 points; 4th, Rosberg, 11 points; 5th, Mansell, 9 points.

Mansell needed to attack – and soon. Next was Spa, and he duly attacked. In the closing laps Williams' concern was not so much the opposition as the fuel read-out. Mansell judged it perfectly and had his first win of the season. Senna was second. There was no elation for Mansell. His former team-mate de Angelis had died just ten days earlier. He dutifully attended a press conference, then slid quietly away.

In Canada Mansell was simply magnificent, in command all week-end. He was fastest in qualifying and showed enormous discipline in pacing his race to suit his own requirements. He was not panicked by Rosberg's charge to the front, rationed his fuel and won the race in his own good time. What is more, all the other big boys stayed the course. He took on the lot and beat the lot. Prost was second, Piquet third, Rosberg fourth and Senna fifth. That made it all the more satisfying.

Now the Championship table read: 1st, Prost, 29 points; 2nd, Mansell and Senna, 27 points; 4th, Piquet, 19 points; 5th, Rosberg, 14 points.

Over the border in Detroit, Mansell had the scent of another win. He brushed aside Senna and eased away. He seemed unstoppable. But then his brakes began to fade and here, of all places, that amounted to a major dilemma. Detroit's concrete walls give no second chances. It was a time for prudent compromise. Victory was out of the question so he nursed home the Williams and accepted what was on offer. He got two points. Senna was first and Prost third. Piquet's car came to grief in the concrete.

Back to Europe and the French Grand Prix at Paul Ricard: the circuit where Mansell had his accident 12 months earlier; the circuit where

Heroes both . . . Mansell and Stewart

Williams had watched his cars testing immediately before his accident; the circuit where de Angelis had his fatal crash. Mansell knew he had to be the cold professional and that is precisely what he was. He and the team decided on a second tyre stop to maintain the pace and the pressure, and the strategy worked. Prost could not contain Mansell, who crossed the line seventeen seconds ahead of the Frenchman. Piquet was third, Rosberg fourth. Senna went off.

Halfway through the season, the standings were:

1st, Prost, 39 points
2nd, Mansell, 38 points
3rd, Senna, 36 points
4th, Piquet, 23 points
5th, Rosberg, 17 points.

Mansell was within reach of the summit and coming up, seven days later, was his home race. Brands Hatch braced itself for an epic British Grand Prix.

Frank Williams appeared at the track that weekend and his drivers did not let him down. Piquet and Mansell put his cars on the front row. The contest enticed 115,000 on race day, and what they wanted most of all was to see Mansell make it four wins in five. Within a few hundred yards Mansell thought the prospect had gone. A broken drive-shaft had disabled the Williams. But to his astonishment the race was stopped. A pile-up at the first corner, injuring Frenchman Jacques Laffite on his record-equalling 176th appearance, would mean a re-start.

157

Mansell had to take the spare, more specifically Piquet's spare, set up by Piquet. Mansell wasn't sure how it would feel, how it would behave. He would ease himself into the race. Piquet was away first, Berger in the Benetton, second, Mansell, third. By the third lap Mansell was comfortable, confident, set to attack. He took the Austrian and tracked his partner. On lap twenty-three Piquet missed a gear and it was all Mansell needed. The cars were so evenly matched that there might not be another opportunity. Mansell pounced.

Everything now depended on the tyre stops. Mansell came out just ahead of Piquet and knew it was vital to hold him. Piquet darted, Mansell covered. As his tyres heated, Mansell was able to increase his pace again. Their ferocious, high-speed duel was on. They traded lap records, but they always came back out of the trees in the same order. Mansell would not be No. 2. Anxiety gripped the great Brands amphitheatre until, suddenly, a gap began to appear between the cars. Piquet was broken. The tension was released in an explosion of cheers.

Mansell took the flag five-and-a-half seconds ahead of Piquet. No other car was on the same lap. Only Prost's McLaren had not been lapped at least twice. Piquet was a disgruntled No. 1, but this was no day for pulling rank. He had been beaten – fairly. Mansell was groggy after the supreme effort. The car had not been equipped with a drink bottle and he was dehydrated. But he could cope with that. After all, he was leading the World Championship.

He was also now a man in demand. He flew to Maranello for talks with Enzo Ferrari and was inevitably impressed. The proposition was very tempting and he might well drive the scarlet car one day – but not now. He wanted the Championship and had no intention of jeopardising his chances. He was staying with Williams for another two years.

Mansell's fortunes dipped over the following weeks and races. He was third in Germany behind Piquet and Senna (the McLarens ran out of fuel) and it was the same order in Hungary, where he was angry that he had not been told about a crucial differential adjustment made by his teammate.

The relationship between the two drivers had never been good. From now on it was to get worse. Piquet was undoubtedly surprised at Mansell's pace and resented his challenge. Mansell, for his part, had no intention of being a meek No. 2 and Williams made no attempt to stifle him. Frank Williams' attitude was: 'We are racers.'

Mansell, Piquet and Senna were all out of luck in Austria, leaving Prost to win with a sick car. The Williams pair were back in charge at Monza. Piquet was first, Mansell second. Prost was disqualified for changing cars too late and Senna was left on the line.

With three races remaining the contenders stood like this: 1st, Mansell, 61 points; 2nd, Piquet, 56 points; 3rd, Prost, 53 points; 4th, Senna, 48 points. Rosberg, on 22 points, was out of the running.

Mansell had a spare car in Portugal and made good use of it. By race day he was thoroughly satisfied with his preparations. Senna beat him for pole but Mansell led into the first corner and dictated the race. His authority was absolute. Behind was the scramble for the places. Eventually it was Prost second, Piquet third and Senna fourth. Now the contenders were down to three: Mansell on seventy points, Piquet on sixty, Prost on fifty-nine.

The title was so close for the Englishman. One more masterful drive would do it, but he knew he could take nothing for granted. Still two races left, eighteen points to go at. Next was Mexico City – high altitude, smog, bumpy track. And a stomach bug. On the start-line, a nightmare – green light and no response from Mansell. 'All I had was a bunch of neutrals.' He crept away in second, the majority of the others already on their way. Fifth place at the end of the day was a reasonable result, particularly as Berger had his first win to keep Prost in second place. Senna was third, Piquet fourth.

Under the eleven-score rule Mansell and Prost were now dropping their lowest scores, so as they headed for the final race, in Australia, the table read: 1st, Mansell, 70 points; 2nd, Prost, 64 points; 3rd, Piquet, 63 points.

Mansell was still clear favourite. Any top three finish would secure him the Championship. It would still be his no matter where he finished if neither Prost nor Piquet won. For the Frenchman and the Brazilian, it was all or nothing.

Mansell set a blistering pace in qualifying to take pole ahead of Piquet, Senna and Prost. But he decided this race was no place for heroics. He took his time, stayed out of trouble and eventually settled into the third place he required. Ahead were Rosberg – having his final race – and Piquet; immediately behind was Prost, who had had a puncture. That early mishap was a blessing in disguise for the defending champion. Goodyear personnel gauged from the relatively little wear on Prost's tyres that the other drivers would be able to go the distance on one set.

Mansell had planned to change at half-distance but his team told him it would not be necessary. When Rosberg's tyre disintegrated less than twenty laps from the end they changed their minds. Mansell would have to be called in. He was still third – now behind Piquet and Prost – and had an advantage of more than a minute over Stefan Johansson, placed fourth in the Ferrari.

He never got the chance to make that pit stop. As he came down the Brabham Straight at almost 200 m.p.h. his rear left tyre exploded. It was all Mansell could do to keep the wickedly-jerking Williams out of the wall. It came to rest at the end of the straight. The tyre was in shreds, Mansell's Championship was in shreds. After sixteen races across the world, he was denied the crown forty-four miles short of the final flag.

Prost resisted a late charge from Piquet – who made it to the pits for his tyre change – and retained his title. He was honest enough to admit: 'It should have been Nigel's. He was the one who deserved it most.'

The 1986 World Championship finished thus:

1st, Prost, 72 points; 2nd, Mansell, 70 points; 3rd, Piquet, 69 points.

Mansell and his wife Rosanne walked away from the Adelaide circuit in total dejection: 'All through my career we had worked together for this day, this opportunity. To have the Championship stolen like that was a terrible blow. It wasn't just a personal disappointment, though, I was disappointed for all the people who had helped us and all those back home who had stayed up to watch the race on television.'

It was a time to draw on the old will-power. He had proved his ability and the Williams Honda would still be the car to beat in 1987. He would pick himself up and go on the attack again.

Britain's other drivers switched camps for the new season. Brundle and Palmer simply swapped places. Brundle, looking for a change, was talked into joining Zakspeed. An agonising year produced two points and convinced him it was time to do something completely different. He joined Jaguar and won the 1988 World Sportscar Championship.

Palmer, glad to see the back of Zakspeed, gratefully took the opportunity to join Tyrrell in 1987. He collected seven points in the Championship proper and won the Jim Clark Cup for drivers of normally aspirated cars. Turbos were being phased out and would be outlawed from 1989. The big prizes, though, would still go to the turbo brigade in 1987 and 1988.

Warwick, after his short spell with Brabham, signed for Arrows. The car was powered by a Megatron turbo engine and the Jersey-based driver was typically optimistic. But apart from an equally typical, bold effort in his home race, where he was fifth, there was little encouragement for him. At the end of the season he had just three points.

So, it was down to Mansell again to carry British hopes. He was soon in his stride, taking pole in Rio. His Brazilian luck did not change, though. He had an overheating problem and a painful reminder of his last race – a puncture. The day's hard labour earned him one point. Prost was first, Piquet was second, Senna retired.

Piquet crashed heavily in qualifying and was refused a medical certificate to race in the San Marino Grand Prix. He could only watch as his team-mate won with economy of effort and fuel, ahead of Senna. Prost's McLaren had an alternator belt failure. Only two races gone, but Mansell enjoyed the feeling of leading the Championship again.

In Belgium he was on pole and confident of another win. But as he attempted to take the lead from Senna they collided and slid off the track. Senna retired immediately and eventually Mansell, too, had to call it a day. He reckoned he still had some unfinished business with Senna. He sought out the Brazilian and had him by the throat before three Lotus mechanics were able to drag him off. Piquet had a more mundane turbo problem, leaving Prost to equal Jackie Stewart's record of twenty-seven Grand Prix wins.

Mansell channelled his aggression into driving at Monaco and was irresistible. In qualifying he was seven-tenths of a second faster than second-placed Senna, 1.7 seconds quicker than third man Piquet. It was, in Mansell's opinion, a lap of 'near perfection'. So was his performance in the race. Mansell, like Clark, had always yearned to win Monaco, the great challenge, and, like Clark, had always been frustrated. Now, surely, the Principality was Mansell's. But no. His exhaust broke, ending his race. Senna won, Piquet was second, Prost, in more trouble, came nowhere.

Detroit followed a similar pattern: Mansell beat Senna for pole, led comfortably, then hit trouble. This time he had cramp and toiled to finish fifth. Senna took over the race and the Championship lead. Mansell had another pole in France – and a relatively trouble-free run to victory. He

The British Racing Hero

Opposite page

Above: Mansell's breathtaking win in Hungary, 1989

Below: New partners . . . Prost, Mansell and Ferrari

outfoxed Piquet to leave the title table like this:

1st, Senna, 27 points; 2nd, Prost, 26 points; 3rd, Piquet, 24 points; 4th, Mansell, 21 points.

The Championship was again beautifully poised as they made for the British Grand Prix, which this year and for many years to come would be held at Silverstone. Once again it was to be a Mansell–Piquet duel. The Brazilian stoked the fires with a few jibes about his stable-mate having already lost a Championship, and then edged out Mansell in an absorbing contest for pole.

Piquet seemed also to be on his way to victory in the race as Mansell struggled to compensate for a lost wheel balance. The Englishman changed tyres and had thirty laps to make up twenty-eight seconds. Surely it was too much to expect, especially after last year. It was not. Mansell gnawed away at the lead and the crowd began to realise all was not lost. Down Hangar Straight, with two-and-a-half laps left, Mansell sent Piquet the wrong way, dived inside and led through Stowe. According to his fuel read-out his tank was empty, but nothing was going to spoil this day of unabashed patriotic fervour, and he somehow made it to the line. An emotional Mansell kissed the ground where he had made that decisive, breath-taking manoeuvre.

Senna's third place kept him at the top of the Championship but now Mansell and Piquet were just a point behind. In Germany, pace-setters Prost and Mansell dropped out, handing Piquet his first win. His second, in Hungary, was also fortuitous. Mansell was coasting home until, thirteen miles out, a wheel nut popped out and the Williams was crippled.

Events off the track were going Piquet's way, too. He negotiated a deal that would take him to Lotus at the end of the year. Lotus would retain Honda engines but Williams would lose them – to McLaren. A gloating Piquet declared that he had turned over Mansell and Williams.

Mansell feared as much and would complain about his engines being down on power compared with Piquet's. But he had no intention of throwing in the towel, as he demonstrated in Austria. He swatted away Piquet like a fly and celebrated his hundredth Grand Prix with a majestic win. Piquet retaliated in Italy, taking advantage of Mansell's struggle and Senna's late error to give the active-ride Williams a winning debut. In Portugal Mansell's car died on him, Prost had his record-breaking twenty-eighth win and Piquet gained a useful third place.

With four races remaining Mansell faced a near impossible task. Piquet was on sixty-seven points, Senna on forty-nine, Mansell on forty-three, Prost on forty. The Englishman needed wins, nothing less. In Spain he produced a performance reminiscent of his drive in Portugal the previous year, taking control and leaving the rest scrapping in his wake. Mansell's pole in Mexico gave him a record fifteenth consecutive front row position. The Grand Prix was held in two parts because of Warwick's accident at the infamous Peralta Curve and Mansell took the flag again. It was his thirteenth win in a phenomenal two-year period.

Now the title was between the Williams pair. Piquet led by twelve points, the odds heavily in his favour. But Mansell was on a roll and quite capable of winning the last two races. Alas for him, he was not able to

Opposite page

Above: Martin Donnelly faces up to Formula One, Paul Ricard, 1989

Below: Rising star? Allan McNish on the glory trail

161

compete. He crashed during the first qualifying session in Japan, seriously injuring his back. His season was over, and with it another Championship bid. He had won six races, twice as many as Piquet, but the Brazilian had the title for a third time.

The final table was:

1st, Piquet, 73 points; 2nd, Mansell, 61 points; 3rd, Senna, 57 points; 4th, Prost, 46 points.

The British Racing Hero

After the dramas of 1986 and 1987, Mansell would find 1988 thoroughly unspectacular. Despite restrictions on turbos in this, their final year, the best of them were still too much for the normally aspirated runners. The Marlboro McLaren Honda won fifteen of the sixteen races, Senna taking the individual title by three points from Prost.

The Williams was powered by a Judd engine and although Mansell pedalled it for all his worth, it was no match for the heavyweights. His brightest days were in the wet and gloom of Silverstone, where he was second to Senna, and on the meandering Jerez circuit, where he was second to Prost. They were his only finishes of the season. Twelve points gave him joint eighth place in the Championship.

Palmer, still with Tyrrell, scored five points. His new partner, Julian Bailey, an Englishman not afraid to enjoy himself off the track, found the pressure of qualifying one of the worst cars ever made by Tyrrell so intense he never gave of his best and drifted from the Formula One scene at the end of the year.

The top Brit of 1988 was Warwick, in the Arrows Megatron turbo. He was fourth in Brazil and went on scoring fairly consistently without ever being able to move up a notch. He completed the season with seventeen points and joint seventh place.

Warwick and Palmer stayed on for a final season with their respective teams in 1989. Warwick managed seven points in the Arrows Ford while Palmer had an utterly miserable year in the Tyrrell Ford, not helped by the pace and audacity of his young partner, Frenchman Jean Alesi.

Brundle was back, with Brabham, the team also returning after a year in exile. The Judd-engined car graduated from the pre-qualifying class mid-season but results were hard to come by. A flat battery denied Brundle a place on the Monaco podium and he finished the season with four points.

Totally new to Formula One was Johnny Herbert, a chirpy lad from Essex signed by Benetton Ford despite smashing his feet in a Formula 3000 accident the previous summer. He laid down his crutches to take fourth place in his debut at Rio, but from then on he clearly struggled and was dropped after failing to qualify in Canada.

Britain looked, yet again, to Mansell. And, now, so did Italy. The man who rejected Ferrari in the summer of 1986 was more receptive when they came back two years later. John Barnard's car, complete with semi-automatic, seven-speed gearbox, needed all the time and attention they could lavish upon it. They knew that. It had potential but the Brazilian Grand Prix was upon them and in warm-up Mansell managed just one lap. He booked an early flight home and confidently expected to be on it.

To his amazement, the Prancing Horse kept on prancing. Then it was galloping away with the race. Mansell shot outside Riccardo Patrese –

driving the No. 5 Williams he had left behind – then took Prost in more orthodox manner. McLaren's problems undoubtedly helped, but it was still a remarkable debut success. Mansell brought the No. 27 home to an ecstatic welcome from the Ferrari camp. The British hero had become an Italian hero as well.

Ferrari's season changed dramatically and almost tragically at Imola. Mansell's partner Berger went straight on at the Tamburello, his car smashing into a wall and bursting into flames. Thanks to the strength of the monocoque and the efficiency of the emergency crews, Berger not only survived but missed just one further race.

The team confronted a long struggle for reliability and Mansell's disqualification amid confusion at the start of the Canadian Grand Prix didn't help the cause. Ferrari were in need of a lift. Mansell was about to give it to them.

He was second after starting from the pit-lane in France, second in Britain and third in Germany. He went to the winding Hungaroring in optimistic mood. Here the acceleration of the McLaren Honda would not be such a potent weapon, while the Ferrari would surely be extremely effective. Practice confounded his prognostication. His Ferrari was not effective at all. He spent the final qualifying session working on a race set-up and was relegated to twelfth place on the grid. It proved a wise, as well as courageous, strategy.

From the start he instantly flashed past four cars and then patiently awaited his opportunities to advance. When he came up to Prost the little man admitted defeat. Senna would not be so co-operative. Mansell's chance came on lap fifty-eight as they lapped Johansson's Onyx. Senna was drawn in a little too close and although he went to the right to overtake, the Ferrari had the momentum and the space – just – to go wider still and snatch the lead. 'It was,' said Mansell, 'one of the most satisfying wins of my life, if not *the* most satisfying.'

He followed up with a cavalier drive through the wet of Spa to third place, but then the flow of results dried up. In Portugal he was snugly on course for victory until he came into the pits for a change of tyres and overshot his crew. In his anxiety he reversed, and reversing in the pit-lane is not permitted. As he went out to retrieve the lead officials brandished the black flag of disqualification. Mansell, who later insisted he had not seen the flag, eventually collided with Senna and both went off.

Mansell was fined $50,000 and banned from the next race – a punishment made all the more severe because he had high hopes of success in that next race, the Spanish Grand Prix. Driver and team contested the decision in the FIA Appeal Court but withdrew their case. The authorities caught up with Senna after his collision with Prost in Japan. He was disqualified – a decision which cost him his chance of beating Prost for the title – and then fined $100,000 and given a suspended six-month ban for 'dangerous driving'.

Mansell had nothing to show for his trips to Japan and a wet Australia. He finished the season on thirty-eight points and was nudged out of third place in the Championship by Patrese.

11

... There's a Way

Nigel Mansell's stature at the end of the 1980s served to remind everyone that a drivers' World Championship title is not the only badge of greatness. In the minds of the vast majority, he ranked alongside Senna and Prost – even in the minds of those who had dismissed him out of hand during the first half of the decade.

There were some who always gave him a chance, Pat Mennem for example: 'From the outset he had fantastic guts and determination. I was struck by that from the time he came into Formula One. I admired him enormously. He has deserved everything he's achieved since then.'

Peter Collins, who worked at Lotus when the young Mansell was striving to make an impression in Formula Three, was another. Collins was sufficiently impressed to recommend Mansell to Colin Chapman. He, too, recognised the raw qualities that gave Mansell the will to succeed, but he also saw the driving potential that would blossom in the late 1980s.

In 1987, when Collins was team boss at Benetton, he watched from the back of the paddock in Hungary as Mansell set fastest time in qualifying. He said: 'People go on about Nigel's courage and determination but that lap was also about skill and precision driving. It was brilliant.'

Relieved of the pressure and anxiety to prove himself, Mansell had, by then, begun to give fuller expression to his talent. Confidence lifted his driving to a new plane. Not only self-confidence but the confidence he generated around him. People were believing in him and he responded. The move to Williams came just when he needed it. They gave him the car and the opportunity to win races, and he repaid them. When the team lost Honda engines he felt betrayed and neglected.

Enter Ferrari, again just at the right time. Apart from an association with the greatest name in motor racing and all the public attention that entailed, they offered him a warm embrace. They were willing to cosset him, even to spoil him a little. Mansell, still basically a down-to-earth family man, was made to feel at home, wanted, and he liked that. He was content and relaxed. It showed in his driving and it showed in his manner out of the car.

Ferrari is no charity refuge for waifs and strays. Mansell gave them – and indeed all Italy – what they demanded in return. They had a man at the peak of his powers: fast, aggressive and bold, but also controlled, cunning and mature. All these qualities were evident at that unforgettable 1989 Hungarian Grand Prix. On a circuit where overtaking is difficult, he forfeited a reasonable grid position to fashion a winning car. In the race he was forceful when he had to be and cautious when he had to be. Then came the final, showman's flourish to take Senna for the lead.

The style and spectacle were in keeping with the Ferrari tradition. The *tifosi* loved it and the team loved it. Ferrari chief Cesare Fiorio was moved to say: 'It was one of the greatest drives I have ever seen and Nigel is one of the greatest drivers Ferrari have ever had.'

The thoughts of one of the greatest team bosses in the history of Formula One, Ken Tyrrell, are typical: 'I couldn't understand what Frank Williams was up to when he took on Nigel. He used to go off and make mistakes. Then he won the Grand Prix of Europe at Brands and it was like turning a switch. All of a sudden he became a racing driver. I can't explain it but now he's a fantastic driver. That win in Hungary proved the point.'

Innes Ireland is another who has revised his opinion: 'I didn't rate him very highly in his earlier years but he's certainly got himself together and now he can be as quick as anybody. And I mean as quick as Senna on a hot lap – though I wouldn't care to be sitting next to him on that lap. He has to have very good reflexes and very good car control.'

Rob Walker was at least served notice of Mansell's emergence: 'I was told way back that he was a good driver to watch for, so I kept an eye on him and he has, indeed, become an extremely fast, extremely good driver. I think what impresses me most of all about him is his passing. He passes the way Surtees used to when he first came into car racing. He still defeats me, though. Family man, wife pushing a pram while he's winning an important race. Not the way you usually think of a racing driver. But there's no doubt about it, he's extremely good.'

At the climax of the 1986 season James Hunt stirred up a hornets' nest with the assertion that Mansell would not be a suitable champion. He now sees a different Mansell: 'It's unfortunate that Nigel's two chances of winning the Championship came when he wasn't ready. I don't think he had the right persona then. But things have changed. He's a better driver now and a different person. He came of age in 1989. I noticed a new maturity in him. It was there in the car and it was perhaps even more noticeable out of the car, when talking to him. Anyone who has known him over that period of time will agree. Now he's ready and capable of winning the Championship – if he has the car with which to do it.'

Mansell's domestic 'rival' Derek Warwick could be forgiven a touch of envy. After all he, too, had talks with Williams about a drive in 1985, but chose to stay at Renault. Warwick says: 'It was the right decision at the time and even now I can justify that decision, but as Nigel went on to win thirteen races with Williams you obviously have to say it was the wrong decision. But all credit to Nigel. He deserves it.

'People ask me if I get hacked off because Nigel, another British driver, has won all these races. I get hacked off when *anybody* beats me. It doesn't matter who he is or what his nationality is. Yes, I'd rather it had been me winning those races, but there are no grievances on a personal level at all.

'Nigel has probably done more for British motor racing than anybody. I hope he doesn't go through his career without becoming World Champion because he deserves to be Champion. The way he is driving he can still do it. He has time.'

Mansell's driving has provided inspiration for a younger generation of British hopefuls. Johnny Herbert, planning a more successful second attempt at Formula One, says: 'There have been certain drivers I've looked up to, heroes really. Lauda was one, Villeneuve was one, and Nigel is one.'

165

Nigel Mansell – true Brit

Julian Bailey's ill-starred venture into Formula One in 1988 left him with mixed feelings about the sport's upper classes, but it gave him a sharper appreciation of the leading drivers: 'Nigel has made himself special. He and Senna are the best and fastest drivers in the world. I like drivers who drive hard and fast and that's the way these two guys drive all the time.'

Mansell himself acknowledges the benefits of maturity and a more relaxed manner. He talks of his 'new perspective' and his 'sense of values'. But don't run away with the idea that the beast has become a pussycat. He remains a ferocious, hungry competitor. He has made more than enough from the sport, and from his business interests outside, to retire and keep his wife and three children in luxury for the rest of their lives. But into the 1990s, the familiar ambition and willpower still lure him to the track: 'I go on because I feel I am driving as well as, if not better than, at any time of my career. I still enjoy racing, I still enjoy competing. And I would still like to win the Championship. It is not an obsession, but it is my remaining ambition in racing.'

Mansell went into the 1990 season with a new partner, reigning champion Alain Prost, and an old travelling companion, determination. 'When I joined Ferrari in 1989 I had a definite two-year plan. The first year went fairly well. I won a couple of races and with better reliability might have been able to challenge for the Championship. The plan was to be ready for the onslaught in the second year.'

He had had to carry the burden of not only his own Championship expectations but those of an entire nation. He arrived at the fortieth anniversary of the World Championship with little prospect of being able to share the load. Seven years had passed since another Briton – John Watson – had won a race.

Warwick embarked upon his tenth season in Formula One with Lotus, the team he wanted to join four years earlier. The passage of time had done nothing to dull his enthusiasm, or his yearning for that first Grand Prix victory: 'I've won in every form of racing I've ever done – from go-karts to stock cars, Formula Ford, Formula Three, Formula Two and sportscars. Everything, that is, except Formula One, and my career won't be complete if I don't win at this level. I know I have the ability, I just haven't had the opportunity. That's not sour grapes. I'm not that sort of person. It's what I honestly believe.

'Had I made different decisions in my career I'm sure I would have been winning Grands Prix and would have been World Champion by now. I know that, although I haven't proved it yet. I am every bit as good as Ayrton Senna, Alain Prost, Nigel Mansell and Gerhard Berger.

'Apart from wanting that first win I keep going because I still love motor racing. If there are drivers out there who don't enjoy it – and I think there are – I just feel sorry for them. I get a buzz every time I sit in a racing car, every time I start up the engine. After well over 100 Grands Prix I still have 110 per cent commitment. If I was earning £1 a race I'd still be a racing driver – just a poor one.

'In fact the sport has given me a good standard of living and a lot of fond memories. Winning the Super-stocks World Championship was my ambition as a boy. Any thoughts of Formula One in those days would have been pie in the sky. You always remember your first wins in the various formulas and then of course those first F1 points at Zandvoort. Winning with the Jaguar at Silverstone was a big thrill, and so was driving the Brabham BMW turbo at Monza with 1300 b.h.p. That was an unbelievable experience.

'And I have led Grands Prix. There was that first race for Renault, in Brazil, and more recently, with the Arrows in the wet in Canada. People don't realise how easy it is to win in a good car, but it's bloody difficult to finish tenth in a bad car. Hopefully I can get that good car and get that first win. Obviously time is running out, but I'm younger than Nigel and still have plenty left in me yet.'

The only other British driver in the 1990 starting line-up was Martin Donnelly, alongside Warwick in the Camel Lotus Lamborghini colours. The Ulsterman distinguished himself in Formula Three and Formula 3000 before landing a test and reserve driver contract with Lotus. He actually made his Formula One debut in 1989, ironically taking over the Arrows from the injured Warwick in France. It was Lotus, though, who signed him up for a full-time drive.

Test and reserve duties were given to Herbert, who by the turn of the year had travelled well down the road to full recovery. Jonathan Palmer and Martin Brundle returned to sportscars. Palmer completed a deal to drive a Porsche and Brundle went back to Jaguar.

They are all reluctant to let go, of course. Formula One, the great goddess, has always seduced them and they hope to receive the call again. Brundle was due to continue with Brabham, but uncertainty about the team's future – and his income – made him opt for the security of Tom Walkinshaw's operation. At the age of thirty he felt he still had time for Formula One – third time lucky, perhaps.

. . . There's a Way

Derek Warwick, embarking upon a new challenge with Lotus

Palmer, too, planned to go back. He intended to reinforce his claims with winning performances in sportscars and sound test work with McLaren. His new package, he figured, would serve him better than another season scratching around with an uncompetitive car.

His place at Tyrrell went to Japan's Satoru Nakajima, a signing patently not based on ability alone. It brought into focus an issue that constantly exasperates British drivers and may explain, to some extent, the nation's relatively indifferent showing in the drivers' Championship since Hunt's 1976 title triumph. At the end of the 1980s Britain was still awaiting his successor and only two drivers, Watson and Mansell, had won races during the interim. The Ulsterman had five victories, the Englishman fifteen. The issue: sponsorship.

Palmer says: 'Sponsorship has always been a problem for British drivers but now the situation is worse than ever. It used to be the South Americans and Italians who came in with money. Now it's the Japanese as well. The drivers at the very top of Formula One are there on merit, but all midfield drivers find their careers are influenced by sponsorship. If you can be part of the package, fine. If not, hard luck. It's up to British teams to educate British industry about the benefits of Formula One.'

Tyrrell concedes: 'There is no doubt that a lot of foreign drivers have got in by having sponsors. It is very difficult indeed for a British driver to find the money to get into a good Formula Three team and then a good Formula 3000 team, where he can show his talent.'

Martin Donnelly joins the 1990 Camel Lotus team

Watson takes a similar view: 'There is no question about Britain having the talent, but we seem to like this sadistic initiation or blooding. You not only have to be a good racing driver, you have got to be able to go out and raise the money in a country where raising money for sport is exceedingly difficult. Great Britain has got so much sport at such a high level that the sponsorship is spread so thin. Motor racing is not a sport that involves a set of golf clubs or a tennis racket, it involves a very expensive piece of equipment.

'You can say the cream always rises, but there are occasions where the cream needs a little assistance in motor racing. It seems that our sports sponsorship strategy is different from that of other countries. In Italy, for instance, there are great advantages in sponsorship as far as off-setting tax is concerned. Sponsorship is an attractive business proposition.'

One man who raised the money for a Formula One drive, alongside Palmer at Tyrrell, was Bailey. He gathered some sponsorship but, unbeknown to Tyrrell, sold a pub he and his brother owned to get the bulk of the £500,000 he promised. That solitary 1988 season cost him £370,000 of his own money.

Bailey says: 'Ken couldn't believe that a British racing driver could come up with that sort of sponsorship. As it turned out, it wasn't all sponsorship, of course. It cost my brother and me £370,000. I have no regrets, though. I would do it again because it gave me my chance. Nobody wanted the car to be as bad as it was. It was just unfortunate that it worked out that way. It was an experience I'll never forget, though. Formula One is a very unfriendly place. It's as cold as ice. There's a lot of back-stabbing. I suppose that's because there's so much money at stake. I became disillusioned. I'd always wanted to be an F1 driver and when I got there it wasn't all it was cracked up to be. I didn't need to be that unhappy in life. There's no point being in F1 just for the sake of it. I'm better off out of it for the time being.'

Bailey has followed the familiar trail into sportscars, driving a second season for Nissan in 1990: 'I'd rather be at the front in sportscars than at the back in F1. I'm enjoying life much more and I'm earning more than I would in F1. Over the last couple of years I've just about got back what I lost. I want to go back to F1, but I want to go back at a different level.'

The desire still burns in most of them, stoked by Mansell's example. After all, they point out, he was thirty-two when he won his first race. Derek Bell, an earlier Formula One refugee, believes too many teams are obsessed with youth: 'I can understand Nigel coming to the forefront in the middle thirties. The problem is that as soon as some young bloke in Formula Three looks any good the attitude is "wow, we must get him," but to get him you've got to shuffle another bloke out. There's no guarantee the younger bloke can do the job any better and often he can't. In sportscar racing they appreciate the value of experience. Had Mansell got his big break at twenty-two instead of thirty-two he would have been out by now.'

Martin Brundle . . . changing course

For all the tales of hardship, Jackie Stewart has another theory. He bemoans the scarcity of hungry fighters: 'You have to consider whether this dry period has come about because we are now too lethargic and over-confident. It's possible there was a feeling that because we were British we had to succeed without the sweat and the tears. I think we became over-comfortable, over-rich. We had so many race tracks, so many teams. Foreign drivers had to make the effort to come to Britain. So if you were from Europe, or South America or Australia you got your economy ticket, came to Britain and lived out of a suitcase or in the back of a van or in some creepy flat in London because this is where the teams were. Our lot were living in style, jumping into the car at 9 o'clock and slipping down to Brands Hatch or up to Silverstone. There was no pain.

'I don't think we were hungry as a nation and it's a real malady when that happens. The lethargy sets in not only in sport but in all other spheres of life. You always get people who want to enhance their experience of living and moving into new areas. I do and I love it. I find it a challenge and I find it very stimulating. But I have always preferred to be a little hungry, literally. When I was driving it kept me alert, made me concentrate. The same still applies in a wider context.'

Stirling Moss believes a lack of discipline is undermining the development of young drivers: 'I have competed in touring car racing in recent years and the standard of driving leaves a lot to be desired. I've seen drivers do really appalling things and not have their licences lifted. I think the ethics of driving today are much lower and there is very little discipline. I think that is bad and inclined to breed drivers who don't feel for a car.

'Motor racing isn't supposed to be an easy sport. Jack Brabham and Graham Hill weren't easy to pass. They were tough guys. But they also had ethics. That's the difference. People didn't go around in those days deliberately putting you into a position of considerable danger.'

Warwick sees it another way. He – like Watson – feels British drivers

Jonathan Palmer in the Tyrrell at the 1987 Hungarian Grand Prix

aren't arrogant and pushy enough: 'There are drivers no better than we have who somehow have bigger reputations. Maybe that's our fault, a bit of British reserve. We don't beat the drum enough for ourselves because we think that would be big-headed. I think that's my problem. If I'd beaten my drum harder earlier in my career maybe I'd have been a bigger star.'

Brundle goes along with that: 'British drivers tend not to shout about themselves. If anything, we put ourselves down. Put any of the leading British drivers in a good car and he will win races. No doubt about it. It's the old problem, getting that good car.'

Most agree that Britain still has the raw driving talent, and that given time, opportunity and backing, it can be refined to become a match for the best in the world. So who are the bright young men capable of carrying the flag all the way to the summit of Formula One?

Herbert could certainly be one. He has already been exposed to the treacherous slopes, but was clearly ill-equipped. His feet and ankle injuries were far too great a handicap. That marvellous opening drive in Brazil led everyone to believe that the damage was not so bad after all, even though it was obvious he could barely walk. The circuits that required harder braking found him out. He began to suffer not only physically but also psychologically. He knew he was not giving of his best. He knew he could not.

In Canada his confidence was decimated, his driving woefully off the pace. He might well have performed more positively in the new Benetton but he never got the chance. He went away to rest, to clear his mind, and to start all over again. Ken Tyrrell offered him the chance to stand in for Alesi – who was still pursuing the European Formula 3000 Championship – and was instantly impressed: 'When I called Johnny and asked him if he'd like to drive in Belgium he said he'd love to. He never hesitated or asked what sort of deal it would be. As a team boss I see that as a good sign in a driver. He saw the chance and he went for it. It's important to remember the circumstances. He had just been, in effect, sacked and if he hadn't done well people would have said that was the end of Johnny Herbert in Formula One. He knew he would have very little time in the car and that he was taking a chance.

'His performance in the wet, when he suddenly put in a lap two seconds quicker, convinced me he'll make it. Absolutely. I asked him if it was the car but he said it wasn't, it was him. He said he just stopped pussy-footing and got on with it. The boy's honest. He has the right attitude. That's important. When I'm looking for a young driver I want to know what sort of person he is, whether he is really serious and understands what is at stake. If, for example, he says he wants to do some saloon car racing as well, I'd realise he didn't know what he was talking about because you can't mix the two.'

Hunt is extremely positive in his assessment of Herbert: 'He is an absolute natural. I think he's very very talented and has considerable maturity already. He hasn't been rounded off in Grand Prix racing yet but he has come on to the scene with very good credentials. He has a lot of experience of leading and winning races. He's not frightened of winning. I just hope he gets fully fit again and gives of his best in Formula One.'

There are some famous names coming up through the racing ranks. There's Justin Bell – 'He's coming on really well,' says proud father Derek. There's Damon Hill – 'I know he's good enough for Formula One,' says proud mother Bette. There's Paul Stewart – 'He did a lot better in his first Formula Three season than I anticipated,' says proud father Jackie. And there's Paul Warwick – 'I think he's got tremendous potential,' says proud brother Derek.

There are many, many more not so famous names out there, desperate for the opportunity, desperate to succeed. Some time in the 1990s, a few of them may emerge as Formula One title contenders. Perhaps one of them will be David Coulthard, who, at the age of eighteen, completed a Formula Ford Championship double in 1989. That sort of achievement takes ability and makes motor racing teams take note. In the years to come, Coulthard might well be one of the sport's famous names.

Allan McNish, many are convinced, will be another. Scottish talent is coursing along the race tracks of Britain and Europe, and it did not take the pigeon-holers long to tag McNish the new Clark or the new Stewart. Those tags may yet prove to be millstones for the wee man, but so far he has taken all the publicity in his stride and there appears little doubt that he is exceptionally gifted.

McNish, born on 29 December 1969 in Dumfries, was brought up surrounded by cars. His father owns a BMW dealership. Young Allan started competing in motor cycle scrambling but at the age of eleven ventured into the less physical racing of karts. The pattern of his early sporting life was soon established. Victories and titles came with his every move: three Scottish Junior Championships, Junior British 100 National Super Championship, then the Senior Championship.

Three months after earning his full driving licence, in 1987, McNish launched his car racing career. Driving an Ecurie Ecosse Van Diemen, he won five out of six Formula Ford British Novice Championship races that summer. A senior win at Snetterton guaranteed him a little extra attention. He completed his first season in cars with second and third places in the novice series and, for good measure, was fifth overall in the highly competitive Brands Hatch Formula Ford Festival.

In 1988 Marlboro took him under their wing for the new Vauxhall-Lotus challenge, a dual contest that assured him quality opposition at home and in Europe. He responded with five British wins to take the domestic title, and one win on the Continent. His progress was recognised when he was named Young British Driver of the Year in the Cellnet Awards.

The progress continued the following season, in Formula Three. He joined the West Surrey Racing camp and, driving a Marlboro Ralt, fought a fascinating duel with David Brabham, youngest of Sir Jack Brabham's three racing sons. Wranglings over engine regulations, disqualifications and appeals tarnished the British Championship yet did not detract from the driving of McNish, or indeed, of Brabham.

They came to a last race decider at Thruxton, and although Brabham's early shunt took the heat off McNish, the Scot produced an immaculate winning performance worthy of the title – provisional, of course. (The following spring their disqualifications were overturned and Brabham was named champion.) It was reminiscent of the young Senna's conclusive drive on the very same track six years earlier. McNish pulled clear of danger, gave himself a buffer, and steered through the rest of the race with the minimum of fuss.

Among the first to congratulate McNish as he stepped down from the podium were Stewart and Hunt. Stewart says: 'Allan's the best British hope we've had for a very long time. He's not only got great natural skill, but for a boy of his age enormous maturity. Above all, of course, he's Scottish! I've no doubt he'll go all the way to the top. I don't like too much to be expected of young drivers, but Allan so clearly has great potential.'

Hunt is in total agreement: 'McNish is a genuinely outstanding talent. He's very much in the mould of his two countrymen, Clark and Stewart. You see it in his intellectual approach, his methodical approach to it.

'My one reservation about him was that he might not have the flair to match his brains. I was trying to persuade him to relax and throw it about and have a go more. You see, because he was intelligent he was getting his wins on brain-power. He wasn't having to draw on his full driving talent. Luckily a failed clutch when he was on pole at Brands meant he had to start in the pit-road. The lack of pressure and the adrenalin and the annoyance of being in the pit-road conspired to make him drive in a way that he hadn't driven before and he managed to keep that level going right through his Formula Three season.'

Soon McNish was flexing his muscles in the Formula 3000 ring – a bit of useful sparring before the real contest in 1990 – and trying out the McLaren Formula One car. Hunt had no doubts at the end of that Formula Three season: 'He's ready for Formula One now. There's no doubt he's good enough. But he has to go through the Formula 3000 stage first and he'll be better still in 1991.'

McNish is grateful for the help and advice he has received from the two former champions: 'Jackie has always taken time to speak to me, he's always given me encouragement. James has been more forthright [now there's a surprise]. He's always given me constructive criticism when he's felt it necessary. He's pointed out areas where I could improve, that sort of thing. It's all been very important for me.'

McNish, small, bright, courteous and remarkably assured for one so young, has the credentials to fulfil Marlboro's expectations inside and outside the cockpit: 'I have high expectations of myself, but in the end you have to deliver,' he says. 'If you are good enough, you make it. I regard it as a great honour when people mention my name along with Jim Clark and Jackie Stewart. It certainly isn't a burden.'

Stewart rates the British Formula Three Championship the most competitive arena in racing and McNish identified the benefits in his driving: 'There are new guys coming in all the time, ready to take you on and push you out. It really is dog eats dog. In terms of driving ability I learned an awful lot from Formula Three. I also leapfrogged in a technical sense, which is equally important in racing now. But I know better than anyone that I have a a long way to go.'

Just how far remains to be seen. What he can count on is an audience out there ready to welcome him, invigorate him, exalt him.

They do like their British heroes. Ask Stewart and Hunt. Ask Moss and Mansell.

Driver	Races	Wins	Points	World Champion-ships	Date of Birth	Died
George Abecassis	2	0	0	0	21.3.13	
Kenny Acheson	3	0	0	0	27.11.57	
Cliff Allison	16	0	11	0	8.2.32	
Bob Anderson	25	0	8	0	19.5.31	14.8.67
Peter Arundell	11	0	12	0	8.11.33	
Peter Ashdown	1	0	0	0	16.10.34	
Ian Ashley	4	0	0	0	26.10.47	
Gerry Ashmore	3	0	0	0	25.7.36	
Bill Aston	1	0	0	0	29.3.1900	4.3.74
Richard Attwood	17	0	11	0	4.4.40	
Julian Bailey	6	0	0	0	9.10.61	
John Barber	1	0	0	0	–	
Don Beauman	1	0	0	0	26.7.28	9.7.55
Derek Bell	9	0	1	0	31.10.41	
Mike Beuttler	28	0	1	0	13.4.40	29.12.88
Eric Brandon	5	0	0	0	18.7.20	8.8.82
Tom Bridger	1	0	0	0	24.6.34	
Tony Brise	10	0	1	0	28.3.52	29.11.75
Chris Bristow	4	0	0	0	2.12.37	19.6.60
Tony Brooks	38	6	75	0	25.2.32	
Alan Brown	8	0	2	0	20.11.19	
Martin Brundle	70	0	14	0	1.6.59	
Ivor Bueb	5	0	0	0	6.6.23	1.8.59
Ian Burgess	16	0	0	0	6.7.30	
John Campbell-Jones	2	0	0	0	21.1.30	
Jim Clark	72	25	274	2:'63+'65	4.3.36	7.4.68
Peter Collins	32	3	47	0	8.11.31	3.8.58
Piers Courage	28	0	20	0	27.5.42	21.6.70
Chris Craft	1	0	0	0	17.11.39	
Jim Crawford	2	0	0	0	13.2.48	
Tony Crook	2	0	0	0	16.2.20	
Geoff Crossley	2	0	0	0	11.5.21	
Colin Davis	2	0	0	0	29.7.32	
Martin Donnelly	1	0	0	0	26.3.64	
Ken Downing	2	0	0	0	5.12.17	
Johnny Dumfries	15	0	3	0	26.4.58	
Guy Edwards	11	0	0	0	30.12.42	
Vic Elford	13	0	8	0	10.6.35	
Paul Emery	1	0	0	0	12.11.16	
Bob Evans	10	0	0	0	11.6.47	
Jack Fairman	12	0	5	0	15.3.13	
Ron Flockhart	13	0	5	0	16.6.23	12.4.62
Philip Fotheringham-Parker	1	0	0	0	22.9.07	15.10.81
Joe Fry	1	0	0	0	–	29.7.50
Bob Gerard	8	0	0	0	19.1.14	26.1.90
Peter Gethin	30	1	11	0	21.2.40	
Dick Gibson	2	0	0	0	16.4.18	
Horace Gould	14	0	2	0	20.9.21	4.11.68
Keith Greene	3	0	0	0	5.1.38	
Mike Hailwood	50	0	29	0	2.4.40	23.3.81
Bruce Halford	8	0	0	0	18.5.31	
Duncan Hamilton	5	0	0	0	30.4.20	
David Hampshire	2	0	0	0	29.12.17	
Cuth Harrison	3	0	0	0	6.7.06	22.1.59
Brian Hart	1	0	0	0	7.9.36	
Mike Hawthorn	45	3	127.5	1:'58	10.4.29	22.1.59
Brian Henton	19	0	0	0	19.9.46	
Johnny Herbert	5	0	5	0	25.6.64	
Graham Hill	176	14	289	2:'62+'68	15.2.29	29.11.75
David Hobbs	7	0	0	0	9.6.39	
James Hunt	92	10	179	1:'76	29.8.47	
Innes Ireland	50	1	47	0	12.6.30	
Chris Irwin	10	0	2	0	27.6.42	
John James	1	0	0	0	10.5.14	
Leslie Johnson	1	0	0	0	–	8.6.59

173

Driver	Races	Wins	Points	World Champion- ships	Date of Birth	Died
Rupert Keegan	25	0	0	0	26.2.55	
Chris Lawrence	2	0	0	0	27.7.33	
Geoff Lees	5	0	0	0	1.5.51	
Les Leston	2	0	0	0	16.12.20	
Jackie Lewis	9	0	3	0	1.11.36	
Stuart Lewis-Evans	14	0	16	0	20.4.30	25.10.58
Ken McAlpine	7	0	0	0	21.9.20	
Mike MacDowel	1	0	0	0	13.9.32	
Lance Macklin	13	0	0	0	2.9.19	
Damien Magee	1	0	0	0	17.11.84	
Nigel Mansell	133	15	252	0	8.8.53	
Leslie Marr	2	0	0	0	14.8.22	
Tony Marsh	4	0	0	0	20.7.31	
John Miles	12	0	2	0	14.6.43	
Dave Morgan	1	0	0	0	7.8.44	
Stirling Moss	66	16	186.5	0	17.9.29	
David Murray	4	0	0	0	28.12.09	5.4.73
Brian Naylor	7	0	0	0	24.3.23	
Tiff Needell	1	0	0	0	29.10.51	
Rodney Nuckey	1	0	0	0	26.6.29	
Jackie Oliver	50	0	13	0	14.8.42	
Arthur Owen	1	0	0	0	23.3.15	
Jonathan Palmer	82	0	14	0	7.11.56	
Mike Parkes	6	0	14	0	24.9.31	28.8.77
Reg Parnell	6	0	9	0	2.7.11	7.1.64
Tim Parnell	2	0	0	0	25.1.32	
David Piper	2	0	0	0	2.12.30	
Dennis Poore	2	0	3	0	19.8.16	12.2.87
David Prophet	2	0	0	0	9.10.37	29.3.81
Tom Pryce	42	0	19	0	11.6.49	5.3.77
David Purley	7	0	0	0	26.1.45	2.7.85
Ian Raby	3	0	0	0	22.9.21	7.11.67
Brian Redman	12	0	8	0	9.3.37	
Alan Rees	3	0	0	0	12.1.38	
John Rhodes	1	0	0	0	18.8.27	
John Riseley-Prichard	1	0	0	0	17.1.24	
Richard Robarts	3	0	0	0	22.9.44	
Tony Rolt	3	0	0	0	16.10.18	
Roy Salvadori	47	0	19	0	12.5.22	
Archie Scott-Brown	1	0	0	0	13.5.27	19.5.58
Brian Shawe-Taylor	2	0	0	0	29.1.15	
Mike Spence	36	0	27	0	30.12.36	7.5.68
Alan Stacey	7	0	0	0	29.8.33	19.6.60
Ian Stewart	1	0	0	0	15.7.29	
Jackie Stewart	99	27	360	3:'69, '71+'73	11.7.39	
Jimmy Stewart	1	0	0	0	6.3.31	
John Surtees	111	6	180	1:'64	11.2.34	
Henry Taylor	8	0	3	0	16.12.32	
John Taylor	5	0	1	0	23.3.33	8.9.66
Mike Taylor	1	0	0	0	24.4.34	
Trevor Taylor	27	0	8	0	26.12.36	
Eric Thompson	1	0	2	0	4.11.19	
Leslie Thorne	1	0	0	0	23.6.16	
Desmond Titterington	1	0	0	0	1.5.28	
Peter Walker	4	0	0	0	—	1.3.84
Derek Warwick	115	0	64	0	27.8.54	
John Watson	152	5	169	0	4.5.46	
Peter Westbury	1	0	0	0	26.5.38	
Ken Wharton	15	0	3	0	21.3.16	12.1.57
Graham Whitehead	1	0	0	0	15.4.22	15.1.81
Peter Whitehead	10	0	4	0	12.11.14	21.9.58
Bill Whitehouse	1	0	0	0	1.4.09	14.7.57
Robin Widdows	1	0	0	0	27.5.42	
Mike Wilds	3	0	0	0	7.1.46	
Jonathan Williams	1	0	0	0	26.10.42	
Roger Williamson	2	0	0	0	2.2.48	29.7.73
Vic Wilson	1	0	0	0	14.4.31	

INDEX

Hampton hill Charity Shop

June 5th Wednesday about
11 H o Clock.